EXPLORING
RESEARCH
METHODS
IN
PSYCHOLOGY
USING

JAMES D. ST. JAMES
MILLIKIN UNIVERSITY

Exploring Research Methods in Psychology Using PsychMate
Copyright © 2006, Psychology Software Tools, Inc.

Publisher:
Psychology Software Tools, Inc.
2050 Ardmore Boulevard
Suite 200
Pittsburgh, PA 15221-4610 USA

Printed in the United States of America.

ISBN 1-880374-83-8

dedicated to marsha
with marsha knows what
and marsha knows why

Table of Contents

Preface

Exploring Research Methods in Psychology Using PsychMate is my effort to provide a background concerning science in general, and the conduct of research in the science of psychology in particular. No textbook of research methods can hope to be complete—the many areas of psychology make such a book a near impossibility. I have chosen instead to provide general information about many aspects of the research process, rather than trying to detail special areas.

There are many topics that I can treat only lightly in a book such as this, but the serious student will want to know more. I have tried to provide references that can guide you to more thorough treatments of the various topics.

PsychMate, the laboratory manual that accompanies this textbook, will provide you with hands-on experience in psychological research as a subject in many of the classic experiments that have shaped the science of psychology. But I hope that you will go beyond that experience to devise your own research. The *Psychology Experiment Authoring Kit* that accompanies *PsychMate* provides you with a powerful tool for computerized experimentation (though obviously much research in psychology does not require a computer).

There is an enormous satisfaction in completing a research project, even an undergraduate effort. I hope that this textbook will help you work your way through that process.

Acknowledgements

Exploring Research Methods in Psychology Using PsychMate has come about through the efforts of several individuals. Amy Eschman served as project manager, overseeing all aspects of the project. Textbook design and layout, and cover and figure artwork were provided by Jeannie Schott. Content/copy editing were provided by Lori Wetzel Morris. Kristi Carter provided valuable proofreading services. Thanks to Millikin University for support during a sabbatical leave. Walter Schneider helped develop my interest in teaching research methods as his teaching assistant many years ago, and has also given his personal support to this project. Charles W. Eriksen also encouraged my study of research methodology in psychology. I must also thank a legion of students who have endured my research methods course and helped shape these chapters.

About the Author

James D. St. James is Chair of the Department of Behavioral Sciences at Millikin University in Decatur, Illinois, where he has taught since 1986. He received his PhD in Experimental Psychology from the University of Illinois at Urbana-Champaign in 1988. He is coauthor of *PsychMate* and of its predecessor, *MEL Lab*. His current area of research involves detection of validity of effort in human motor performance testing. He teaches introductory psychology and advanced courses in statistics and research methods.

Exploring
Research Methods
in Psychology
Using PsychMate

Chapter 1

Science and Psychology

The intent of this textbook is to acquaint you, the student, with science, emphasizing the application of science to psychological issues. I begin with a definition of science turning not to a dictionary but to a scientist. Ragnar Granit was awarded the Nobel Prize in Physiology in 1967 (along with George Wald and Haldan Hartline) for his work on the electrophysiology of vision.

Science is the art of acquiring knowledge in such a manner that coherent structures of understanding can be erected on the basis of a critical evaluation of evidence.

Ragnar Granit
The Purposive Brain (p. 21)

Consider the parts of Granit's definition. Science is an art—that is, it is in part a creative act. Scientific theorizing sometimes involves leaps of imagination as daring as any fine art. But science has its specialty, just like any other art—it is "the art of acquiring knowledge." How does that differ from other ways of acquiring knowledge (such as everyday experience)? It differs because scientific knowledge is acquired "in such a manner that coherent structures of understanding may be constructed." That is, we build up better, more complete, more coherent theories and explanations of the nature of the world. But there is a right way to do that. Proposed explanations (hypotheses, theories) are evaluated by examining the evidence. That evaluation of evidence must be a *critical* examination. We do not just accept evidence; we check it out and see if it meets the standards for scientific reliability.

This book is intended to expose you to some of the basics of how to do the science of psychology. Much of what follows applies to science in general. But while all of the sciences can recognize themselves easily in Granit's definition, they differ vastly in the methods particular to their subject matter. Even within a science the methods can vary widely (in psychology, compare the methods of psychophysics and operant conditioning; in biology, compare the methods of population genetics and molecular biology). Within psychology, we have methods for studying memory and methods for investigating the effectiveness of therapy. Neither this nor any other textbook can introduce you to all of those methodologies. Nor are most individual psychologists acquainted with more than a few of them. The laboratory section of this course should acquaint you with specific research methods in psychology. The discussions of library research (see Chapter 4) will help you find information about areas beyond those covered in this textbook or in your particular course.

Students in the research methods course often ask, "Why do I need to know this stuff? I plan to be a clinical psychologist or a counselor, not a researcher." But practitioners in even the most applied areas of psychology must remain aware of advances of knowledge in their area. Even if you do not go on to do research yourself (and most of you will not), you must be able to *read* research if you are to remain professionally competent. The "critical evaluation of evidence" requires that you have a reasonable familiarity with the methods of the science of psychology and an appreciation for what can (and cannot) be inferred from data. You probably realize that this course cannot give you a complete education in research methodology. You may ask, "So why bother?" For one thing, extravagant claims are common in the areas of mental health, therapy, and counseling. If you know something about what constitutes reliable data, you can at least detect the most egregious blunders. And that makes you better armed than most people. The more you know about how reliable information is gathered, the better you can determine when information does not meet the standards needed for reliability.

A concept currently in vogue in higher education is "critical thinking." Much current writing and thinking in higher education concerns how we (faculty) can promote critical thinking in you, our students. This discussion recognizes a fundamental issue for education. Too often professors teach, and students learn, as if the process of education was a transfer of information from professor to student: "Memorize this stuff and we will be satisfied." But that is more and more seen as a hollow process. If students are to be successful in college and beyond, they need to be able to learn on their own. Learning on your own means doing critical thinking—evaluating evidence yourself and reaching conclusions based on evidence. One purpose of this book is to teach you the type of "critical evaluation of evidence" that is implicit in Granit's definition. Critical evaluation of evidence is not the only kind of critical thinking, but it is an important one.

An unfortunate aspect of teaching students about science is that much of the layman's "common knowledge" of science is a badly distorted caricature of the real process of generating reliable information. Part of teaching about science is teaching what it is not. These distortions will be discussed as the appropriate topics come up later in this book.

One distortion that needs to be dealt with here is the widespread belief that science is characterized by the cold application of a rigid logic—the scientific method.[1] Related to that is the notion that science is somehow antithetical to an artistic spirit. But science is a highly creative endeavor, and those students who fear that imagination will have to be sacrificed for some mechanical application of logic may be pleased to learn that it just isn't so. The development of scientific theories requires you to have thoughts that no one ever had before! Science requires discipline and clarity, but that discipline and clarity must be in the hands of persons of piercing imagination. Logic is used to confirm discoveries, not to make them (a theme to which I will return at length). Artists also require discipline and clarity in order to make their imaginative products available to others through performance, painting, and the like. They must know what they are trying to do (clarity) and how to do it (gained by discipline). Of course, achievements in the fine arts are not judged against a standard of evidence. It would be absurd to ask whether abstract expressionism is "correct." That marks a difference between art and the sciences. But the fact that scientific evidence plays no part in judging artistic achievements does not imply that imagination plays no role in science.

Relationships among Variables

Science is concerned with the relationships among variables. *Such relationships provide the starting point for many scientific investigations.* Why is recognition typically better than recall? Why are males faster at rotation of mental images and more likely to be dyslexic than females? Here, a known relationship becomes a fact to be explained. We have at best a poor idea of how memory works if we cannot explain why recognition is (usually) better. We are missing a piece of the puzzle of sex differences if we cannot account for differences in imagery.[2]

Relationships among variables also provide us with tests of our explanations for various phenomena. Theories and hypotheses usually predict certain relationships among variables, and evaluation of those hypotheses often rests on whether or not the predicted relationship holds. In 1973, Ewald Tulving and D. M. Thomson (see *PsychMate 2.7: Recall, Recognition, and Encoding Specificity*) showed that a prediction from one type of explanation for the superiority of recognition—that subjects would be unable to recall words that

---

[1] Mr. Spock of *Star Trek* is a fine caricature of this view of science.

[2] Sex differences in cognition are about evenly balanced between those favoring males and those favoring females. Males are faster at rotation of mental images (see *PsychMate 1.3: Rotation of Mental Images*), but are also about four times as likely to be dyslexic.

they could not recognize—was false. Because the relationship did not hold, the hypothesis was probably wrong.

Issues of how we can test theories or hypotheses are addressed throughout this book—indeed, theories and hypotheses are how we produce reliable knowledge. My aim is that, after studying this book, you will find that you think more clearly about variables and their relationships.

I begin with a brief delineation of ways that people know about things, and some of the limitations to those ways of knowing. Next is a discussion at some length of the issue of *control*, which is a basic issue for science. That topic will recur frequently throughout this book. Next is a comparison between scientific discovery and the process of a criminal trial. Like all analogies, this one does not lead to a perfect parallel, but it does lead to some insight. The chapter ends with an example of a real, scientific detective story.

Ways of Knowing

Science is but one of the ways that we gain knowledge of the world. It is used by few people, and they (us!) use it sparingly.[3] It is, however, the only way that produces reliable knowledge. When I write that science produces reliable knowledge, I do not mean perfect knowledge. Any knowledge derived from experience (and there is no other kind) is subject to error. But there are many things we can do to rule out error, and those things make up science. It is worth contrasting it with other ways of knowing.

Casual observation and anecdotal evidence.

Probably most of what we know of the world comes through casual observation. By *casual* observation I mean simply what we notice as we go about our daily lives. Casual observation has many pitfalls. Humans are not usually very good observers—especially when they are not prepared to observe. The problems of eye-witness testimony are well known (Elizabeth Loftus, 1993, provides an introduction to this literature). A serious problem with casual observation is that you are not usually expecting to make an observation—you may not be looking in the correct direction or paying attention to the appropriate part of the scene before you.

In addition to errors of observation, errors of memory plague casual observation. We often store in memory our *interpretation* of something we see

---

[3] When you decide which bread to buy or which soap, are you making an informed, scientific decision? I doubt it. Most of our everyday decisions are grotesquely unscientific, even among scientists.

or hear, rather than the actual experience.[4] Jacques Barzun (2000), a cultural historian, put the affair nicely: "The mind is an impressionable organ rather than a recording instrument" (p. 224). *PsychMate 1.8: Change Blindness* discusses at greater length the problems of casual observation.

To make matters worse, observers may be deliberately misled. A magician's greatest tool is misdirection—getting people to look away at a critical point in a magic trick. Of course, this is aided enormously by the combination of our poor peripheral vision, as demonstrated in *PsychMate 1.1: The Filling-In of Blind Spots: Induced Scotomas,* and our usual unawareness of how poor our peripheral vision is. In the heyday of the "materialist" spiritualist mediums, who produced "ectoplasmic" forms of the dead, the séances were typically held in near-darkness—not the best conditions for investigation![5] Chemists and physicists have an advantage over psychologists in that nature does not try to deceive (though it also doesn't try very hard to reveal itself!). But psychologists, insofar as they study humans, have subjects who sometimes lie and cheat.[6]

Anecdotal evidence is evidence by story-telling. If someone tells you about the behavior of a friend and speculates about why the person behaved that way, that is anecdotal evidence about that behavior. Unfortunately, we can seldom rely on such evidence. Anecdotal evidence is usually *somebody else's* casual observation! That does NOT mean that it is wrong. It does mean that it is weak evidence at best and meaningless unless there is supporting evidence. That having been said, a good anecdote can help make an argument vivid and memorable. Many popular discussions of disorders such as dyslexia begin with a description of a single case of the disorder—an anecdote. The discussions then go on to present information. In such a case, the anecdote serves a legitimate purpose—it puts a human face on the disorder and serves as an "advanced organizer" (David Ausubel, 1960) that lets the reader or listener know what is coming, hence improving comprehension and memory (see *PsychMate 2.6: Organization in Memory as an Aid to Recall*).

Though casual observation and anecdotal evidence can seldom provide reliable evidence, they do often provide the hints needed to begin a more

---

[4] William Brewer (1977) presented a fine example of this with a study of what he called "pragmatic implications." He presented subjects with sentences such as "The clumsy chemist had acid on his coat." After a few minutes, subjects cued with "The clumsy chemist..." frequently falsely recalled "*spilled* acid on his coat." Of course, the pragmatic (practical) implication of a clumsy chemist having acid on his coat is that he spilled it, but that was not stated.

[5] For a fascinating account of the materialist mediums, and some photographs of ectoplasmic materializations, see Carl Murchison's (1927) *The Case For and Against Psychical Belief,* especially the chapters by Joseph Jastrow and Harry Houdini.

[6] Lying, incidentally, is not limited to humans. Guy Woodruff and David Premack (1979) reported experiments in which they induced chimpanzees to lie—though not verbally.

formal investigation. Casual observation (whether by yourself or someone else) can *suggest* the importance of variables and the relationships among those variables, but it cannot establish them.

Authority.

> However little authority may be depended upon, it possesses, nevertheless, a name of honor, and habit is more strongly inducive to error than authority; but popular prejudice is more forceful than either of them. For authority merely entices, habit binds, popular opinion makes men obstinate and confirms them in their obstinacy.
>
> Roger Bacon
> *Opus Majus* (1267/1928, p. 10)

Much of what you believe about the world has come from authority — someone you recognize (correctly or not) as more knowledgeable than you. We *must* gain much of our knowledge from authority. We don't live long enough to become experts in all the areas that affect our lives. We entrust the care of our bodies and cars to our physicians and mechanics, often with little personal understanding of how they were fixed. We rely on scientific authorities for (sometimes confusing) advice about what to eat or what not to eat.

The problem with authority as a way of knowing is that not all authority can be trusted. Many persons who set themselves up as authorities are either honestly mistaken or outright charlatans.

In the sciences, we must rely on research reported by others. We cannot independently verify every discovery. (This issue is addressed again in the discussion of replication of research findings in Chapter 7.) And while outright fraud is probably relatively rare in the sciences, experimental results can be wrong for many reasons other than dishonesty. Perhaps the best approach to authority as a source of knowledge is summed up in a phrase that came out of the nuclear arms negotiations between the United States and the Soviet Union during the Cold War — "Trust, but verify."

Religious revelation.

An important source of knowledge for many people is religious revelation. In a sense, this is knowledge given by the highest authority — the word of God. But there is a problem with religious revelation; most of it is wrong. I assert that boldly because it is undoubtedly so. Many religious claims, based on religious revelation, contradict each other. Therefore, they cannot all be correct. The problem is in knowing *which* religious revelations are correct. Though religious issues are of considerable importance to people's lives (Is there a heaven? How do I get there?), science offers little by way of help in deciding among religious claims. The essential problem is that most religious claims are not subject to falsification, which is discussed in more detail in Chapter 2. Science cannot dispute religious revelation. It is simply powerless to decide among competing religious claims. Consider, for example, how you would test the competing claims concerning infant baptism versus adult baptism—a very serious doctrinal dispute among Christians with both sides claiming Biblical sanction (religious revelation) for their views.[7]

Systematic observation.

While casual observation serves as our principal way of knowing about the world, we gain far greater reliability in our knowledge when we observe systematically. Essentially, this means observation that is conscious and deliberate (as opposed to accidental). Systematic observation implies that some variables of interest have been identified, and that those variables are being measured or classified. There is a contemporaneous recording of the data so memory lapses are less of a problem. With systematic observation, then, we enter the realm of science.

Experimentation.

Experimentation relies upon, but also improves upon, systematic observation. One improvement is to make events happen when we can best observe them. When we rely on naturally-occurring phenomena, they may not oblige us by happening when we are looking, when we have the right measuring instruments, or when other conditions are controlled. But when we *cause* the phenomenon to happen and know when it will happen, we have aides to observation at hand (a microscope to see something small, or a computer to record a reaction time) and can control for other factors that might affect the phenomenon.

A second improvement is that we actively manipulate a variable or variables to see what effect they will have. We are no longer at the mercy of waiting around until an event occurs—we make it happen.

Both systematic observation and experimentation represent a scientific approach to gaining knowledge. They have real checks on the quality of the

---

[7] An Internet search for "infant versus adult baptism" will quickly find the arguments on both sides.

evidence and, hence, produce *reliable* knowledge. This does not mean that they are invariably correct. Indeed, the history of science is a history of frequent error. Nevertheless, a better and better approximation to what O. Kempthorne (1976) called a "validated model of the world" (p. 32) is a tremendously valuable asset.

Robert S. Woodworth (1938) was one of the first psychologists to comment on the difference between the "experimental method" and the "correlational method," with the latter based on systematic observation but lacking experimental manipulation. He also pointed out that the correlational method *"does not directly study cause and effect.* The experimentalist's independent variable is antecedent to his [sic][8] dependent variable; one is the cause (or part of the cause) and the other effect. The correlationist studies the interrelation of different effects" (p. 3, emphasis added). You will often see this phrased as "correlation does not imply causality."[9] Indeed, it does not. But the basic problem for correlational studies—based on systematic, scientific observation and measurement, but lacking experimental manipulation of at least one variable—is that it is usually easy to suggest alternative explanations of cause and effect. Experiments do a better job of ruling out alternative explanations. (Thomas Cook and Donald Campbell (1979) provide an excellent discussion of the difficulties of *causality,* what it means that one thing causes another, and how to establish causality.)

Note that the role of experimentation is to rule out two kinds of alternative explanations. One kind of alternative explanation is the kind that challenges the integrity of the experiment itself (confounds or threats to internal validity—see Chapter 5). Another kind of alternative explanation challenges the theory being tested—i.e., alternative explanations for the phenomenon.

---

[8] "Sic" is from the Latin meaning "thus." It indicates that the original is quoted exactly as written, and is used where the original was ungrammatical or, as here, is now dated. It is no longer customary to assume that all persons are male. The square brackets—[ ]—indicate something has been added to a quote.

[9] This phrase is sometimes (especially in Introductory Psychology and Statistics textbooks) taken as implying that when we analyze data using a correlation we cannot make causal inferences. A correlational study—one that establishes a relationship between variables but does not manipulate them—does not imply causality. But a correlational study may or may not be analyzed using the statistical technique of correlation. And an experiment—which does manipulate the variables—may well be analyzed with a correlation. For example, Sternberg's measure of the speed of search of short-term memory (see *PsychMate 2.2: Scanning Short-term Memory*) relied directly upon the slope of the regression line, when the correlation between RT and memory set size was very high.

Control

One of the most important concepts in regard to scientific investigation is that of *control*. We speak of *control groups*, *control conditions*, and simply *controls*. They are related by the fact that they all address one of the fundamental aspects of scientific investigation—ruling out alternative explanations.

The following discussion owes much to Edwin G. Boring's (1954) classic discussion "The nature and history of experimental control." I will begin by quoting at some length his account of an early experiment with very modern controls.

> The concept of control is pretty old and was quite obvious once the Renaissance had turned men's thought from theological fiat to experiment as the means for penetrating into nature's secrets. Here is a story that makes the whole matter clear.
>
> In 1648 the Torricellian vacuum was known to physics in general and to Pascal in particular. This is the vacuum formed at the upper closed end of a tube which has first been filled with mercury and then inverted with its lower open end in a dish of mercury. The column of mercury falls in the tube until it is about 30 in. high and remains there, leaving a vacuum above it. Pascal was of the opinion that the column is supported by the weight of the air that presses upon the mercury in the dish (he was right; the Torricellian tube is a barometer) and that the column should be shorter at higher altitudes where the weight of the atmosphere would be less. So he asked his brother-in-law, Perier, who was at Clermont, to perform for him the obvious experiment at the Puy-de-Dôme, a mountain in the neighborhood about 3000 ft. ("500 fathoms") high as measured from the Convent at the bottom to the mountain's top. On Saturday, September 19th, 1648, Perier, with three friends of the Clermont clergy and three laymen, two Torrecellian tubes, two dishes and plenty of mercury, set out for the Puy-de-Dôme. At the foot they stopped at the Convent, set up both tubes, found the height of the column in each to be 26 old French inches plus 3 1/2 Paris lines (28.04 modern inches), left one tube set up at the Convent with Father Chastin to watch it so as to see whether it changed during the day, disassembled the other tube and carried it to the top of the mountain, 3000 ft. above the Convent and 4800 ft. above sea-level. There they set it up again and found to their excited pleasure that the height of the mercury column was only 23 French inches and 2 Paris lines (24.71 in.), much less than it was down below just as Pascal had hoped it would be. To make sure they took measurements in five places at the top, on one side and the other of the mountain top, inside a shelter and

outside, but the column heights were all the same. Then they
came down, stopping on the way to take a measurement at an
intermediate altitude, where the mercury column proved to be
of intermediate height (26.65 in.). Back at the Convent, Father
Chastin said that the other tube had not varied during the day,
and then, setting up their second tube, the climbers found that it
too again measured 26 in. 3 1/2 lines. These are reasonable
determinations for these altitudes, showing about the usual one
inch of change in the mercury column for every 1000 ft. of
change in altitude.

> In this experiment there was no elaborate design, and it took
> place 195 years too soon for the experimenters to have read John
> Stuart Mill's Logic, but the principle of control and of the
> Method of Difference is there. How important it was for them
> to have left a barometer at the base of the Puy-de-Dôme to make
> sure that changes in the tube that they carried up the mountain
> were due to elevation and not to general atmospheric changes or
> to other unknown circumstances! How wise of the party at the
> top to have made the measurement under as many different
> conditions as they could think of with altitude constant! How
> intelligent of them to take a reading on the way down and thus
> to turn the Method of Difference into the Method of
> Concomitant Variation! (pp. 577-578)

Indeed, these were wise decisions. A barometer's reading can change over
the course of a day as a result of changes in the atmosphere (though that was
unknown to the participants). That might have led to an erroneous conclusion
but for the knowledge that the barometer at the foot of the mountain had not
changed. Furthermore, showing that the readings were unaffected by changes
in location that were not accompanied by changes in altitude helped to test
what I will later call the "boundary conditions" of the phenomenon.

The Method of Difference and Method of Concomitant Variation
mentioned in Boring's quote are two of the formal scientific methods proposed
by James Stuart Mill, the great British philosopher, in his *A System of Logic,
Ratiocinative and Inductive* published in 1843. Mill was not the first to
describe these scientific methods—being anticipated by David Hume in1739
and Francis Bacon in 1620—but Mill wrote when science was becoming more
formalized and developed the ideas more completely. Mill proposed several
methods of scientific inquiry, which are outlined briefly.

First is the Method of Agreement. "If *A* is always followed by *a*, then *A* is
presumably the cause of *a*" (Boring, 1954, p. 574). But this really will not do, as
Mill himself noted in remarking that mere agreement would lead us to conclude
that night causes day and that day causes night. Indeed, this sort of logical

fallacy has a Latin name: *post hoc, ergo propter hoc* ("after it, therefore because of it").

Ambrose Bierce, an American author and wit, provided the following example of the weakness of the Method of Agreement in his *Devil's Dictionary* (first published about 1911): "Effect, n. The second of two phenomena that always occur together in the same order. The first, called a Cause, is said to generate the other—which is no more sensible that it would be for one who has never seen a dog except in pursuit of a rabbit to declare the rabbit the cause of the dog" (1946, p. 229). Mill noted that this method is strengthened considerably if we can vary *A* "at will." When we cannot, we have what we now call a correlational study. Boring put it this way: "Mere agreement does not furnish rigorous proof, although you may be limited to it when you lack the voluntary variation of events—the independent experimental variable—and are reduced to description only. For this reason the establishment of causal relations in biography, history, geology, paleontology, and even astronomy is less sure than in experimental science" (1954, p. 574).

Mill's second method is the Method of Difference. "If *A* is always followed by *a* and not-*A* is always followed by not-*a*, then *A* is certainly the cause of *a*" (Boring, 1954, p. 574). If *A* is dichotomous (that is, it has only two values—present or not present), then we have the Method of Difference. But when *A* can take on a range of values (for example, varying the amount of study time in a memory experiment, or varying dosages of a drug), then we use the Method of Concomitant Variation. Here the value of *a* is shown to vary concomitantly with changes in the amount of *A*. It is precisely this method that was used in Pascal's experiment, when readings were taken with the barometer at three different altitudes.

Pascal's experiment also illustrates what I will term "control conditions." The barometer left at the base of the mountain served as one kind of control. The repeated readings taken at varying heights and at varying locations at the same height provided another. Other uses of "control" refer not to control conditions for explicit comparison, but rather to any techniques used to avoid variation in experimental conditions. Testing all subjects at the same time of day or calibrating laboratory instruments against known standards are examples of this kind of control. These I will refer to as "experimental controls."

The use of a "control group" in its modern sense is actually relatively recent. R. L Solomon (1949) wrote, "If one is interested solely in the concept of Control Group in the history of psychology, Twentieth Century psychology contains that history. We have not been able to find a single case of the use of control group design, as we use it today, before the year 1901. Control group designs seem to have awaited the development of statistical concepts which allow for the characterization of group performances in terms of measures of central tendency; and psychologists seem to have been slow to combine statistical sophistication with experimental design" (p. 137). Solomon noted that early experiments on training typically used a pretest followed by training and then a posttest with the difference between pre- and posttest scores indicating the amount of learning. According to Solomon, the first adequate experiment on training was that of Winch (1908) who used two groups of subjects.[10] One group received a pretest, then training, then a posttest. The other group was the control group. They received the pretest, then *no* training, then the posttest. Boring notes the interesting coincidence that "the statistical techniques for measuring the significance of group differences were being invented or discovered just about the time group controls came into general use" (p. 585). Indeed, "Student's" paper detailing the *t*-test for mean differences was published the same year as Winch's experiment on training (though Winch did not take advantage of Student's test).[11]

An analogy

A useful analogy to the process of scientific discovery is the process of a criminal trial. Both processes are ultimately concerned with finding the truth, and both processes have more than a few pitfalls. In a criminal proceeding, a prosecutor, based on evidence developed by the police, presents a theory of the crime to a jury or judge. That theory is that the accused committed the crime in some specific manner. Note that it is up to the prosecutor to provide evidence in favor of his or her case (theory). That is the sense in which the accused is "innocent until proven guilty"—if the prosecution does not make its case, the jury must acquit. As a case is presented, the judge acts as a referee and can rule out certain evidence (such as most hearsay testimony) that does not meet the proper standards.

The role of the attorney for the accused is to try to demonstrate any logical or evidential flaws in the prosecutor's case. The judge or jury then makes a decision concerning guilt. A verdict of "guilty" indicates that they found the

---

[10] "The control group in transfer experiments was employed in a small way by Thorndike and Woodworth (1901)..." (Woodworth, 1938, p. 178).

[11] "Student" was the pseudonym of Edwin Gossett, a pioneer of statistics, who was employed by the Guinness brewery of St. James' Gate, Dublin, Ireland, makers then and now of Guinness Stout and other fine products of the brewer's art. Gossett was an early and successful developer of what is now termed *statistical quality control*. Company rules forbade him from publishing under his own name, (lest his publications somehow reflect poorly on the company?), so he was required to use a pseudonym. He chose marvelously—what better for a scientist than "Student"? The small community of researchers in the newly-developing field of inferential statistics was mostly British, and was, of course, well aware of the identity of "Student."

evidence for the prosecution's case against the defendant persuasive "beyond a reasonable doubt." A verdict of "not guilty" is more complex. It may indicate that the jury did not find the evidence persuasive at all, and they believe the defendant to be innocent. It may, however, merely reflect that the jury did not find the evidence compelling—they may feel that it is somewhat likely that the defendant is guilty, but there is still reasonable doubt.

Let us examine the analogy to a scientist trying to persuade others of the soundness of a theory. If you present a theory of why or how some phenomenon occurs (e.g., the cause of schizophrenia or the nature of different memory systems), it is your responsibility to show that your theory is correct. The "jury" of other scientists can quite reasonably refuse to accept your theory unless you have evidence to back it up. Scientists favor evidence based on the results of experiments, as opposed to the eye-witness testimony and circumstantial evidence of a courtroom, but otherwise the logic is the same. Who acts as judge, deciding what evidence is admissible? To a considerable degree, that role is played by peers, who review articles submitted for publication and by the editors of the scientific journals. The body of scientists who deal with the area in question will serve as both defense counsel and jury. Some may reply to the published article, pointing out flaws in the "case," thus acting as defense counsel. Others will decide whether they find the case sufficiently compelling that they will accept the theory (at least provisionally). These scientists are playing the role of the jury. If they find the evidence compelling, they will make that theory a part of their intellectual equipment, and try to find ways to fit the new theory with older ones (or modify older ones to adapt to the new knowledge). They may also incorporate that theory into their teaching. But if other scientists do not find the evidence compelling, they may either reject the theory altogether (the defendant did not commit the crime) or hold a decision in abeyance until more evidence is available—there is still reasonable doubt.

There are some differences between scientific theory-testing and a criminal trial, of course. One important one is that a scientific case is never fully settled. In a criminal trial, new evidence discovered after the trial does not automatically re-open the case, but, at least in principle, a scientific theory is always subject to an appeal due to new evidence. Another difference is that a jury must reach a unanimous decision or the whole trial is just thrown out. Scientists are not required to reach agreement as a jury is. Some may find the evidence compelling and teach the theory or incorporate it into their own work. Others may reject it.

One very important way in which jury decision-making is like that of the body of scientists is in the fact that "proof" is never absolute. It is beyond a *reasonable* doubt, but not beyond all doubt. As noted in Chapter 2, empirical evidence simply cannot prove beyond all doubt. Data (evidence) can suggest, support, and even convince, but it cannot prove beyond any possible doubt.

Much of the rest of this book is about scientific detective work—finding the evidence that can both help create a coherent theory of a phenomenon and provide evidence to support that theory. Just as in police work, careful collection of evidence is required. Some leads will turn out to be false, just as most hypotheses about a phenomenon may be wrong. Sometimes the evidence will seem to be very clear, but still turn out to be wrong. While no path to knowledge is perfect, a careful respect for the quality of the evidence will eventually lead to something pretty close to the truth.

Science: An Example

It may be useful at this point to consider an illustrative example of scientific research. Because of the clarity and importance of his work, I choose John Snow's investigation of the cause of cholera during the London epidemic of 1854.[12]

Cholera is a water-borne bacterial disease usually contracted from water supplies contaminated by feces. Direct person-to-person contact rarely spreads the disease, though poor sanitation in caring for patients with the resulting diarrhea often aids the spread of the contamination. The disease produces gastro-intestinal symptoms of diarrhea, cramps, and vomiting. Patients die of dehydration—sometimes within hours. Cholera is now largely unknown in Western Europe and the United States. There, water treatment and filtering almost completely eliminate the bacterium that causes the disease. However, outbreaks of the disease can occur when flooding overwhelms water treatment plants and ground water becomes contaminated by mixing with sewerage. In poorly developed countries, cholera remains a threat. It should also be noted that nursing care, in the form of rehydration via intravenous fluids, is the normal method of treatment. At the time of the early pandemics, however, intravenous rehydration was not yet known.

Cholera began historically as an endemic disease on the Indian sub-continent.[13] It spread in a series of pandemics beginning in about 1816 when it spread across India. A second pandemic, beginning in 1829, saw it spread to

---

[12] This discussion is largely based on information from the UCLA medical school web site on John Snow (www.ph.ucla.edu/epi/snow.html) and the web site of the John Snow Society (www.johnsnowsociety.org).

[13] An *endemic* disease is one restricted to a particular locality, while a *pandemic* disease is one spread over a wide area with a higher rate of infection. An *epidemic* disease is one with a sudden, rapid spread.

Europe, reaching London and Paris by 1832. There were more than 23,000 deaths in England and more than 100,000 in France. By mid-century, the pandemic had spread to North America. As recently as 1994, an outbreak beginning in Peru killed 10,000 and infected more than one million. The improved methods of rehydration have reduced the death rate enormously in areas where adequate nursing care is available.

John Snow (1813-1858) was a London-educated physician of broad interests. He was one of the first British physicians to pursue the use of the new anesthetics developed in the United States in the 1840s. He made improvements in administration of the anesthetics and, in 1853, administered obstetrical anesthesia to Queen Victoria during the birth of Prince Leopold. Snow began his investigations of cholera during an outbreak in London in 1848-49. During that epidemic, there were at least 250,000 cases and 53,000 deaths in England. Noting that the symptoms were intestinal, Snow argued in his 1849 book, *On the Mode of Transmission of Cholera*, that it was a water-borne disease. Medical opinion on the cause of the epidemic was largely in favor of some kind of air-borne pathogen. Note that at that time the role of bacteria in infectious disease was only beginning to be understood.

It should be noted that, especially in the poorer parts of London (and most other cities), sanitation was dreadful. Sewers were often just open trenches that ran down the middle of streets into which people dumped their "night soil" in the morning. Sewerage ran off into the River Thames untreated. The waste of cattle and horses was largely left in the streets for the rain to wash away.

Another outbreak of cholera occurred in the Soho district of London in August of 1854. Over a very hot summer, there had been a few cases of cholera in the area, but on August 31, the disease reached epidemic proportions with 56 new cases in a single day. By the next day the death toll was 70 with 143 new cases within an area of a few blocks.

Snow began to investigate the latest outbreak on his own as he had no official standing. Snow's approach has become standard for epidemiology—he drew a map. This is sometimes cited as the beginning of modern epidemiology. Snow reasoned that if the prevailing theory of transmission by a mist or miasma—essentially by bad air—were correct, there should be a relatively uniform distribution of cases along the streets of the affected areas. Snow's map plotted the number of deaths for each building in the affected area. The data initially challenged the theory of transmission by air and appeared to support Snow's own theory of transmission by contaminated water because the overwhelming majority of cases occurred within walking distance of the Broad Street pump—a hand pump available to the public. An inspection he made of the pump, however, failed to find contamination. Snow consulted the Register of Deaths and plotted more cases. In doing so he found details that seemed to undermine his theory. A 500-inmate workhouse in the neighborhood (where the homeless could find shelter and a bit of gruel in return for a loss of freedom and hours of manual labor) had only five deaths by cholera. At a large brewery adjacent to the pump, there had been no cases. Even worse, deaths were reported in the rural villages of Hampstead and Islington some distance away.

Snow went on to ask people who remained in the district about details of the outbreak. He discovered that the workhouse had its own well and did not use the Broad Street pump. Also, the workers at the brewery drank only their own product at work. When Snow visited the village of Hampstead, where a death had occurred far from the pump, relatives of the dead told him that the deceased had a jug of water delivered regularly from the Broad Street pump because she preferred its flavor. On further inquiry, he found that her niece had visited her, drank from the jug, and later died at home—in Islington.

Snow's map provided another clue. Cholera was worst around the Broad Street pump, which pumped ground water. But cases of cholera occurred in other parts of London, as well. In much of London, water was supplied to homes and businesses by one of two commercial suppliers. They pumped water from the Thames—the great river that flows through London. Although the pumping of water in this manner is not unlike much of today's water supplies to many cities, the treatment plants used today were absent and water was not treated with chlorine or filtered. The two company's operations differed in a crucial detail, however. The Lambeth Company drew its water from the Thames upstream from London, while the Southwark and Vauxhall Company drew its water from local wells and from the Thames in central London. Snow found an astonishing difference in death rates from cholera when comparing households that used water from the two companies. The death rate per 10,000 households was 37 for areas supplied by the Lambeth Company. It was 315 per 10,000 for those supplied by the Southwark and Vauxhall. Water taken from wells and from the Thames in London was regularly contaminated with London's sewerage.

Armed with these facts, Snow persuaded the Board of Guardians of St. James Parish to remove the handle from the Broad Street pump. There was an immediate reduction in cholera cases, though in par that was probably due to the fact that many people had already fled the neighborhood.

Snow did not, of course, solve the problem of the cause of cholera—it would be several decades before the bacterium *Vibrio cholerae* was identified as the culprit by the great bacteriologist Robert Koch in 1883.

Today, the John Snow pub stands on Broad Street (now Broadwick Street). Nearby, a granite slab marks the location of the original Broad Street pump.

The second edition of Snow's *On the Mode of Communication of Cholera* (1855) is a deserved classic in science in general and epidemiology in particular. It is available online through the UCLA medical school web site listed in the footnote at the beginning of this section. Both editions are republished in Snow (1845, 1855/1965).

The history of epidemiology is full of great detective stories. Careful observation and the interplay of hypothesis and data, a willingness to stick with a theory when some data appeared to contradict it, a willingness to challenge received wisdom (authority), comparisons and controls, and willingness to put a theory to experimental test (by removing the pump handle) are admirably displayed in John Snow's work. In much scientific work, only a partial answer is found, and some of the causal mechanisms may remain hidden—just as the bacterial cause of cholera remained hidden in Snow's time. But even an incomplete understanding can be enormously better than none. To know that contaminated water produces cholera can prevent the disease even when the specific bacterial pathogen remains unidentified. In the rest of this book, I will have occasion here and there to draw parallels with John Snow's investigation of cholera.

Chapter 2

Some Nuts and Bolts of Science

In this chapter, I develop several areas of background knowledge concerning science—some necessary terminology, some of the logic of science, and the relationship between science and technology.

Some Terms and Definitions

Regularities in relationships between variables: Laws and Effects

Law and effect are terms to describe known regularities or facts about the world (in our case the world of psychology). An issue of major concern for any of the sciences is the discovery of relationships between variables. Lawful relationships among variables provide both regularities to be explained and tests of those explanations since theoretical explanations typically predict relationships.

An excellent example of a law was discovered when pumps were first invented, and it was discovered that water could not be raised more than about 32 feet by a pump. That caused a real problem with trying to pump water out of flooded mines and the like. The eventual correct explanation (that the air pressure exerted on the pool of water could not raise the water more than 32 feet, at which point the weight of the water in the column equaled the air pressure) made a signal contribution to the understanding of the physical world. (This finding and its explanation are addressed again later in this chapter in the discussion of technology and science).

BOOK VI.   185

A—SHAFT. B—BOTTOM PUMP. C—FIRST TANK. D—SECOND PUMP. E—SECOND TANK. F—THIRD PUMP. G—TROUGH. H—THE IRON SET IN THE AXLE. I—FIRST PUMP ROD. K—SECOND PUMP ROD. L—THIRD PUMP ROD. M—FIRST PISTON ROD. N—SECOND PISTON ROD. O—THIRD PISTON ROD. P—LITTLE AXLES. Q—"CLAWS."

From De Re Metallica by Georgius Acricola (1556)

Other examples of laws are Boyle's Law, relating the temperature and pressure of a gas, and Fourier's Law, stating the frequencies of the overtones of a fundamental frequency of vibration such as the overtones of a plucked string on a guitar or piano. Maxwell's Equations, named after James Clerk Maxwell (1831-1879), a Scottish physicist, described the lawful interrelationships of magnetism, electricity, and light. That work set the stage for measurement of the speed of light and the notion of light as an electromagnetic wave.

Psychology possesses few such quantitative laws. In the study of perception, *Steven's Power Law* relating the physical intensity of a stimulus to its perceived magnitude is one such quantitative law. The *Hick/Hyman Law* is another. W. E. Hick (1952) and Ray Hyman (1953) independently demonstrated that reaction time is linearly related to the log (base 2) of the number of stimulus-response choices. This is a somewhat intermediate case since the slope and intercept of the line differ from one subject to the next. But a straight line provides an excellent fit to the data for each individual. (See *PsychMate 5.1: Reaction Time Procedures* for a more detailed discussion of the Hick/Hyman Law.)

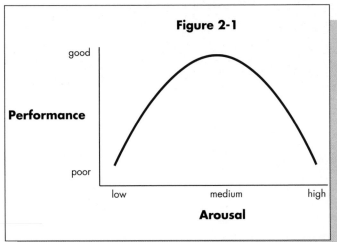

Figure 2-1

The Yerkes-Dodson Law: Performance as a function of arousal.

Robert Yerkes and J. D. Dodson (1908) reported an experiment with mice in which they showed that learning of a sensory discrimination improved as the intensity of a shock increased. This improvement was evident up to a point. Further increases in the shock caused a deterioration of performance. If this finding was limited to shock and mice, it would be of only passing interest. However, a wide variety of situations show the same essential relationship—increases in arousal improve performance up to a point. Further increases in arousal cause a decrement in performance (see Figure 2-1). This has come to be called the *Yerkes-Dodson Law.* Daniel Kahneman (1973) reviewed this literature and discussed its implications for theories of attention and memory.

The term *law* is usually reserved for those relationships that yield relatively exact numerical predictions. As stated previously, psychology has few such quantitative laws, but it is certainly not lacking in regularities. These regularities are usually best expressed as qualitative relationships and are often called effects.   (The Yerkes-Dodson law is perhaps better called the *Yerkes-Dodson Effect,* but these terms are not always used with precision.) For example, it is easily demonstrated that the reaction time (RT) to a stimulus increases as the probability of the stimulus decreases (see the Probability of a Stimulus section in *PsychMate 5.1: Reaction Time Procedures*). That general statement is true, but it is hard to pin down an exact number to produce a quantitative law—individuals differ in RT, and also in the differences in RT produced by changing the stimulus probability. As far as I know, this regularity has never been given a formal name, but it could easily be styled the stimulus probability effect.

Effects are named in various ways. Some are named after their discoverer. The Stroop Effect refers to the slowing in the time needed to name the colors in which words are printed when the words are the names of other colors. If you see "red" in green, you will take much longer to say "green" than if you saw a row of X's in green. This may be the best-known "effect" in psychology, with a literature of more than 1,000 articles since J. Ridley Stroop first described this in 1935 (see *PsychMate 1.5: Attentional Interference and the Stroop Effect*).

Some effects are named descriptively. Charles Eriksen (1995) used the term *Flankers Effect* to refer to the slowing in RT to a target letter if it is flanked by another, response-incompatible target letter. That slowing is assumed to occur because the flankers are too close to the target letter to be blocked by selective attention, and thus partially activate a competing response (see *PsychMate 1.6: Selective Attention and Response Competition*). The Serial Position Effect refers to the finding in memory research that the first and last few words on a list are almost invariably recalled best, with poorer recall in the middle of the list. When psychologists studying memory began to think in terms of a long-term and a short-term memory, Murray Glanzer and Anita Cunitz (1966) suggested

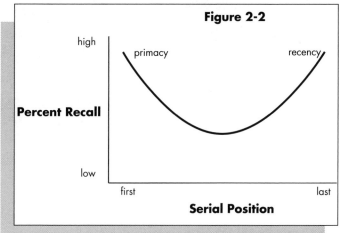

Figure 2-2

high

primacy   recency

Percent Recall

low

first   last

Serial Position

The Serial Position Effect: Recall as a function of position of an item in the list.

primacy (the good recall of the first few words) was due to effective rehearsal that resulted in long-term memories for those words, while recency (the good recall of the last few words) occurred because those words were still in short-term memory. Words in the middle of the list cannot be rehearsed well enough to form long-term memories and have been pushed out of short-term memory by later words. (But see Greene, 1992, for a different view. Nairne (2002) provided a recent discussion of the theoretical swamp of how to properly conceptualize the phenomena of brief and lengthy periods of memory retrieval.)

Another well-known effect was named for a foundational finding for industrial psychology. Elton Mayo, F.J. Roethlisberger, and William J. Dickson studied factors affecting productivity at the Hawthorne Plant of the Western Electric Company in Cicero, Illinois, in the early 1930s. They manipulated a number of variables, such as lighting, which led to improvements in productivity, but they soon discovered that the improvements depended more on the fact that the workers appreciated the attention paid to them than to the actual changes. This is now referred to as the Hawthorne Effect. (See Franke & Kaul, 1978. For other interpretations see Parsons, 1974, and Bramel & Friend, 1981.)

Western Electric Company – Hawthorne Works (Tower) Cicero, IL, August 1956.

As noted, regularities in the relationships between variables provide important starting points for scientific investigation. They often can be seen as catalysts for problem-solving—why this regularity and not some other? Indeed, in the case of the serial position effect, one can hardly be said to have a science of memory if one cannot explain so important a regularity. The attempt to explain *regularities* (whether formally named as laws or effects or not) is often an important step in science. Indeed, the very existence of regularities (known effects) in the data provides the beginnings of any science. W. I. B. Beveridge (1957, p. 10) quoted the 19th-century neurologist John Hughlings Jackson to the effect that "the study of the causes of things must be proceeded by the study of the things caused."[1]

I now consider a variety of explanatory mechanisms and the terms used to describe them.

---

[1] One of the principal difficulties in the study of paranormal phenomena, such as extrasensory perception, telepathy, and telekinesis, is the lack of a replicable phenomenon. Scientists are reluctant to seek an explanation for a phenomenon until they are quite sure there is a phenomenon to be explained. James Alcock (1981) develops this notion at some length, noting that parapsychology "is best described as ... belief in search of data rather than data in search of explanation" (p. ix).

Hypotheses, theories, Theories, and Models

The terms to be discussed below suffer (if that is the right term) from an inexactness of usage. Each term conveys different meanings in different contexts and perhaps conveys different meanings to different people. We lack a systematic determination of the meanings of words—there are no "word police" to dictate "the" meaning of a word. This is one of the reasons that physicists try to reduce their theories to mathematical symbolism, where there is a far more precise usage. But little of psychology permits this so you just have to get used to it!

Hypothesis

I begin with *hypothesis,* which has, it seems to me, three related meanings. One meaning is a tentative suggestion that a phenomenon exists. While watching children at play, it might seem to you that little boys play more aggressively than little girls. That suspicion would constitute a rather low-level hypothesis. In order to test that hypothesis, you would need more formal observation. If you went beyond casual observation to formulate operational definitions (see Chapter 3) of aggression, and then formulated a plan for systematically observing boys and girls, you might confirm your hypothesis, changing a speculative guess into an "effect."

A second, slightly higher-level meaning of hypothesis would be for a tentative explanation for a phenomenon. As discussed in Chapter 1, John Snow noticed a large number of deaths from cholera around the Broad Street pump, and suspected that it might be the source of the disease. He went on to test this hypothesis by systematically collecting data on deaths building by building around the area.

At the highest level, a hypothesis represents a prediction from a fairly well-developed theory. Endel Tulving and Donald Thomson (1973) noted that Walter Kintsch's (1971) generation-recognition theory of why recognition is (usually) superior to recall predicts that recall can be equal to recognition, but not superior. They then tested the prediction (hypothesis) and showed that, under the right circumstances, subjects can easily recall words that they failed to recognize just a few seconds earlier. In this case, the failure of the prediction challenges the theory, but also suggests an alternative explanation for the usual superiority of recognition—namely, that recall tests usually have poorer retrieval cues than recognition tests. See *PsychMate 2.7: Recall, Recognition and Encoding Specificity.*

In this third, best-developed, sense of hypothesis, a theory generates hypotheses (makes predictions) that go beyond what is already known.[2] In this case, confirming the hypothesis seems to strengthen the theoretical explanation for the phenomenon, while falsifying the hypothesis seems to weaken it. (The ins and outs of verifying and falsifying theories are treated in more detail later in this chapter).

The interested reader is referred to Peter Lipton's (2005) discussion of the issue of prediction versus accommodation. "In the case of 'accommodation,' a hypothesis is constructed to fit an observation that has already been made. In the case of 'prediction,' the hypothesis…is formulated before the empirical claim in question is deduced and verified by observation….Well-supported hypotheses often have both accommodations and successful prediction to their credit. Most people, however, appear to be more impressed by predictions than by accommodations" (p. 220.) He gives as an example Edmond Halley's hypothesis, published in 1705, that the comets that appeared in 1531, 1607, and 1682 were a single comet. But his correct prediction of the comet's return in 1758 was what made it really Halley's comet.[3] Here, one prediction was far more convincing than three accommodations. But is this really justified? The arguments are a bit complex and beyond the scope of this text, but Lipton argues that there is—sometimes—a justification for preferring prediction to accommodation. Whether or not prediction is truly more effective than accommodation in testing theories, there is certainly a human bias to favor prediction.

Theory and theory

Another area in which the inexactness of usage can be bothersome involves the word *theory*. The word is applied to a range of levels of certainty: Sometimes synonymous with hypothesis in the sense of a tentative suggestion of the existence of a phenomenon; sometimes meaning a suggestion of an explanation of a phenomenon; and sometimes meaning a well-known and thoroughly documented explanation of a phenomenon. Scientists typically use the word *theory* to mean only the second and third of those meanings, relying on context to make the meaning clear. I will suggest a difference between a "little-t" theory (a suggestion of causal relationship) and a "big-t" Theory (a known causal relationship).[4]

---

[2] For reasons that are as much aesthetic as logical, scientists are especially fond of "counter-intuitive" hypotheses. If a theory predicts a relationship among variables that had never been previously suspected, and that runs counter to established thought, a demonstration of that relationship provides an especially powerful boost to the credibility of the theory.

[3] Halley's comet continued to appear faithfully every 78 years. In 1910, it was still bright enough to excite wonder. At its last appearance, in 1988, it had been reduced in size to a degree that it was no longer so impressive a sight in the night sky.

[4] When you see an article titled "Toward a Theory of X" or something similar, read that as a little-t theory.

One place where this confusion is evident is in the way opponents of Charles Darwin's theory of evolution often dismiss it as "only a theory." This is suggesting the first of the meanings above—equivalent to a lower-level hypothesis. "Darwin's theory is just a theory, and so other theories [usually meaning the account of creation in Genesis] should be taught as equally good." This reasoning makes a couple of mistakes. "Darwin's theory of evolution" is often taken by those making this argument to suggest that Charles Darwin originated the idea of evolution. But biologists of his day widely accepted that species change had occurred. Indeed, Darwin's grandfather, Erasmus Darwin (1794), had proposed a theory of evolution, though with little empirical backing. And an important rival theory existed—Jean Lamarck's theory, published in his *Zoological Philosophy* in 1809, based on the inheritance of acquired characteristics.[5] In "Darwin's theory of evolution," the emphasis is misplaced—instead of stressing the word *theory*, emphasize instead, "*Darwin's* theory of evolution." What was new with Darwin was not the theory *that* evolution had occurred, but rather his theory about *how* it occurred. When Darwin (1859) first offered his theory, it was of the second variety—a suggestion of an explanation for speciation. He had evidence to support his theory, but it could hardly be taken as established. The development of biology since that time has been a magnificent triumph of that theory. We must now read "Darwin's Theory of Evolution" (all caps and no serious doubt), and the biologist Theodosius Dobzhansky (1973) could write that "nothing in biology makes sense except in the light of evolution."

Theories can also differ in scope. There are small-scale, "local" theories. An example would be Tulving and Thomson's (1973) theoretical account of why recognition is (usually) easier than recall. Darwin's theory of evolution is quite the opposite. It is concerned with explanation on a grand scale—how do species arise?

Properties of good theories:

A general principle enunciated in the 14th century by the English philosopher William of Ockham (known as *Ockham's Razor*) was first stated in Latin: *Pluralitas non est ponenda sine necessitate*, which is translated most directly as "Plurality must not be posited without necessity." Later versions have expressed the idea as "Thou shalt not needlessly multiply explanatory entities." In other words, don't add variables to your explanation that aren't needed. If Y can be explained by A and B, and C adds nothing to the explanation, then leave it out!

---

[5] Lamarck postulated that changes in an organism due to experience could be transmitted to their offspring. His theory did not survive the development of modern genetics, which makes it clear that this kind of genetic transmission cannot occur.

Ockham's Razor has sometimes been taken a further step to imply that "the simpler of two theories is to be preferred," where simplicity refers to the number of "explanatory entities" or variables. This simplification is not justified, except in a limited instance. Certainly if theory A states that $y = f(a, b)$ and theory B states that $y = f(a, b, c)$, and both do an equal job of predicting y, then theory A is preferred because theory B has needlessly multiplied explanatory entities.[6] That is, adding variable c did not improve the theory. But suppose that theory C states that $y = f(a, c, d)$, and both theory A and theory C are equally good predictors of y. It seems to me to be far from justified in this instance to say that theory C is more likely to be right than theory A just because it is simpler. We really cannot choose between theory A and theory C (at least until one theory or the other is refined so as to make a more accurate prediction). William Jefferys and James Berger (1992) give an interesting account of issues in deciding the degree to which a simpler theory should be preferred.

The fact that our minds want simple laws is no reason for supposing that nature must be simple.

Stuart Chase, *The Tyranny of Words*, p. 137.

Theories have other uses as well. A theoretical point of view is sometimes a strong determiner of what data one finds to be of interest. B. F. Skinner, in his pioneering work on operant conditioning (1938), dealt almost exclusively with data that were counts of the frequency of bar-presses by rats. Because of Skinner's theoretical claim that reward and punishment are the most potent contributors to learning, this emphasis on the frequency of bar-presses seemed reasonable—at least to him. Other aspects of behavior, such as the rats gnawing on the steel bar early in extinction, were thus of little interest to him—Skinner describes that the rat simply bar-pressed less and less often. It is wise to avoid blinding oneself to relevant data, but it is very much the case that "without a good theory there is no way to tell fundamental facts from irrelevant ones" (Bela Julesz, 1995, p. 11.)

A. F. Chalmers (1976) discusses at length what he calls the theory-dependence of observation. He gives the example of measuring the weights of a variety of human earlobes, and carefully recording and characterizing them.

---

[6] This is read as "y is a function of a and b." That is, the value of y can be predicted if we know the values of a and b. In this usage, y is the dependent variable, or outcome measure and a, b, c, etc. are the independent variables that were manipulated in the experiment.

Would these observations be of any scientific value? No—unless some theory had been proposed that made them relevant, such as a theory proposing some reason for a relationship between earlobe size and incidence of cancer.

Finally, theories (and models), even if ultimately unsatisfactory, provide a means for organizing data. Note the powerful effect of organization on memory, as illustrated in the *PsychMate 2.6: Organization in Memory as an Aid to Recall*. Good theories thus aid memory.

Models

Models represent another class of explanatory device. If you think of the everyday uses of the term *model*, you will capture much of what scientific models are about. A scale model of a car, airplane, or other object is a smaller version that is intended to be like the real thing in some ways. A model airplane may not have a working engine but does have the same shape as the real thing. Such models can be quite useful. The Wright brothers used a crude wind-tunnel to test the lift of various types of airplane wings, using scale models of those wings. Thus, they could fairly easily test many different designs without needing to make full-size versions of them. That type of testing is still used by engineers for airplanes, cars, and hulls of boats (though mathematical, computerized modeling has begun to replace physical modeling).

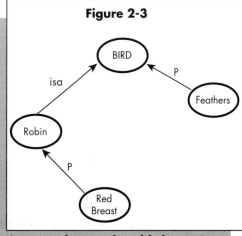

Figure 2-3

A portion of a network model of semantic memory.

The essence of a model, then, is to capture some important aspect of a situation. But unlike theories, which are intended to be statements of fact (though test may prove them otherwise), models are analogies. They act in an "as if" manner. One does not ask of a model, "Is it true?" Rather, one asks of a model, "Is it useful?" A few examples from psychological research will clarify the idea of a model.

Allan Collins and M. Ross Quillian (1969) developed a network model of semantic memory, or memory for basic knowledge about the world. Their model had nodes or location, with links between some nodes. Figure 2-3 shows a part of such a network. In that figure, nodes are the rectangles with the links represented by lines connecting them. Note that there are two types of links: *isa* links and property links. Isa links indicate category membership. For example, "A robin is a bird," is represented by the nodes for "robin" and "bird" and their connected isa link. Property (P) links denote such things as "A bird has feathers." In their model, nodes can become activated. For example, if you hear the word "bird," the bird node becomes activated. Activation then spreads to other nodes connected to the activated node. (See *PsychMate 2.1: Lexical Decisions.*)

This network model has been tested by a number of experiments that have shown systematic differences in reaction time for sentence verification. In a sentence-verification task, subjects are asked to indicate as quickly as possible whether a sentence they see is true or false. If asked to verify the sentence, "A robin is a bird," the model suggests that you seek a link between robin and bird. If asked to verify the sentence, "A robin has feathers," you would need to find a link from robin to bird, and then from bird to feathers. Indeed, tests routinely find that it is faster to verify "A robin is a bird" than "A robin has feathers."

Note that this model has been elaborated by many researchers, and I will not review that literature here. Any cognitive psychology textbook will discuss these models, including John Anderson's ACT model and its subsequent development. Network models of semantic memory have proven to be quite powerful and useful in studying human memory. But note their essentially "as if" flavor—no one is suggesting that memories are really stored in point locations (nodes) with direct connections (links). However specific memories are stored, it does not appear to be in point locations (Karl Lashley, 1960). But the notion of links of some kind between memory representations is neurologically quite plausible, as is the further idea that the links can vary in strength (Donald O. Hebb, 1949). While the models do not assume a specific nature of what *activation* may mean, it is neurologically plausible that it involves literal activation (increased firing rates) in sets of neurons.

Another example of a model in psychology is the model of sentence-picture comparison developed by Herbert Clark and William Chase (1972), which is discussed in *PsychMate 2.4: Sentence-Picture Comparison.* The model of semantic memory sketched previously is a relatively informal model. It predicts differences in reaction times in sentence verification, for example, but does not predict exact values. Formal models are often purely mathematical in nature, especially in more mature, physiologically grounded areas such as perception, where the fit between predicted data and actual data can be marvelously close. This difference between formal, mathematized models and informal, qualitative models parallels the difference between (quantitative) laws and (qualitative) effects. But there is here, also, a continuum, rather than a dichotomy—there are intermediate levels between informal models and mathematically specified models. Douglas Hintzman (1991) provides a useful discussion of formal models and their role in psychology.

Logic and Science

> He did not arrive at this conclusion by the decent process of quiet, logical deduction, nor yet by the blinding flash of glorious intuition, but by the shoddy, untidy process halfway between the two by which one usually gets to know things.
>
> Margery Allingham (1964, p. 129).
> *Death of a ghost.* London: Heinemann

Deduction and Induction

Let me begin with common definitions of deduction and induction — two methods of logic. *Deductive logic* is reasoning *from the general to the particular*, while *inductive logic* is reasoning from the *particular to the general*. If that doesn't move you with the thrill of understanding, don't feel alone. A few examples will make the matter clear.

Consider a simple example of deductive logic:

All Greeks are mortal.
Socrates is a Greek.
Therefore, Socrates is mortal.

This *syllogism* (one form of deductive argument) was first used by Aristotle (384-322 BCE) in his *Prior Analytics.*[7] It is a valid argument — if the premises (the first two statements) are true, then the conclusion *must* be true.[8] We literally need no further investigation to know that Socrates is mortal, if we accept the premises. Formal logical arguments, including mathematical ones, can thus be said to *prove* their conclusions. If the premises are true, whether in

---

[7] Before the Common Era. This is the standard terminology of modern history, which designates dates from the year 1 as CE. The early fathers of the Christian church, working in the 5th century to determine the dates of biblical events certainly erred, and their designation of the year 1 (note their Roman ignorance of zero!), based on historical events such as the death of Herod, is at least four years off from the year of Jesus' birth (see Stephen Jay Gould, 1999). It should be noted that at the time of those calculations, the church was using a system based on the founding of Rome. The year 1 AUC (*ab urbe condita* — from the founding of the city) corresponds to 753 BCE. Other calendars date from the beginning of the world (Byzantine-5508 BCE and Jewish-3761 BCE), and the Hegira (Moslem — the year of Muhammed's flight from Mecca-622 CE). Take your pick.

[8] Note two other uses of the term "valid" in this book. A logical *argument* is valid if the premises compel belief in the conclusion. A *measurement* is valid if it measures what it claims to measure (Chapter 3). An *experiment* is valid if there are no experimental confounds (see Chapter 5).

a simple syllogism such as this one or in a more complex logical argument involving many premises and their relations, then the conclusion is *compelled*— it cannot *not* be true. There is a fly in the ointment, however, since the conclusion is proven *if and only if* the premises are true.[9] That point is elaborated later in this chapter. Perhaps it is clearer to write the syllogism as:

> *If* all Greeks are mortal,
> and *if* Socrates is a Greek,
> then Socrates is mortal.

Note that the deductive argument proceeds from a *general* statement— *all* Greeks are mortal—and proceeds to a conclusion about a *particular* Greek—*Socrates* is mortal.

Inductive logic proceeds in a different way. Suppose I observe a number of particular instances of a phenomenon—the classical example is observing one white swan after another. If I observe enough of them, then I will begin to suspect that perhaps all swans are white. I will reason from the *particular* (swan A and swan B and swan C are all white) to the *general* (All swans are white). But there is a very real problem for inductive logic, which is pretty obvious—even a large number of cases, each showing the same particular finding, cannot *prove* that the generalization based on them is true. That logical problem lies at the very heart of the use of logic in science—I will return to this shortly.

White swans are all very fine and good for a philosopher, but a scientist is more interested in the replicability of a relationship among variables. For example:

> I put a cup of water in the freezer, and it became ice.
> I repeated this several times.
> Water freezes when put in my freezer.

Water does freeze when placed in my freezer. But suppose the power fails, and my freezer thaws. Does this failure of the theory *prove* that it is wrong? Hardly. There are *boundary conditions* to the demonstration of any phenomenon. Exploring those, or showing that a well-known effect fails under a particular restraint does not prove that effect invalid but rather suggests more variables to explore in future research.

In this regard, Rom Harré (1960) contrasts what he calls the "disconfirming instance" in logic and science. "In logic a single contrary instance is sufficient to falsify the generalization from which it was derived [one black swan falsifies the generalization that all swans are white], but in science the appearance of a

---

[9] If-and-only-if is sometimes abbreviated as *iff*.

contrary instance is not a signal for a rejection of the generalization but rather for more intensive investigation into the [boundary] conditions under which the generalization holds. Scientists are the misers of logic who throw nothing away but rather try to find how to fit the restricted knowledge of their predecessors into the wider knowledge they themselves possess" (pp. 156-157).

We certainly do a lot of inductive reasoning in daily life—we have to. If you have enjoyed several books by the same author, you are likely to watch for his or her new one. If you have tried Brussels sprouts repeatedly and found them inedible, you may decide not to give them another chance.

Returning to the classical syllogism that all Greeks are mortal, note that the premise is itself derived from induction—the observation of instances. But no matter how many Greeks die, that does not establish it as absolute fact that they have to keep doing so (though, unfortunately, it looks like the statement generalizes beyond just Greeks). Not all Greeks have died, and so we cannot have absolute certainty that there isn't a really old one hiding somewhere. But how old would she have to be to challenge the generalization? In fact, induction is the way we establish the premises from which deduction can flow. To the degree that our induction is correct, our deduction (if it is valid) will also be correct.

W. I. B. Beveridge (1957), in his marvelous book, *The Art of Scientific Investigation*, sums up the problems of deduction and induction for science this way: "Since deduction consists of applying general principles to further instances, it cannot lead us to new generalizations and so cannot give rise to major advances in science. On the other hand, the inductive process is at the same time less trustworthy but more productive. It is more productive because it is a means of arriving at new theories, but is less trustworthy because starting from a collection of facts we can often infer several possible theories...In biology every phenomenon and circumstance is so complex and so poorly understood that premises are not clear-cut and hence reasoning is unreliable." (Beveridge, 1957, p. 85). In psychology, too, I might add.

Francis Bacon, who tried hard to codify science and make the scientific enterprise self-consciously *scientific* remarked that "Men are rather beholden ... generally to chance, or anything else, than to logic, for the invention of arts and sciences" (cited in Beveridge, 1957).[10]

---

[10] If any readers are bothered by the use of "men," let them take it in the sense of "all men, male or female."

Logic and Scientific Discovery

> Our conception of science has been given us by teachers and authors who have presented science in logical arrangement and that is seldom the way in which knowledge is actually acquired.
>
> Beveridge, 1957, p. 82.

The presentation of a formal mathematical proof proceeds from premises to conclusion by a series of formal logical steps. Scientific thinking requires the application of deductive logic. There must be a valid series of arguments connecting theory to data (does the theory really predict this outcome of an experiment?). However, as Beveridge (1957) noted, "Reason seldom can progress far from the facts without going astray" (p. 82). The *presentation* of a scientific result usually involves, in part, a demonstration of why the data are logically predicted by the theory. But, in fact, scientific advances are seldom made by reasoning from first principles. Even advances in mathematics, where there is a precise chain of logical reasoning from premises to conclusion, are usually made by an intuitive leap beyond what is known (a hypothesis, or little-t theory), and then an effort to fill in the gap logically. G. K. Chesterton, a British writer of the early 20th century, who is still worth reading, noted that "You can only find truth with logic if you already found truth without it" (1905/1963, p. 104).[11] Chesterton was speaking of theological truth, rather than mathematics or science, but the point holds just the same. Logic helps confirm discoveries; it does not make them. We find truth by conjecture and test. You must make an inspired leap and then hope you were right!

---

[11] Chesterton's Father Brown mysteries are among the best of that genre, though he was far more than a mystery writer.

[12] While Arthur Conan Doyle's Sherlock Holmes stories reflect the assumptions and prejudices of their age, they are among the marvels of English literature. The student who has not read them has weakened his or her education. Your library or bookstore doubtless has one of the many collections of the stories and novels.

Testing theories

It is a capital mistake to theorize before one has the data. Insensibly one begins to twist facts to fit theories, instead of theories to fit facts (1928, p. 7).

A Scandal in Bohemia
The Adventures of Sherlock Holmes[12]

How can we test theories and hypotheses? A straightforward approach seems to be to seek confirmation of predictions from the theory. If the theory predicts certain results of experiments, and the experiments come out as predicted, does that not confirm the theory? Yes, but don't be too impressed. Consider the claim that all swans are white. Every white swan you find is a confirming instance. But so, too, is every green telephone and every purple chair! The latter may seem rather counter-intuitive, but follows from the fact that, if every swan is white, then everything that is non-white must be a non-swan. If you find something green, and then discover that it is not a swan, it confirms the prediction based on the claim that all swans are white. Look around you at all the non-white objects you can see. Probably none of them are swans. But does that really make you more certain that all swans are white? Unfortunately, a large pile of confirming instances cannot compel belief in a claim.

Another difficulty is that alternative theories may make similar predictions in which "confirming" the prediction lends added credence to a whole group of theories.

Unfortunately, there is a pervasive tendency of humans to seek confirmation rather than falsification (which is treated below), whether in science or everyday life. Research has repeatedly demonstrated this *confirmation bias* (see Amos Tverksy & Daniel Kahneman, 1972). A well-known example is the Wason four-card problem, shown in Figure 2-4. You should try to solve this problem before continuing.

Peter Wason and Phillip Johnson-Laird (1970) showed that subjects will usually choose to turn over the E and the 4, even though the 4 tells them nothing.[13] Mike Oaksford and Nick Chater (1994) confirmed this finding, though they offer a different analysis of the reason for the error. It has also

---

[13] The correct solution is to turn over the E and the 7. If the E does not have an even number on the other side, the rule cannot be true. If the 7 has a vowel on the other side, that would also disconfirm the rule. It doesn't matter what is on the back of the K or the 4—the rule says nothing about what is on the other side of a consonant or of an even number.

Figure 2-4

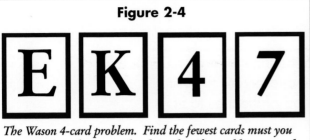

The Wason 4-card problem. Find the fewest cards must you turn over in order to test the claim that if a card has a vowel on one side, it must have an even number on the other side.

been shown that people are far less prone to this confirmation bias when the task is less abstract. You should try this version taken from Robert Griggs and James Cox (1982): Imagine that you are a policeman charged with enforcing the 21-year-old minimum age for drinking alcoholic beverages. Four persons are sitting at a table. You know the following: Betty is drinking beer, Al is drinking cola, Jane is 16 years old, and Bob is 22 years old. From which two do you need to seek more information in order to decide whether the law is being broken? The correct answer appears at the bottom of the next page.

Falsification

Karl Popper (see Popper, 1935/1959, for an overview of his work) pointed out that the basic problem of induction is also the basic problem of science—you can pile up observations of white swans *ad nauseum*[14] without proving that all swans are white, and you can pile up facts that support your theory *ad nauseum* without proving that your theory is correct. He then argued that the proper emphasis of science in evaluating theories should be on efforts to *falsify* theories, rather than confirm them.[15] A single black swan can, after all, prove that *not* all swans are white. A single failure of a prediction from a theory thus can prove the theory wrong (though, as will be noted shortly, this is a severe overstatement).[16]

> Those among us who are unwilling to expose their ideas to the hazard of refutation do not take part in the scientific game.
>
> Karl Popper (1935/1959), p. 280.

I must note a problem for falsifiability, already hinted at in the discussion of inductive logic. This problem was described independently by two

---

14 *Ad nauseum:* [L.] Until you are sick.

15 You may be familiar with a more common meaning of the word *falsify*, which is to make something false by altering it, An example would be, "She falsified the document." As used in the context of testing scientific theories, to falsify is to show that a scientific claim is false.

16 You will likely have encountered the phrase "The exception proves the rule." No—the exception *falsifies* the rule. But the phrase actually comes from an earlier, now archaic meaning of "prove," namely "test." An exception does, indeed, test the truth of a rule. That older meaning of "prove" also survives in the phrase, "The proof of the pudding is in the eating." Yes—the only way to test ("prove") the pudding is to eat some.

philosophers, Pierre Duhem (1962) and Willard Quine (1961), and is sometimes styled the Duhem/Quine thesis. Popper's formulation is quite simple—a theory predicts certain experimental outcomes. If a prediction is falsified (if an experiment produces a different outcome than expected) then the theory must be wrong. But this won't quite do. Should a theory be abandoned because a single predicted experimental result fails? Hardly. Duhem and Quine pointed out that it is not the case that a theory predicts certain data. Rather it the theory *plus its accompanying auxiliaries and mappings* that predict the data. By *mappings*, I mean the mapping of theory to data by logic. There may be a flaw in the logic tying theory to data that is not apparent. Perhaps the theory doesn't really predict these data at all. In the case of a complex theory and predictions logically derived from it, this can be a very real possibility. *Auxiliaries* are the minutiae of the experiment—the details of how the experiment is carried out. Note that in most experiments there are a large number of auxiliary assumptions concerning how instruments (including the human senses) work. It is not always clear, when a predicted result does not arise, whether the theory is wrong or whether the experiment failed for some unrelated reason. If the specifics of the experiment (e.g., size of stimuli or timing of presentation) move it outside the boundary conditions for the phenomenon, then the expected result may not appear, even though the theory is sound. Thus, if we do not get the expected data, either the theory is wrong *or* the mappings are wrong *or* the auxiliaries are wrong. Thus falsification is not as simple as it first seems. A. F. Chalmers (1976) presents the logic of falsification and its difficulties particularly well.

Historically, the issues of falsification and confirmation have been framed by philosophers, and their examples often are of no interest to scientists. As a scientist, you will probably never be concerned with propositions as simple as "All swans are white." More recently, there have been interesting studies of what is styled the "cognitive psychology of science." One of the traditional areas of cognitive psychology has been problem solving, and science is certainly a variety of problem solving. Clifford Mynatt, Michael Doherty, and Ryan Tweney (1978) reported a study in which their subjects (advanced under-graduates, graduate students, and working scientists) tried to explain the motion of particles in a computerized "universe." They conducted experiments by "firing particles" at objects on a computer screen and recording the results. They could spend up to 10 hours experimenting to try to find the laws of motion of the particles in this artificial universe. Tweney (1998) describes the

In Griggs and Cox' study using undergraduates in Florida, who were familiar with the 21-year-old drinking age, 74 percent correctly chose the beer drinker (Betty) and the 16-year-old (Jane).

successful subjects as those who "were flexible in their use of both confirming and *disconfirming* [falsifying] information....Our subjects seemed to do best if they ignored disconfirming evidence early in the task, and made deliberate efforts to disconfirm their hypotheses only after they had a good deal of confirmatory evidence in hand. This procedure seemed to protect weak hypotheses from premature falsification, allowing opportunity for revision and refinement" (p. 151).

Tweney (1998) continued: "Note that the confirm-early/disconfirm-late strategy explains what has sometimes been a puzzling aspect of scientific thinking, namely, the dogged persistence of some scientists, even in the fact of evidence against their ideas. To be sure, the heuristic is not foolproof; dogged persistence in the face of disconfirmation is sometimes a bad idea. But sometimes it is just what the problem demands" (p. 151).

Dmitri Mendeleev, a Russian chemist, wrote out the properties of the then-known 60 elements on cards and tried to find an arrangement that would make sense. That pattern became the basis for the modern periodic table of the elements. At the time, Mendeleev realized that there were gaps in his scheme, but he thought (correctly) that they corresponded to as-yet-undiscovered elements. Within 20 years, several of those gaps were filled. But his scheme had a problem—several of the atomic weights did not fit his table. Mendeleev apparently decided that if the data contradicted his theory, then so much for the data! Later, more accurate measurement of the atomic weights showed them to fit exactly as predicted by his theory. It should be noted, though, that Mendeleev had good reason to suppose that the estimates of the atomic weights were crude and likely to have some error.

A related issue for science, and one that may have a larger effect on day-to-day scientific work, is that of pet theories and hypotheses. Scientists get attached to their ideas, just like other people do. Sometimes they refuse to give up an idea even when the facts suggest that they should. But is that altogether bad? Ian Mitroff (1974) reported on the results of interviews with a group of 42 lunar scientists (this was only a few years after samples of lunar rocks had become available for direct study). Among other things, Mitroff was interested in whether these scientists saw themselves as purely objective in pursuing their work.

Of the 42 scientists Mitroff (1974) interviewed, every one indicated that he [sic] thought the notion of the purely objective, uncommitted scientist was naive. To the credit of these scientists, they not only freely acknowledged their biases but argued that in order to be a good scientist, one had to have biases. The best scientist, they said, not only has points of view but defends them with gusto. Their concept of a scientist did not imply that he would cheat by making up experimental data or falsifying it; rather he does everything in his power to defend his pet hypotheses against early and perhaps unwarranted death caused by the introduction of fluke data. The objectivity of science is a result, the scientists said, not of each individual scientist's unbiased outlook, but of the scientific community's examination and debate over the merits of respective biases (p. 65).

I am convinced that interviews with scientists in any other branch of science would yield the same result. So when do you say, "Enough is enough," and abandon your pet theory? In the final analysis, you must be the judge. But it is not uncommon for theories eventually accepted by the scientific community to initially be rejected because they do not seem to fit. They are not within the current *paradigm*, to use a term that will be formally introduced later in this chapter. An example is the proposal by Alfred Wegener in 1912 that the land mass of the earth had begun as a single continent that broke apart and drifted into the current positions of the continents. There was some evidence to back the idea such as similar fossilized plants and animals from South America and Africa. Lacking any mechanism that could account for the drift, however, his theory was widely ignored—it just didn't fit with what was known. Since then, of course, the theory of plate tectonics has become well-established and is supported by abundant evidence, including measurements of the speed of that drift.

Another example comes from psychology and the work of John Garcia and Robert Koelling (1966) on learned taste aversion (this is also discussed in Chapter 5). They showed that rats could easily learn to avoid a novel taste if it was followed—even several hours later—by sickness, but could not learn to avoid a novel taste followed by a painful shock. The prevailing point of view in psychology simply didn't permit such a finding, and the work was rejected out of hand by the journal editors. It is now a well-accepted finding, and led the way to an understanding of the importance of biological preparedness for learning certain kinds of associations. Note something, though. Despite the fact that each of these ideas was rejected, the scientists who rejected them were willing to rehear the case when more or better evidence was available. The logic has to work this way: If you want me to believe your claim (especially if it flies in the face of what I think are the facts), then it is up to you to make your case. Until you do, I will reject your claim. I do not have to show that you are wrong. You have to show that you are right.

Falsifiability, existence claims, and the burden of proof:

I need also to point out one more limitation to falsifiability, and that concerns the falsifiability of *existence* claims. An existence claim is simply a claim that something exists. For example, suppose that someone claims that there really are such things as unicorns—little white horses, each with a single, spiral horn growing from its forehead. An existence proof is easy—all they have to do is produce a unicorn.[17] (Obviously, it would need to stand up to scrutiny—no tell-tale signs of surgery or SuperGlue™.) If the proponents can produce a unicorn under conditions that preclude cheating, then I would be inclined to join them in their belief. But note that the person making the existence claim—here, that unicorns exist—has the absolute burden of proof. Until they show me a unicorn, I can reasonably refuse to accept their claim. One reason for the burden of proof falling on the claimant is that I cannot prove that there are no unicorns. There is no way logically to prove the non-existence of *anything*. I can search high and low for unicorns, but my failure to find them does not prove they do not exist. There may always be one on some distant planet that I have not yet explored. Or perhaps the unicorns scatter when I look here, and then return when I look over there. As unlikely as I think that is, I cannot disprove it.

A further note on confirmation and falsification

It may occur to you that confirmation and falsification are not necessarily different acts. If I show that my theory makes a certain prediction and test that prediction, I am giving my theory a chance to be falsified. If the data are as predicted, my theory has passed a test of falsification, lending at least a small degree of credibility to my theory.

Summary

So, if we cannot *prove* with evidence, if no amount of confirmation can absolutely compel belief in a theory, if falsification does not provide absolute disproof, and if the history of science is littered with failed theories, why should we continue with this rather grubby enterprise? Lewis Wolpert (1992), an embryologist who writes frequently on general issues of science, wrote, "Science is progressing in that the truth is being approached, closer and closer, but perhaps never attained with certainty. But very close approximation can be a great achievement and is infinitely better than error or ignorance" (p. 100).

---

[17] Some years ago, the Barnum and Bailey circus advertised that they had a real unicorn in their show. On examining pictures of the creature, it was clear that they had grafted a horn on a goat. Even if the horn were real, that's no unicorn. A goat! Bah!

[18] A theory might not be falsifiable for purely practical reasons, but still be properly scientific. When Einstein proposed his general theory of relativity, it made predictions that could not be tested because the equipment needed did not yet exist—the theory was still scientific. Another example would be a prediction in developmental psychology that childhood sexual abuse puts a person at risk for becoming a psychopath. Such a theory is testable and thus logically falsifiable, but it would be unethical in the extreme to conduct the relevant experiment and randomly assign children to be abused or not. A lack of a *practical* means to test a theory does not remove it from the realm of science.

Popper on what it means for a theory to be scientific

Karl Popper also argued that falsifiability is a necessary condition for any theory to be taken seriously as science, saying that there must be some experimental outcome that would cause one to abandon the theory.[18] Obviously, if a theory is true, it cannot be falsified, but Popper meant that a theory must be *potentially* falsifiable. If it is not, then the theory is simply not a part of science. It might be true, but the methods of science cannot help us determine whether or not it is true.

To illustrate, consider a theory that states that intercessory prayer is effective.[19] One could test such a theory by randomly assigning sick people to be prayed for or not, and see whether those prayed for have a better outcome (for example, a shorter recovery period or lower death rate) than those not prayed for. But suppose that there was no difference in the outcomes. Would persons whose religious belief includes a belief in the efficacy of intercessory prayer change their belief? That is, would they abandon belief in intercessory prayer? Probably not. They might simply argue that their god did not see fit to participate in the experiment. Thus, no negative outcome could reasonably cause one to abandon the theory. Does that prove that intercessory prayer is not effective? Certainly not. It simply is not a part of the reality that can be examined scientifically. If a theory is not falsifiable, then science has nothing to say about whether or not it is correct. Belief in such theory is a matter of faith. That faith may or may not be justified, but it is beyond the scope of science.[20]

Statistical generalization

Let us return to the problem of induction—that no number of correctly predicted outcomes can furnish proof of a theory.

First, let's note a probabilistic assertion—not "All swans are white," but rather "70% of swans are white." Here we have enormously better ground than traditional logic provides us. Suppose I test you in an experiment on the

---

[19] "Lord, won't you buy me a Mercedes Benz?" (Janis Joplin, Mercedes Benz, from the album *Pearl*, 1971). *Intercessory prayer* is prayer in which one asks a god to intercede on behalf of oneself or someone else. Praying that you win the lottery, or that a sick friend recovers, are each examples of intercessory prayer.

[20] Despite this, the federal government has spent $2.3 million on studies of intercessory prayer in medical cases. Benedict Carey (2004) reported on the controversy, and quoted Rev. Raymond Lawrence, Jr., a director of pastoral care at New York-Presbyterian Hospital/Columbia University Medical Center: "There's no way to put God to the test, and that's exactly what you're doing when you design a study to see if God answers your prayers. This whole exercise cheapens religion, and promotes an infantile theology that God is out there ready to miraculously defy the laws of nature in answer to a prayer." It should be noted that the published research in this area is generally severely flawed. Many report so many different measurements of the patients that the statistical likelihood of finding *some* difference becomes a near certainty, even if no effect occurs.

relation between reaction time (RT) and the number of stimuli or responses from which to choose, and I discover that you have shorter RTs with fewer choices.[21] The results would tell me something about you, at least within the limited context of this experiment. If I then test another person and find that she, too, is faster with fewer choices, I would know something about her. If I keep testing people, and find the same relationship every time, I am likely to be tempted to make a *general* claim — "RT is faster when there are fewer choices"—based on the *particular* data of each subject. If I find a pattern repeated across individual cases (humans, dogs, or rock formations), I will begin to suspect that the general statement about all cases is also true.

In doing an experiment on RT as a function of the number of choices, I am likely to find at least one subject who gives me very different data—faster RTs with *more* choices. What am I to make of this occasional failure of the theory? In a later chapter, I discuss the "screw-you effect," Joseph Masling's (1966) term for the situation in which a subject simply makes it her business to mess up the experiment. The discussion of deletion of data in Chapter 6 contains an account of the subject from hell. Humans are humans, and have a variety of motivations in any study. Would I regard a single failure in this study, over a large number of subjects, as falsifying my claim? Hardly.

Another limitation can be easily accommodated. Suppose that I get a sample of swans and find that 96% are white. I ask around and review the literature and find that others who are equally obsessed with the color of swans report values of 94%, 98%, and so on. I could then surely be justified in claiming that "about 96% of swans are white." (Statistically, I could use the various estimates to get a highly accurate range and report that it is highly likely that between 94% and 98% of swans are white.) Thus, I can make a rigorous statement about the color of swans that is probably very close to the "real" percentage. If I can't claim exact knowledge, I am still certainly better off than if I simply said the theory, "All swans are white," has been falsified.

---

[21] By the way, this would be very easy to set up using the PsychMate Experiment Authoring Kit. See *PsychMate Appendix A*.

Philosophy of science

> There is a vast literature dealing with the philosophy of science and the logic of scientific method. Whether one takes up this study depends upon one's personal inclinations, but, generally speaking, it will be of little value in doing research
>
> Beveridge, 1957, p. 7.

The following quote is from embryologist and science commentator Lewis Wolpert (1997) as part of a debate with Anthony Gottlieb, executive editor of *The Economist*. It originally appeared in the February 1997 edition of *Prospect* and was excerpted in *The Chronicle of Higher Education* (Feb. 28, 1997).

I will not spare your convictions—this century you philosophers have contributed nothing to the understanding of science. Certainly nothing that is of the slightest relevance to practicing scientists such as myself.

This is a great pity as science is the foremost achievement of our culture. It is the best way to understand the world. But it involves ideas that are "unnatural" in that they do not conform to common sense. Just consider the Earth going round the Sun or the big bang. I looked to the philosophers of science for illumination as to what, for example, is meant by a scientific understanding and why science works. Alas, I found nothing but obscurity and lack of interest. They seem to be interested in philosophy, not science.

I would like help with problems such as the nature and limits of reductionism (according to which scientific explanation proceeds by reference to ever more basic entities, such as DNA in the case of genes) and how to distinguish science from non-science. But philosophers of science seem to be much more interested in problems related to realism: is there a real world out there that we scientists study? How boring. I am a crass and naïve, even militant realist, which I know I could not defend philosophically, but for my science it is totally irrelevant. Practicing scientists have no interest in the philosophy of science and, in Gerald Holton's phrase, view philosophy as a "debilitating befuddlement." (p. A19)

That having been said, any student of science should be acquainted with Thomas Kuhn's (1970) highly influential work, *The Structure of Scientific Revolutions,* which is discussed in the following paragraphs. Rom Harré's (1960) *An Introduction to the Logic of the Sciences* contains an excellent discussion of that topic in more detail than this short book can include.

It should be noted that the logic of science discussed previously is very much a part of the philosophy of science, so I am not as dismissive of it as the two quotes may suggest.

Because of its wide impact, you should have some acquaintance with Kuhn's (1970) work. It is one of the most widely read (and widely misinterpreted) works in the philosophy of science. Kuhn's broad argument is that scientists generally work within a prevailing *paradigm*—a conceptual framework and body of assumptions that guides their scientific work. An example is the Ptolemaic paradigm in astronomy, which operated under the assumption that the earth is motionless at the center of the universe (the *geocentric* or "earth-centered" view). Note that casual observation seems to clearly show the sun and stars moving relative to earth. Indeed, we still speak of the sun "rising" and "setting!"

Kuhn saw two kinds of science: normal science and revolutionary science. *Normal science* is that accumulation of knowledge that occurs within a paradigm. By far the greatest amount of science is normal science. *Revolutionary science* occurs when there is a paradigm shift forced by the accumulation of so many discrepancies that the old paradigm loses credibility. An example of a paradigm shift was the "Copernican revolution." Early scientists, trying to understand the movements they observed in the "heavens," developed elaborate explanations for some other wise discrepant phenomena (such as the retrograde motion of the planets). In 1530, Nicolas Copernicus completed *De Revolutionibus*, in which he proposed a *heliocentric* (or "sun-centered") theory, which had the sun unmoving at the center of the solar system. Though not without its own problems (Copernicus assumed circular orbits, which did not match the known observations very well), the new theory challenged the old. Retrograde motion (the fact that the planets at times seem to move "backwards") required some elaborate theorizing to fit it into the geocentric view but was easily understood within the new paradigm. After Johannes Kepler amended the theory in 1609 to use elliptical orbits, the heliocentric theory simply accounted for the data far better than the geocentric theory. There was much religious resistance to Copernicus' theory. As noted later in this chapter, Galileo, who had published in favor of the theory, recanted when shown the instruments of torture in 1633. But among scientists, the new theory quickly replaced the old.

Kuhn argued that scientists treat discrepant data as errors or irrelevancies when they cannot be made to fit the prevailing paradigm. What counts as a fact to be explained scientifically is partly determined by the prevailing paradigm.

There has been much argument over the validity of Kuhn's argument. Some of the argument has centered around his rather loose use of the core term, *paradigm*. Others dispute the general theme that paradigms shift only by revolutionary change. A middle ground is possible and, I think, likely to be true. Paradigms (at several levels) do guide our research and thinking, and our interpretation of what counts as a fact. Paradigm shifts may not always have the high drama of revolution, but there clearly have been, and continue to be, relatively sudden shifts in how scientists in certain areas do their business.

Are there paradigms in psychology? The best candidate is Behaviorism, surely. John B. Watson first proposed Behaviorism in 1913, in a famous article in the *Psychological Review*. He noted a problem with the prevailing psychology of his day—its strong reliance on trained introspection as a method of scientific inquiry. Trained introspection involved presenting some stimulus to an Observer, who tried to report the resulting contents of consciousness in a strictly bottom-up fashion, rather than relying on higher-level interpretation. From these data, psychologists hoped to work out the elemental feelings, perception, thoughts, etc., that make up consciousness. But Watson noted a severe problem. When people disagreed about their introspections, there was no way to resolve the matter. The problem, Watson argued, was that introspection is fundamentally private—I cannot experience the contents of your consciousness, and, thus, I have no way to independently verify your experience. He argued that we must restrict ourselves to the study of behaviors—movements—because they are subject to direct verification—they are "public" data. Within a decade or so trained introspection was largely relegated to the dustbin of history. Psychologists then spent a half century or so working within that new paradigm. Note one way in which that changed the contents of psychological research. The study of learning had certainly existed prior to Watson's Behaviorism, but Watson put the study of learning at the center of psychology. The goal of psychology, Watson argued, was to determine the circumstances under which a stimulus comes to control a response. The general answer is that most responses to stimuli are learned, and learning thus took center stage in the concerns of psychologists. Thus, a change in paradigm led to a change in research emphasis.

Behaviorism, however, came under increasing fire, and, by the 1960s, its own basic assumptions were being seriously challenged. One assumption was that the laws of learning are general—that is, the same laws of learning apply to all types of learning. One law of learning, well established empirically, is that reward and punishment are less effective if there is a delay between the behavior and its consequence. That can certainly be shown in rats learning to bar-press for pellets of food, or almost any organism learning almost anything it can learn.[22] Note that this assumption is embodied in the title of the Behaviorist B. F. Skinner's first book, *The Behavior of Organisms* (1938), in which he reported mostly experiments with white rats learning to press a steel bar for pellets of food. This issue is discussed in Chapter 5 in the section on external validity.

Some claim that cognitive psychology provides a new paradigm for psychology, but I find that hard to accept. Abram Amsel (1989) put the point nicely: "Cognitive psychology does not refer to a coherent theory but to areas of research—attention, perception, language, memory, imagery, and problem solving—that have expanded rapidly as the advent of small computers made them easier to study" (p. 51). In my view, it may be asking too much for an overall paradigm that will guide research in areas as disparate as those covered by cognitive psychology, let alone the whole of psychology. Add to Amsel's list the additional areas of personality, development (in all its aspects), skills testing, clinical diagnosis, and physiological psychology (to name only a few), and you may begin to see why I don't expect a general paradigm for psychology. We may be too many disciplines to ever have an effective umbrella theory of paradigmatic dimensions. Certainly, though, we have local paradigms that guide research within many of these areas.

T. X. Barber (1975) wrote that "the prevailing paradigm determines not only what questions are asked but also what kinds of data are considered relevant and how the data will be gathered, analyzed, interpreted, and related to theoretical concepts" (p. 5). Paradigms can thus shape our research in ways that we are not (at the time) completely aware of. Research within a paradigm may well be fruitful and important, and we probably cannot anticipate when our research will turn out to challenge a current paradigm. Barber suggests that awareness is the best answer. Know the history of your science and you will see where your research fits into a larger pattern. John Ziman (1968) put it nicely: "The major task, and the corresponding problem of scientific education is easily defined; it must teach the consensus without turning it into an orthodoxy. The student must become perfectly familiar and at ease with the current state of knowledge and yet ready to overthrown it from within" (p. 69).

Some critics of science, after a cursory reading of Kuhn (1970), have taken the existence of revolutionary science to mean that normal science is a waste

---

[22] The assumption of the generality of the laws of learning does not, of course, imply that all organisms can learn the same things. You cannot teach a pig to sing. It does nothing for music and it annoys the pig. But if a pig could learn to sing, according to this assumption, it would do so by the same laws that govern all types of learning.

since it may become irrelevant following a paradigm shift (as the geocentric theory in astronomy did). But the argument is wrong. When we reject a paradigm, we should not assume that we have rendered every observation made under that paradigm irrelevant. Nor would we imagine that there will be no need for any of the previous constructs. As an example, in psychology, the widespread abandonment of Behaviorism did not lead to an abandonment of research on operant conditioning or the forsaking of learning as a central issue for psychology. Even though the interpretation of operant conditioning has changed, the facts of conditioning remain. I return to the criticisms of science in the last section of this chapter.

Reductionism and Levels of Explanation

Reductionism refers to the goal, assumed by some to be the major goal of science, to explain every phenomenon in terms of the "deeper" mechanisms of a more-basic science. The argument for reductionism goes something like this: "After all, mind (or consciousness) clearly emanates from brain, so we should seek explanations for mental phenomena in the underlying biology. Biological phenomena, of course, arise from the complex chemical organization of cells, cell membranes, etc., so we should seek explanations for biological phenomena in the underlying chemistry. Chemical phenomena arise from the nature of the atoms and sub-atomic particles that make up the stuff of physics, so we should seek explanations for chemical phenomena in physics."[23]

There are those who argue that a phenomenon is not understood at all until it is reduced to particle physics. At the other end of the spectrum, I know scientists who visibly sneer when they mention reductionism, as if it were a grave moral fault. My own view is that neither argument holds much water. Reductionism is sometimes useful and sometimes not. After a couple of examples, I will argue that the real issue is to determine the appropriate level of analysis and decide whether a phenomenon is best explained at the psychological, biological, chemical, or physical level (or somewhere in between).

First, I present a highly successful example of reductionist thinking — explaining the dark-adaptation curve. You are aware from your own introspection that when you first enter a dimly-lighted room you can see almost nothing. But over time you begin to see more and more by the little light that is available. Is getting used to the dark physics, chemistry, physiology, or psychology? Figure 2-5 shows the psychological measurement of the phenomenon, expressed as the threshold of light (the faintest light that can be

---

[23] I am giving each discipline very short shrift, and over-simplifying dreadfully. In fact, there are levels within each of the four disciplines.

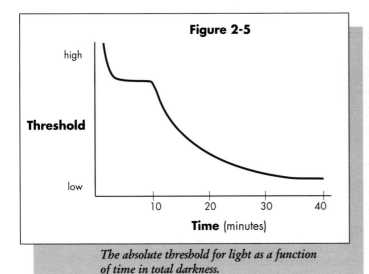

Figure 2-5

high

Threshold

low

10   20   30   40

Time (minutes)

The absolute threshold for light as a function of time in total darkness.

reliably detected) repeatedly measured across time. It has an interesting shape, since it drops to a plateau after about six minutes, then at 10 minutes begins to drop again, with the full adaptation taking about 40 minutes. Can we explain this psychological phenomenon in purely psychological terms? Hardly. In fact, the explanation of this phenomenon leads in a rather elegant reductionist way to the physics of light.

When the two types of cells called rods and cones (from their shapes) were discovered in the vertebrate retina there would have been no clear understanding of why these two types of cells existed except that it was known that cones are less numerous in the eyes of nocturnal animals and more numerous in animals who are principally active during daylight (see Ragnar Granit, 1977, for this history). We can then "explain" the scalloped shape of the dark-adaptation curve by the different properties of rods and cones. Rods take about 40 minutes to reach full adaptation, but when they do, they are far more sensitive than cones. Cones become dark-adapted in only about 10 minutes.

The operations of the rods and cones themselves require an explanation at the level of chemistry. Essentially, light breaks down certain chemicals in the rods and cones, thus making them more likely to start a neural signal. The pigments are continually re-generated within the rods and cones, but that process cannot fully keep up with the rate of breaking down, so the cells become less sensitive to light. In the dark, the regeneration process continues, unopposed by breakdown due to light, and the cells eventually reach their maximum sensitivity.[24]

---

[24] The confirmation of rhodopsin as the photopigment for the scotopic (rod) system for low-illumination vision is an interesting piece of science for a psychologist. The spectral-absorption curve for rhodopsin is obtained by passing lights of varying wavelengths through a solution of rhodopsin and measuring the amount of light absorption. One can also measure the absolute threshold for vision using varying wavelengths of light. When George Wald and his colleagues compared those two curves (after suitable manipulations to express them in the same units), they found a near-perfect fit, confirming rhodopsin as the substance that begins the photochemical process of changing light striking the retina into a neural signal to the brain (Morgan, 1965). (The slight discrepancies in the two curves are known to be due to transmission losses in the fluid media of the human eye.) Wald later received the Nobel Prize in chemistry for this and similar discoveries in color vision. Note that it was the agreement of the absorption spectrum of rhodopsin with the *psychological* data of threshold measurements that confirmed rhodopsin as the "light-catcher" for the rods.

The chemistry of how rhodopsin (and the corresponding chemicals in the cones) is broken down by light resulting in increased firing rates and then regenerated within the cell is now very well understood, though beyond the scope of this discussion. The dark adaptation curve matches the rate of regeneration of those chemicals when they are no longer being broken down by light—the chemicals in the cones regenerate completely after about 10 minutes, but rhodopsin requires about 40 minutes to fully regenerate. The quantum nature of light as revealed by physics makes it possible to measure the relevant aspects of the photochemical process.

So the explanation of the dark-adaptation curve really does rely on a reductionist approach.

Another example of a reductionist argument concerns the issue of whether mental images are really picture-like analogues of direct visual representations, or whether they are built up of propositions (essentially descriptions) that are not themselves visual analogues. That debate was a lively one in the 1970s, but is now largely settled in favor of images as visual analogues. Resolution of that debate, however, required the demonstration that the parts of the brain involved in actual perception are also involved in imagery (LeBihan, et al.; Kosslyn, 1994; Kosslyn, Pascual-Leone, Felician, & Camposano, 1999). In this case, it is useful to reduce the image to a pattern of neural activity in the visual cortex of the brain, but it isn't at all clear that any deeper understanding would be gained by an analysis at the level of the chemical mechanisms of neural activity.

Sometimes, however, our explanations for psychological phenomena seem best left at the level of psychology. Consider the experiment in *PsychMate 2.6: Organization in Memory as an Aid to Recall,* which replicates an experiment by Gordon Bower, Michal Clark, Alan Lesgold, and David Winzenz (1969). Subjects study four lists of 26 words for one minute each and then try to recall the words. For some subjects, the lists are arranged in a logical hierarchy so that each word is clearly related to others. For other subjects, the words are arranged randomly across the four lists. The difference in recall is quite striking—organization has a profound impact. Considering other things we know about memory, we seem to be able to explain this fairly well. Network models of memory (see *PsychMate 2.1: Lexical Decisions*) suggest that a plausible explanation is that each item recalled can serve as a retrieval cue for other items related to it, giving an advantage to organized lists. We can also relate this advantage to the notion of elaborative rehearsal that was developed along with the levels-of-processing approach to memory (see *PsychMate 3.4: Levels of Processing and the Self-Reference Effect*)—each item we study in an organized list is elaborated in the context of the other items. While I have no doubt that we will soon know a great deal more about how networks of memories are instantiated at the level of the brain, we still have a good, viable explanation that does not require us to venture beyond our own department. I fail utterly to see what particle physics can add.

In conclusion, it seems to me that the best approach to reductionism is not to decide whether reductionism is right or wrong, but rather to ask, "What is the best (most appropriate) level at which to explain a phenomenon?" For the dark-adaptation curve, we don't get a satisfactory explanation until we get to the level of chemistry, with some physics mixed in. The imagery debate is pretty well settled at the level of biological neuroscience. The effect of organization on memory seems to be well explained at the level of psychology. To demand reductionism for all phenomena is as silly as denying that it can be useful.

A biologist, John Moore, forcefully showed that explanation at one level does not rule out explanation at another.

> "One may observe and describe the complex movements of a ballet dancer or baseball pitcher, each beautiful and important in its own way. Understanding of this movement is increased when we obtain information about the many muscles and their attachments that make the motions possible. Other sorts of understanding come when we study muscles at the cellular level—when we learn about the activity of myosin, actin, and other molecules involved in the movement of muscles. Knowledge obtained at each level of organization contributes to an understanding of the total phenomenon, *while each retains its own validity*. One cannot completely understand a Waslaw Nijinsky [a dancer] or a Fernando Valenzuela [a baseball pitcher] merely by knowing about the actin and myosin in their muscle cells, any more than one can predict the properties of water from knowing about hydrogen and oxygen" (1993, pp. 265-266, emphasis added).

Science and Technology

Science and technology share many features, and it is not uncommon to hear people speak as if the two were slightly different versions of the same process.[25] It is true that some scientific ideas, such as discoveries in molecular biology, are translated into practical technologies such as pharmaceuticals (drugs to treat disease). It is also true that developers of technologies often use

---

[25] This section is based in large measure on Lewis Wolpert's (1992) chapter "Technology is not Science." I quote him from time to time when his own words are most compelling but must also acknowledge a more general indebtedness to his work.

the techniques of science to test their ideas—trials of new drugs use the techniques of random assignment and control groups—and analyze their data with the statistical techniques that were invented for the evaluation of scientific experiments in the social sciences and agriculture.

But science has only informed technology in relatively recent times—perhaps since the middle of the 1800s. Technology is vastly older than science, as well. A self-aware , organized science (when persons knew that what they were doing science) dates to the early 1600s, when scientific societies, such as the Royal Society in England, were formed and their members thought of themselves as engaged in a special kind of enterprise. Technology, on the other hand, is as old as humankind if one thinks of tool-making as technology, which it certainly is. Agriculture involving planting of crops and domestication of animals such as cattle probably dates to about 7000 BCE. Mesopotamian craftsmen, in what is now Iraq, mixed copper and tin to make bronze. Since that requires a temperature of around 1000°C, they had clearly gained considerable knowledge of kilns. The Great Pyramid of Egypt, constructed c. 2560 BCE is rightly one of the wonders of the ancient world.[26] But none of those involved scientific principles such as the basic understanding of plant genetics or the molecular structure of metals. The knowledge of stone-working that lead to the building of the great cathedrals of medieval Europe was based on practical experience and predated by centuries the scientific understanding of the nature of the forces to be controlled.

Three of the most important inventions in terms of their historical impact on the Renaissance of Europe were the magnetic compass (which permitted exploration), printing with moveable type (which improved the dissemination of knowledge), and gunpowder (which permitted people to kill each other more efficiently). All were technologies imported from China, which had an enormously well developed technology long before Europe but failed at that time to develop anything recognizable as science. Note that a needle that points North is a very handy thing for navigation, whether one knows anything about the Earth's magnetic fields or not.

More recent inventions, such as the telescope and the steam engine, were also made without reference to the general principles by which they operate. Galileo, who greatly improved the telescope, wrote that its discoverer must have chanced to look through two lenses of the right kind and find that they made distant objects appear much nearer—a discovery based on trial and error, rather than scientific knowledge of optics. Wolpert (1992) noted that "the

---

[26] "C." is short for "circa", from the Latin *circum*, meaning "around," and is used to indicate an approximate date.

origin of the steam engine can be thought of as owing more to the blacksmith's world than to the Royal Society and its scientists" (p. 30).

There are other differences between technology and science worth noting. One is the difference in motivation. Technology is concerned with solving specific problems—how to grow more food, improve transportation, or make musical instruments.[27] Science, on the other hand, is concerned with general principles. The development of the wheel, which makes the moving of heavy loads enormously easier, occurred thousands of years before there was any understanding of *why* the wheel makes it easier. (Most of the work of moving something involves overcoming friction. A wheel reduces the friction.) But note that wheels work just fine even if you don't know why! A major part of the success of the Wright brothers in achieving powered flight in 1903 was their use of models in wind tunnels—their knowledge of aerodynamics was derived from direct observation rather than general principles.

The products of science and technology are also different. The product of science is information, while the product of technology is an artifact—a thing. The basis for evaluating success differs, as well. A new technology is successful if it fulfills a want or need, but scientific discoveries are successful if they improve our understanding of the world. John Ziman (1981) captured one aspect of the difference between science and technology. "The goal of science is not to solve a succession of immediate problems but to establish a body of knowledge from which good answers to particular questions may ultimately be derived" (p. 153).

As science has matured, and more of the basic facts of how the world works are known, more and more of technology derives from the application of science. That brings with it a set of decisions and judgments that properly involve all of society. What basic science gets done is largely the decision of scientists (unless it involves large sums of money and thus requires government funding). But ultimately, *societies* decide whether to apply basic science and transform it into technology. Those decisions are sometimes shaped by government and sometimes shaped by consumers. At a global level, we currently have discussions among nations concerning global warming. At local levels, we have concerns about how to deal with pollutants. At the individual level, we influence the development of technology through the marketplace—what we choose to buy (or not). Some people who argue for

---

[27] Technological advances have often been exploited quickly by artists. Wolpert (1992) notes the existence of a recipe for a green pottery glaze from 1600 BCE found near modern Baghdad. Even today, such technological advances as the Internet have been exploited for art—downloads of music files! The technology for recording sound and pictures (from the Edison cylinder recording to the DVD) has been used for art and entertainment.

controlling science are confusing science with its application through technology. Scientific knowledge is neutral—it is an understanding of the way the world works. What we can and should *do* with that knowledge is a separate decision to be made by society.

Scientific understanding will be translated into technology whenever it is profitable to do so. The application of knowledge of microbiology to the treatment of infectious diseases is an old example. A striking example is the development of X-ray machines for medical usage, which came about within three to four years of Roentgen's discovery of X-rays in 1895.[28] Currently, there is the promise of new treatments or preventions for many diseases that will come eventually from modern molecular physiology and genomics. Some of that translation of science into technology will be beneficial, such as prevention or treatment of disease. Some of it, inevitably, will be debatable at best. Knowledge of microbiology makes germ warfare possible, and knowledge of chemistry permits the manufacture of poisonous gases. We must all, as concerned citizens, make ourselves heard on these issues. Just because a scientific discovery *can* be turned into a technology does not imply that it *should*, though in specific instances the decision may be a very difficult one. In the U.S., there is a near-moratorium on the building of new nuclear reactors,[29] for example. I won't try to decide the debate, but note that there are those who fear that accidents at nuclear plants could cause devastating harm, as occurred at Chernobyl in the former Soviet Union. Others note that nuclear power is much cleaner than fossil fuels like coal and oil, and that nuclear energy reduces our reliance on foreign sources of energy (especially oil).

Note that there are many enormous technological changes that, though incredible and important, rely only remotely on scientific advances. They, too, can have both good and bad consequences. A good example is the Internet. It puts you just a few mouse-clicks away from accessing the world's literature in psychology, via PsycInfo (see Chapter 3). A few different mouse-clicks and you can find out more about human sexual behavior than you perhaps ever wanted to know.

Some Recent Attacks on Science

Over the last 30 years or so, a loose-knit set of related theories have been developed about the nature of literary criticism. These are usually referred to as "post-modernism" and "deconstructionism." I will not comment on these

---

[28] Roentgen won the first Nobel Prize in physics in 1901 for this discovery

[29] That may be changing. At least two consortia of energy and construction companies have proposed new plants, as reported in *The New York Times* March 31, 2004, p. A17.

theories in regard to their literary merit, and only mention them because certain adherents of these positions have made the amazing discovery that science does not work! Science, they proclaim, has no claim to producing reliable data, and scientific theories and discoveries are simply cultural constructs. To these critics of science, it makes no more sense to ask whether a scientific theory is true than to ask that question of an Impressionist painting.

The weak form of this argument—essentially that our social/cultural backgrounds affect what science we do and how we do it—is certainly true. Science is a human activity and is therefore subject to all the frailties humans bring to our other enterprises. Some examples:

- There are occasional reports of outright fraud—though in important areas of research such fraud is unlikely to remain undetected.

- People are sometimes influenced in their choices of scientific problems to work on by a myriad of factors—individual and societal. For example, medical researchers sometimes choose to study diseases because of the personal experience of a loved one or friend who has the problem. Some areas of research get more funding and recognition than others, for a host of reasons. Research on HIV/AIDS seeking treatments, vaccines, and eventually cures has strong public backing because of the recognition of the gravity of the spread of such a terrible disease.

- Moreover, scientists sometimes cling to outmoded theories in the face of compelling evidence contradicting them.

Are scientists influenced by their cultures? Of course. But the existence of these influences is not a secret to scientists. Indeed, the history of science is in large measure a history of people gradually figuring out how to do their research such that the influence of their personal beliefs and cultural backgrounds are minimized. The existence of textbooks on research methods, such as the one you are currently reading, and the lessons taught in them, are a direct reflection of the fact that all scientists know that the personal and social can influence their decisions about interpreting data and conducting experiments. Topics such as the use of control groups, random assignment of subjects to conditions, peer review of discoveries before publication, and many others are covered in this course precisely because they help us avoid at least some of the errors that humans too easily make.

But there is a strong version of the argument that science is culturally constructed, and it is more problematic. Paul Gross and Norman Levitt (1994) and Gross, Levitt, and Martin Lewis (1997) present the arguments at length. In short, the deconstructionists or post-modernists argue that the very "facts" of science are socially constructed, with no more claim to "truth" than a literary production. They argue that scientific facts are simply the agreement of the powerful (usually, white, male, European). To them, scientific theories are accepted because of the power and prestige of their proponents and not because they correspond to facts. The facts, in this view, are caused by the theory rather than the other way around.

The argument fails along a number of lines. One problem with most presentations of the anti-science position of the deconstructionists is their appalling lack of understanding of the science. The literary philosopher Derrida, for example, provided this: "The Einsteinian constant is not a constant, not a center. It is the very concept of variability—it is, finally, the concept of the game. In other words, it is not the concept of some thing—of a center from which an observer could master the field—but the very concept of the game" (cited in Ernest Gallo, 1991). The "Einsteinian constant" to which he refers is the speed of light in a vacuum (the value of c in $E = mc^2$), which is 300 million meters per second. Examples of this kind of verbal silliness are legion in the writings of Derrida and other deconstructionists.

A second problem concerns the claim that the rich and powerful can make the facts. They can, in some times and places, determine what is publicly dared to be told as fact. In 1633, the Inquisition of the Church (one of the most politically powerful forces ever in human affairs) showed Galileo the instruments of torture and demanded that he publicly retract his claim that the Earth orbits the Sun. Old and in poor health, with the powerful against him and few beside him, and mindful that Giordano Bruno had been burned at the stake for that same heresy by the Inquisition in 1600, sank to his knees and publicly stated "I, Galileo, being in my seventieth year, being a prisoner and on my knees, and before your Eminences, having before my eyes the Holy Gospel, which I touch with my hands, abjure, curse, and detest the error and the heresy of the movement of the earth."[30] Nevertheless, it moves.

When governments trust ideology above science, however, they do not have an enviable record. Consider the Lysenko affair. In the 1930s the Soviet Union instituted agricultural policy based on the views of Trofin Denisovich Lysenko, a Communist Party member who was head of the Institute for Genetics of the Soviet Academy of Sciences. Lysenko rejected Mendellian genetics as not fitting Soviet ideology. Instead, he based his theories of plant genetics on the work of Jean Baptiste Lamarck, who proposed that evolution occurred through the inheritance of acquired characteristics—an antelope that

---

[30] Quoted in White, Andrew (1899), Volume 1, p. 142. In 1980, then-Pope John Paul II appointed a commission of scientists, theologians, and historians to review the case. In 1984 they reported that the original finding was in error.

stretches its neck to get food will have offspring with longer necks, eventually evolving into giraffes. By the 1920s, the understanding of genetics in the West had shown Lamarck's theory to be false. But for reasons too complex for the current discussion, the Lamarckian theory fit better with Marxist thought as developed in the Soviet Union. The agricultural policy resulting from this pseudo-science was a compete failure. Instead of increasing agricultural production, it brought about its collapse.[31] Here, the insistence of the government that genetics worked a certain way led directly to the starvation deaths of millions of people.

The powerful can sometimes force scientists to agree to "facts" that are not true, but they cannot make the facts true. The Earth orbits the Sun, no matter the opinion of the very powerful. And plant genetics works like Mendel said it does, despite the full force of the state proclaiming it is not so.

A third problem can be put quite simply: Science works. Consider some examples, and try to square them with the notion that scientific facts are simply cultural constructs with no "real" basis in reality.

- Reduction in disease due to vaccination. Few of you who are traditional undergraduates have ever had the whooping cough. For my generation (born 1951) it was virtually expected. And nasty, too!

- The predictions from pure physics that led to the development of nuclear energy. Is the electricity flowing from a nuclear power plant socially constructed?

- The development of antiseptic techniques in medicine that reduced infection and the development of antibiotics that kill bacteria and help heal infection. Are germs a cultural construct?

- In our own back yard of psychology, consider such robust findings as the Stroop effect (see *PsychMate 1.5: Attentional Interference and the Stroop Effect*) or the flankers effect (see *PsychMate 1.6: Selective Attention and Response Competition*). Are these well-known effects really just social constructs? Are they true because we believe them?

- Is the blindspot in vision (at the head of the optic nerve) real, or is it a cultural construct? Perhaps in other cultures people do not have such a blind spot. You would make your career if you showed that, but I wouldn't waste my time, if I were you.

---

[31] Forced collective farming under communist ideology also contributed to the agricultural collapse.

A final note

The post-modernist/deconstuctionist view of science is, on any reasonable analysis, silly. Scientists largely regard it (when they know of it at all) as comic relief. Unfortunately, it is also taken quite seriously by a lot of otherwise well-educated people.

As I will illustrate repeatedly in this book, science is indeed a human enterprise, and it is indeed subject to human frailties. But the claim that science produces reliable knowledge remains without serious challenge. The power of science comes from recognizing those frailties and developing mechanisms for overcoming them.

Data can suggest, support, and even convince, but they cannot prove beyond any possible doubt. If you can bring yourself to abandon the need to have an absolute, final, known-for-all-time-to-be-correct answer to your research questions, you can get on with the job of getting a really good approximation to reality.

A comment by Jack Adams (1980) seems apt here: "Some may find theoretical indecisiveness…uncomfortable, but it does not bother scientists very much because the world is clouded with uncertainty in their eyes and they are tolerant of it. At any moment, given the facts available, a scientist will pass tentative judgments on the mechanisms that are required to explain the facts, and then will get on with the job of research to refine the judgments and reduce the uncertainty" (1980, p. 283).

Chapter 3

Variables and Measurements

Data! data! data!...I can't make bricks
without clay (1928, p. 283).

The Copper Beeches
The Adventures of Sherlock Holmes

Relations among variables form the basis of science. In many instances, we seek to explain laws and effects, which are statements about relationships among variables. In other instances, we develop hypotheses and test them. Those hypotheses are statements about variables. So, you must know something about variables. First, what is a variable? A variable is any property that varies from one object to another or from time to time in the same object. This is in contradistinction to constants, or properties of objects that do not vary. Of course, as psychologists, we are most often concerned with the properties of "objects" such as humans and other species.

Abstract definition is often aided by concrete examples. Here are some.

Variables of interest in psychological research (varying from person to person or from time to time in the same person) on humans include reaction time, percent correct recall of a list of words, choices made in a social bargaining study, ratings of painfulness of a stimulus, brightness or loudness of a stimulus, visual acuity, preference for one flavor over another, Intelligent Quotient (IQ), achievement test scores, and scores on personality measures, among many others.

In regard to living organisms, there are many constants (that are the same for everyone or the same across time for individuals), but they are seldom of interest to psychologists. Nearly all humans have two eyes, two arms, one heart, and 10 fingers. Those are (almost) constants. Of course to a developmental biologist, such constants are quite interesting—why is it that most of us end up with two eyes? Developmental psychologists also are interested in understanding some constants, such as the nearly-universal acquisition of language among humans. Most often though, psychologists are concerned with variables rather than constants.

Note that some variables differ from person to person, and some differ from time to time within the same person. We are sometimes concerned with the former and sometimes with the latter. Much of science, including psychology, is concerned with explaining variability. We want to know why people differ in intelligence or attitudes or percent recall. We also want to know why people *change* in intelligence or attitudes or recall. Scientific investigation designed to answer such questions typically makes use of variability. In an experiment, we may manipulate (vary) the conditions under which subjects memorize and then see whether this made any difference in the ability to recall. In a correlational study, we may seek to determine how much the IQ scores of identical twins raised in dissimilar environments differ in order to estimate the degree of influence of heredity and environment on intelligence.

Most of this chapter is devoted to acquainting you with several different schemes for classifying. These schemes are not mutually exclusive, nor contradictory, but simply different ways of talking about variables that are widely used and must be part of your vocabulary if you are to make sense of what you read in the scientific literature in psychology.

Levels of Measurement

The first "scheme" will be familiar to you if you have already completed a course in statistics. S. S. Stevens (a major figure in psychophysics and the inventor of psychophysical scaling) argued that variables differ in the degree to which numbers attached to them are mathematically meaningful. He proposed four such levels of measurement. As I will discuss shortly, this scheme may not be as meaningful statistically as Stevens believed, but it is still a useful way to think about variables and is part of the intellectual equipment assumed of any psychologist. See Stevens (1951), but also Gene Glass and Julian Stanley (1970).

Nominal scales. The least impressive level of measurement is the nominal scale of measurement. A variable has a nominal scale of measurement if the "measurements" simply classify the objects of interest. It has essentially no mathematical meaning. These are *nominal* variables because they *name* [L. *nomen*] the individual or their group membership. For example, soldiers vary in their type of uniform, but there is no inherent ordering—grey uniforms do not signify better soldiers than do blue uniforms. The different uniforms worn by soldiers in a war serve to identify them as friend or foe. Another example is your Social Security Number (SSN). It identifies you, but if your SSN is greater than mine that tells us nothing about our relative worth. A person with a high SSN is no more socially secure than someone with a low one! (The first three digits of your SSN identify the region of the country in which the number was issued, which is also a nominal variable). Nominal variables of interest in psychological research include sex, handedness, and race/ethnicity. Note that while we may assign numbers to the levels of the variables (male=1, female=2, or vice versa), the numbers are completely arbitrary and not properly subject to mathematical manipulation.[1] We cannot meaningfully calculate the "average" sex.[2] The answer we get is determined by the numbers we chose to use as group labels. This is an important property of nominal scales of measurement—if we assign numbers to the levels of the variable, they have no mathematical meaning; they serve only to identify. Note that we could, if we wished, calculate the average jersey numbers of two football teams. But discovering that our team has a higher average jersey number would not be terribly predictive of their success![3]

Examples of nominal variables include the flanker types described in *PsychMate 1.6: Selective Attention and Response Competition* and the word list types in *PsychMate 6.2: Working Memory and the fMRI*. In both of those cases, though, there is a theoretically expected ordering of the mean RT or mean number of items recalled, and they are typically graphed to reflect that expected (and almost always achieved) ordering. But the underlying levels of the variable (flanker types or word list types) are mere labels. The ordering is the result of observation.

Ordinal Scales. The next highest scale of measurement is the ordinal scale, which, as its name suggests, is concerned with *order*. Here, we typically have a set of ranks. If I gave you a list of your classmates ranked from tallest to shortest (but omitting the actual heights), the data would be at an ordinal scale. Such a list might tell us that Jim is taller than Lucy, and Lucy is taller than Andy, but it wouldn't tell us *by how much*. There is no implication that the difference between Jim and Lucy is the same as the difference between Lucy and Andy.

An ordinal variable with which you are likely familiar, involves student ratings of faculty, which most universities ask students to complete at the end of their courses. Typically, these ratings are on items such as "The instructor was well organized," and you indicate a rating on a scale of *Strongly Agree, Agree, Neutral, Disagree, Strongly Disagree*.[4] Questionnaires may differ in the

---

[1] Early computer programs for statistical analysis usually required numerical labels. Most now permit verbal labels, such as "male" and "female."

[2] An exception occurs if we designate two groups by 0's and 1's. If we designate males by 0 and females by 1, then the "average" will give us the proportion of females. If a sample contains 75 females and 25 males, the "average" of 75 1's and 25 0's would be .75—the proportion of females.

[3] See F. M. Lord (1953) for a satirical treatment of football jersey numbers and levels of measurement.

[4] This type of item, often used in attitude research, is called a Likert scale after R. Likert (1932). It typically has either a 5-point or 7-point scale.

number of choices, and certainly in the wording, but they represent ordinal scales. Why are they ordinal? Note that it is not at all clear that the difference between *Strongly Agree* and *Agree* is the same amount of agreement as between *Agree* and *Neutral*. It may be, but we have no reason to believe so and some reason to doubt it. For example, people responding to such surveys tend to avoid the most extreme labels. When that occurs, then the difference between *Strongly Agree* and *Agree* is likely bigger than that between *Agree* and *Neutral*. It is as if subjects were saying, "I agree a little, so I will choose *Agree* instead of *Neutral*, but only when I feel a compelling, overwhelming level of agreement will I choose *Strongly Agree*."

Stevens argued that ordinal variables do not permit the meaningful calculation of means or standard deviations precisely because the "units" of measurement are not all equal—it is as if you measured various objects with an elastic tape measure with the size of an inch varying from moment to moment.

Interval scales. Interval scales are the first at which numbers carry their usual, familiar meaning in terms of mathematics. Interval scales could be called "equal-interval" scales because they have the property that each interval along the continuum is as large as any other. For example, if I gain one pound in weight and you gain two pounds, that is a difference of one pound. If I gain 19 pounds, and you gain 20 pounds, that is also a difference of one pound. A difference of one pound (or other unit of measurement) is the same all along the continuum of an interval scale.

For reasons that will be clear shortly, the distinction between interval scales and ratio scales is usually of little importance, so I will combine further examples of interval scales with examples of ratio scales.

Ratio scales. Ratio scales are the same as interval scales except for one additional property. Ratio scales also have an absolute zero. That is, "0" represents the complete absence of the quantity being measured. That introduces the property of equal ratios, in addition to equal intervals. See Figure 3-1.

What is the level of measurement of temperature in degrees Fahrenheit or degrees Celsius? Both have equal intervals—that is, if we heat a pan of water enough to raise it from 50 to 51 degrees F (or Celsius), and heat another pan with an equal amount of water from 100 to 101 degrees F, we have added the same quantity of heat to each. The change in temperature is the same. One degree equals the same amount of heat energy anywhere along the continuum. But suppose we have two pans of water—one at 50 degrees F and the other at 100 degrees F. Does the second have twice the heat energy as the first? Hardly. Why not? Because 0 degrees F is an arbitrary point along the continuum. In the Celsius scale, we arbitrarily designate the temperature at which water freezes as zero degrees. We could have chosen any other point.

Now contrast that with the third major scale of temperature used mainly in physics. In the Kelvin scale, zero means absolute zero, or the complete cessation of molecular motion. It doesn't get any colder than that. "Heat" is a manifestation of the degree of molecular motion, which increases as temperature increases. In the Kelvin scale, as a consequence, a pan of water at 100 degrees K really is twice as warm as one at 50 degrees (though both are frozen solid and you would destroy the nerve endings in your skin that sense touch if you handled either one of them).[5] The relationships between these scales are illustrated in Figure 3-1.

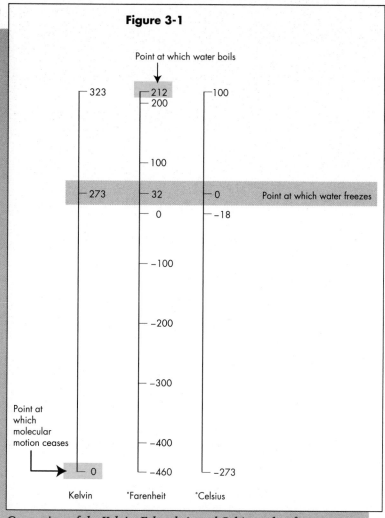

Figure 3-1

Comparison of the Kelvin, Fahrenheit, and Celsius scales of temperature.

Examples of variables in psychology that achieve ratio measurement are the common performance measures of reaction time and error rates (or percent correct), as well as measures such as visual acuity.

Stevens was concerned with what sorts of statistical operations are permissible with different levels of measurement. For "numbers" at a nominal level, normal mathematics is useless, as the example of averaging football jersey

---

[5] You may ask yourself whether I am correct in saying that water at 100 degrees is not twice the temperature of water at 50 degrees. But that confuses the actual temperature (as measured by a physical measuring device (some type of thermometer) with our perception of hot and cold, which has a complex physiology. Note that part of why things feel warm or cold is their ability to conduct heat, rather than their actual heat. A bare wood floor feels colder on a winter morning than a carpeted floor. But that is because the carpet is porous and slows the absorption of heat energy from your foot, even if the carpet and the floor under it are the same temperature.

numbers indicates. When our measurements of a variable are at either the interval or ratio scale, the numbers assigned to those measurements take on true mathematical properties. It is meaningful to average them or calculate standard deviations. Assessing what we do with ordinal measurements statistically is more difficult, and there are fewer statistical techniques available.

The problem is, however, a little trickier than that, and here we see that Stevens' system has some problems. Suppose that you take a 100-item multiple-choice test with each item worth one point. What is the level of measurement? If the variable is "percent correct," then you clearly have a ratio scale. (Zero would mean no items correct, and you can't get worse than that. A score of 80 means twice as many items right as a score of 40, hence we have equal ratios.) That seems unambiguous. But when, I as a professor, make up such an exam, I am not directly interested in "percent correct." Rather, I want to know how much the students learned. If I am measuring *learning*, then I have only an ordinal scale. If someone scores a zero, does that mean they learned absolutely nothing? They didn't learn much, of course, but they may have learned something. And did the student with an 80 really learn twice as much as the student with a 40? The items on such a test will not all reflect the same amount of learning—some items are harder than others. Thus, an 80 may require that you get more of the harder items correct. An 80 may reflect more than twice the level of learning of a 40.

Two of the most common measures in cognitive psychology are reaction time and error rates (percent correct or percent error), both of which are ratio measures. Still, there has long been a concern within psychology about the adequacy of measurements, especially measures of social constructs. Stevens (1951) addressed the issue, but so have others. The student who wishes to pursue this issue further is referred to Joel Michell's (1990) book on psychological measurement, which presents a particularly lucid discussion of the problem of measurement in psychology and elsewhere.

A tempting simplification of Stevens' scheme is to say that nominal and ordinal scales are classifications, and interval and ratio scales are measurements. But this won't really do. Ordinal scales contain more information than mere classifications—i.e., order—though they fail to achieve equal intervals, which is quite a useful property for a measurement. Moreover, we often classify or group subjects based on a ratio variable such as dosage level.

Returning for a moment to the issues of scale items such as those described in the discussion of ordinal scales, a standard way to try to improve the measurement of such variables is to have a number of items on the survey that attempt to ask about the same issue. We then take the average of those items as a *scale score*. For example, to pursue the previous example of research on student opinions about instructors, a standard commercial form, the Student Instructional Report II written by the Educational Testing Service, has students rate their instructor from *Very Effective* to *Ineffective* on a five-point scale on items such as "The instructor's explanation of course requirements" and "The instructor's use of class time," etc. to form a scale called "Course Organization and Planning." Such scale scores are often then treated as continuous, ordered variables and are analyzed statistically as if they were interval-level variables.

Continuous vs. Discrete Variables

Another classification of variables concerns whether the variable is treated as continuous or discrete. All variables are measured discretely, but the choice of statistical tests often depends upon whether we treat the variable as discrete or continuous. Let me make sense of those statements. First, I define discrete and continuous. Then I show why all measurements are discrete, even though some variables are continuous. Finally, I argue that we sometimes choose to treat a variable as discrete for purposes of statistical analysis even though the underlying variable is continuous.

Discrete variables are those that indicate categories, such as race or socio-economic status (SES).[6] Note that discrete variables can be ordered (such as SES—usually Lower, Lower Middle, Middle, Upper Middle, or Upper) or not (such as race).[7] *Continuous variables* are those that can take on (essentially) any value in some range, such as height or RT. But while some examples are quite clear, others are ambiguous; we need to note some issues of interpretation. First, all *measurements* of variables are discrete, whether the variables are discrete or continuous. We have to measure to the nearest something. For example, when measuring height, we can probably measure pretty well to the nearest quarter inch, but we would be hard-pressed to measure to the nearest millimeter (nor would we usually gain anything by that added precision).

How does the classification of variables as discrete or continuous relate to Stevens' levels? Nominal variables are always discrete. But past that statement, things get complicated. An item on a five-point Likert scale (such as student ratings of teachers as discussed previously) would be discrete but ordered. But if we have five items, each intended to tap the issue of course organization, we

---

[6] SES is usually a combination of income, job status, and level of education.

[7] I oversimplify, since few persons are "pure" members of one "race." But I use race as an example here to make just this point—things are often far from clear when examined carefully, and racial classification is certainly one of those, as reflected in the arguments over what classifications to offer on census forms, and whether persons can choose more than one "race." A fascinating discussion of the problem, mainly focusing on definitions of "White" and "Black", is given by F. James Davis (2001).

would average those resulting in values ranging from 1.0 to 5.0, and we would probably treat the resulting numbers as (essentially) continuous.

Measures such as RT are ratio scales and take on a wide range of values if we measure to the nearest millisecond. We would treat them as continuous. But consider a variable such as dosage of a drug. If we examined the effects of caffeine on reaction time, we would likely use three to four dosage levels, for example, 0, 50, 100 mg.[8] Dosage level is a ratio variable with a large range of values (if we measure to the nearest milligram), but since we are only using three of these levels, this would essentially be an ordered, discrete variable. (See Chapter 5 for further discussion of the choice of the number of levels and their spacing.).

Consider also a variable such as income. If we had persons report their income in terms of adjusted gross income from IRS Form 1040, we would have income to the nearest dollar, if not cent—surely an essentially continuous measure. But when we ask survey subjects about their incomes, they are often reluctant to report it that precisely (even if they could remember it). So in practice, most survey research asks subjects to indicate a level of income—$0-$20,000; $20,001 to $40,000, etc. Now the level of measurement is ordinal, and this is a discrete variable.[9]

Consider, too, a variable such as the number of siblings people have—an important issue for some areas of developmental psychology. Here, the most frequent values are going to be 0, 1, and 2, with a few 3's and 4's, but not many 5's and 6's and very few 17's. Because this can take on only a relatively limited number of values, we would probably treat it as discrete.[10] The issue of how many levels of a variable are needed before we treat it as continuous is not one I can settle. It is often a judgment call, but the choice of statistical tests to apply to the data depends on whether the variables are discrete or continuous, so the choice can matter.

---

[8] 100 mg is about the dosage of caffeine in a cup of coffee—though that depends on who's making it.

[9] Note, however, that you should NEVER reduce a continuous variable to a discrete one if you initially measure it continuously. If you knew the adjusted gross income of your subjects, but then reduced it to the scheme above, a person who made $19,999 would be classed the same as someone who made nothing, even though he or she is much closer in income to someone who made $20,000, who was in the higher class. Measure a continuous variable discretely ONLY if you cannot reasonably measure it continuously.

[10] In practice, we might simplify the values to 0, 1, 2, 3 and "4 or more."

Dependent, Independent, and Control Variables

A third classification of variables concerns neither the mathematical nature of the numbers attached to the levels of the variable, nor whether the measurements are continuous or discrete, but rather the way the variables function in our research. In experimental research, we frequently refer to dependent variables, independent variables and control variables. Each is detailed here.

Suppose that we perform an experiment to determine whether the probability of a stimulus affects the reaction time to that stimulus (see *PsychMate 5.1: Reaction Time Procedures*). We present a series of trials in which one of two letters appears, and the subject is instructed to indicate as quickly as possible which letter was seen. We manipulate the probability of a stimulus by presenting a block of trials in which one stimulus occurs 80% of the time, another in which it occurs 50% of the time, and another in which it occurs 20% of the time. (Note that the other stimulus letter would appear 20%, 50%, and 80% of the time during those three blocks.) Because we expect that changing the probability of a stimulus will change the RT, RT is dependent upon the probability of a stimulus. For that reason, RT is the *dependent variable* (DV) in this experiment, while the probability of a stimulus, which you manipulated, is the *independent variable (IV)*. We also talk about the *levels of the independent variable*. In this case, there are three levels of the IV, namely 80%, 50%, and 20% probabilities.[11]

Before turning to some other examples, here is a scheme for remembering these three types of variables:

- Dependent variables are measured.

- Independent variables are manipulated.

- Control variables are controlled.

Dependent variables are measured

"What was your dependent measure?" is a question you hear asked when psychologists are discussing an experiment. "Dependent variable," "dependent measure," and "outcome measure" are interchangeable terms for this type of variable. In experimental psychology, the most common dependent variables are reaction times and error rates. In social psychology, the dependent variables

---

[11] There may be one aspect of this experiment as it is described that bothers you, namely that every subject gets the same order of the levels of the independent variable. We could, of course, test a separate group of subjects at each level of the IV, but in this case that would be wasteful. See Chapter 6 for a discussion of counterbalancing.

might be attitude measures (scale scores on a set of scales reflecting attitudes about college) or the behaviors that people show in certain situations (the number of times someone interrupts the other in a dyadic—two-person—encounter). In other areas of psychology, we might use IQ scores, or ratings of pathology (in clinical areas), or the observed number of instances of apparent hallucination, the amount of change in blood-flow indicating areas of brain activity (using functional magnetic resonance imaging or fMRI), or the number of times a rat presses a bar.

Independent variables are manipulated

Manipulation of the independent variable is at the very heart of experimentation. Experimentation permits us to make causal claims about the relationships among variables (following the example above, changing the probability of a stimulus *causes* changes in RT) precisely because it is actively manipulated by the experimenter. It is important in specifying an IV to specify the number of levels of the variable and what they are.

Examples:

We randomly assign subjects to one of two methods of learning statistics: the method of learning is the IV (here with two levels), with amount learned (probably measured by final exam score) as the DV.

We randomly assign subjects to one of three dental anesthetics and have them give a rating of pain after the dental procedure: the pain rating is the DV and the three types of anesthesia represent the three levels of the IV.

We randomly assign subjects to one of four levels of caffeine to observe the effects on the speed with which they can perform mathematics: speed (correct answers per minute) is the DV, while the IV is dosage, with four levels (for example, 0, 50, 100, and 200 mg.)

We have each subject try to memorize lists of words under three different instructions: the IV is type of instruction, the DV is percent correct recall (or percent errors), and a control variable (CV) is the order in which the instructions were given.

Some things to notice: method of learning, type of anesthesia, and type of instructions are all nominal variables, while dosage level is a ratio variable. (In the case of dosage, we only used a few of the levels of the variable that are possible, as noted above.) The point is that IVs can be of any level of measurement. So can DVs. Percent correct recall, final exam scores, and reaction times are all, at least approximately, ratio measures, while pain ratings are likely to be ordinal, at best. Less frequently, DVs may be nominal, for example if we observe which of several toys a child chooses to play with (DV) after watching different sorts of cartoons (IV).

It is likely to have occurred to you that there are serious issues concerning how we assign subjects to conditions or orders of conditions. If you test every subject in a set of different conditions, and you always do it in the same order, there may be problems. Those problems and some solutions to them are discussed in Chapter 6.

Control variables are controlled

I have already discussed *Controls* in Chapter 1. Some controls are for the purpose of comparison, such as Perier's second barometer left at the base of the mountain to show that the reading did not change when the elevation stayed the same. Other controls are intended to produce uniformity of conditions. In Chapter 1, I gave as an example testing all subjects at the same time of day to remove any influence that time of day might have—though that is seldom actually an issue. But we sometimes include variables in an experiment for other types of control, and these I designate as *control variables*. The use of control variables is illustrated by example.

In general, control variables are introduced into our experiments in an effort to eliminate possible *confounds*, or alternative interpretations. In most cases, we are not directly interested in the effect of the control variable on the DV (though we can usually determine it statistically if we need to). In a study comparing two methods of teaching reading, we might control for the effect of *reading readiness* (how well the students know the alphabet, etc.) by giving all of the children the same reading readiness test. We could then form pairs of children who are nearly the same in reading readiness and assign the pair randomly to one of our two methods of teaching reading. By doing so, we have controlled for reading readiness.

Perhaps the most frequent use of control variables comes in experiments where each subject is exposed to all of the levels of the IV. Such "repeated measures" designs are frequently much more powerful than having separate sets of subjects for each level of the IV (See the section below on Between-Subjects and Within-Subjects Variables. But we almost always have to consider whether order effects (changes in the DV based on the order in which the levels of the IV were presented) are a possible confound. Various schemes for controlling for order effects are presented in Chapter 6.

Control variables may either be manipulated as a part of the experiment proper (such as counterbalancing for order or matching for reading readiness), or they may be measured and then controlled statistically. Because this text is most directly concerned with research methods, I will concentrate here and in later chapters on experimental control rather than statistical control. This choice reflects the priorities of this textbook rather than the actual importance of statistical control, which I do not minimize. Statistical control is more widely used in correlational studies than in experiments.

Cautionary note

Knowing which controls are important and how to deal with them in practice is not something that a text like this can hope to provide. That information comes from experience—much of it is passed down in the laboratory training of graduate students and may never appear explicitly. If you are embarking on research in an area in which you do not have expertise, you should seek expert guidance. The point is not that people hoard private techniques or that they deliberately withhold specific information from the Procedures sections, but rather that researchers get so close to their experiments that they cease to think much about some controls. Those controls are essentially automatic to them—they do them without having to think much about it.

Predictor and Criterion Variables

In correlational research, in which causal relationships are not identified, it is usual to speak of *predictor* and *criterion* variables, instead of IVs and DVs. If your college admissions office uses the Scholastic Aptitude Test (SAT) or the ACT to help predict college Grade Point Average (GPA), the test score is a predictor variable, and the GPA is the criterion variable. We would hardly want to say that GPA *depends* causally on the ACT or SAT.[12]

Between-Subjects and Within-Subjects Variables

One final way to describe variables that you need to be aware of is the designation of IVs as *between subjects* or *within subjects*. Between-subjects variables have different subjects at each level of the IV. Within-subjects variables (also called *repeated measures*) have the same subjects tested at each level of the IV. This important distinction is not pursued further here, but is discussed in more detail in Chapter 6.

---

[12] Most computer programs for statistical analysis simply ignore this distinction and ask you to name a dependent variable The computer doesn't know whether a variable was measured in an experiment or a correlational study. The distinction is important for the interpretation of the statistical result, but not for their calculation.

Measurement and Classification

We have already examined Stevens' (1951) classification of variables according to the mathematical nature of the underlying scales. There are some additional issues in regard to measurement and classification that need to be discussed. I write "measurement and classification." By measurement, I mean a relatively continuous variable, usually at least an interval scale. By classification, I mean a variable that denotes group membership. It may or may not be ordered. (Classification of people as male or female does not imply ordering. Classification of people as short and tall does imply ordering.) From here, I will usually write just "measurement," but "classification" is implicit.

The *reliability* and *validity of measurements* are two extremely important aspects of the measurement of variables.[13] Ann Anastasi and Susana Urbina (1988) provide perhaps the best general discussion of these concepts aimed at the advanced undergraduate level, and the interested student should consult them for a more in-depth presentation of these issues. Reliability is the easier problem, so I will take up that topic first, after a digression to introduce the notion of *correlation*.

Correlation

Assessments of reliability and of validity rely heavily on the notion of *correlation*. If you have had a course in statistics, you will be familiar with the correlation as a measure of degree of relationship, and can probably skip this section. If you have not, this section will give you enough knowledge to follow the discussion.

We can plot a person's scores on two variables as a single point in a Cartesian coordinate space. Typically, the variable plotted along the horizontal axis is designated as X, and that along the vertical axis as Y. As an example, consider Figure 3-2A on Page 70, which plots the heights and weights of five persons. (Note that we are ignoring exact measurements—height ranges from short to tall and weight from light to heavy.) Person a is average in both height and weight. Person b is above average in both height and weight, while person c is below average in both. Person d is below average in height but average in weight. Person e is above average in height but average in weight.

If we measured the heights and weights of a large number of people, we would have a scatter diagram like Figure 3-2B. Note that most points (each designating an individual's height and weight) fall within a fairly coherent "swarm," as indicated by the ellipse. We can mathematically determine the

---

[13] Two other meanings of "validity" are presented in this textbook. The others are validity of a logical argument (see Chapter 2) and validity of an experiment (see Chapter 5).

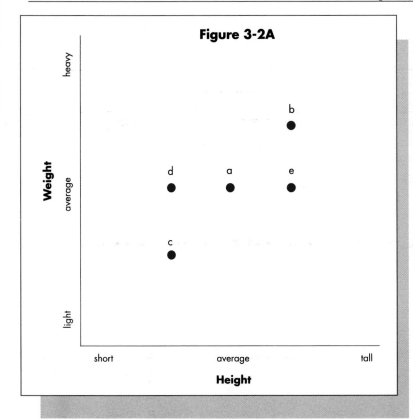

Figure 3-2A

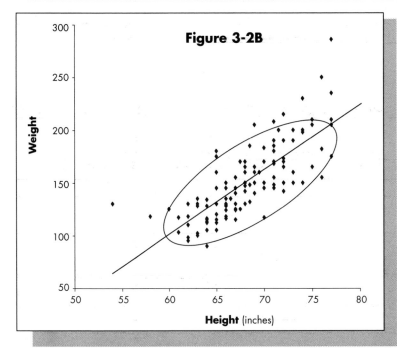

Figure 3-2B

best-fitting straight line through this swarm. That best-fitting line comes closer to all points than any other line we could choose. The measure of the strength of the correlation between the two variables concerns how closely the points fit the line and is designated r. The correlation can take any value between 0.0 (indicating no correlation at all) and 1.0 (indicating a perfect relationship). Correlations can also vary between 0.0 and –1.0, when increases in one variable are accompanied by decreases in the other. For a lot of males, age and amount of hair are negatively correlated. As indicated in Figure 3-2B, the correlation between height and weight in this sample is $r = .776$.[14]

Figure 3-3 shows correlations at four levels. Figure 3-3A shows a correlation between dominant hand grip strength and birth order. Here the correlation is very close to zero—$r = .060$. Note that the points are fairly evenly distributed. A slightly stronger, but still

---

[14] In American Psychological Association (APA) style, no leading zero is used if the value cannot exceed 1.0. Because correlations are bounded by –1.0 and 1.0, we write $r = .776$, instead of $r = 0.776$.

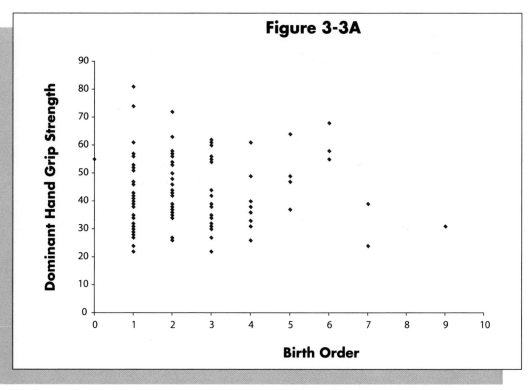

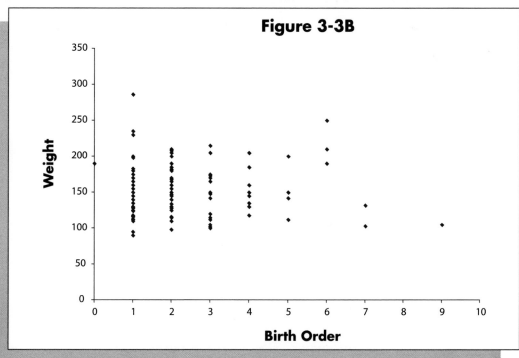

Illustrations of correlations of varying strength.

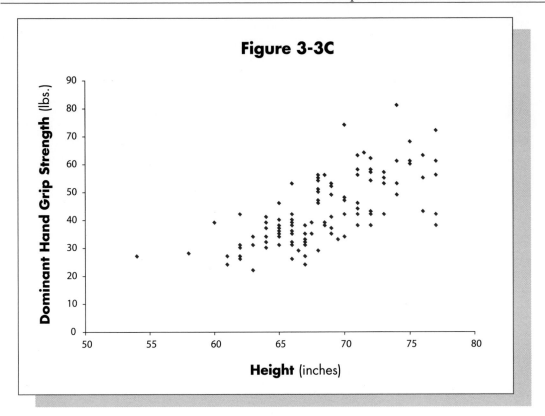

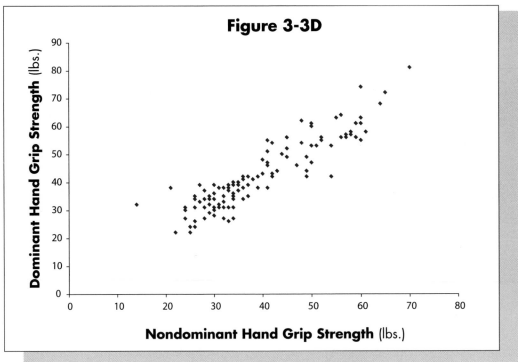

Illustrations of correlations of varying strength.

weak, correlation is shown in Figure 3-3B between birth order and weight. Here, the correlation is $r = .211$. Figure 3-3C shows a substantial correlation of $r = .736$ between dominant hand grip strength and height. Finally, Figure 3-3D shows a very strong correlation of $r = .914$ between the strength of the dominant and nondominant hands.

Reliability

To say that a measurement is reliable is to say that, whatever it is measuring, it is measuring it accurately. Depending on the situation, there are several ways to assess reliability. Proper calibration of instruments, such as EEGs or fMRIs, is important to assure that they are reliable. The reliability of RTs measured using a computer are mainly assured by an enormous amount of testing by the programmers—such was the case with the E-Prime software which is the programming environment underlying the *PsychMate* experiments.

In psychological testing, such as IQ, achievement, and personality tests, two general approaches are used, both of which rely on the use of correlations. Each is detailed, and a somewhat different approach to reliability is discussed— that involving the reliability of human observers.

Test-retest reliability. This approach to measuring reliability is based on the correlation between test scores from the same subjects on two different occasions. If an IQ test is reliable, it should give us just about the same score each time, and the correlation between the first and second test scores should be high. There are circumstances that limit the use of test-retest reliability. If the test might itself constitute practice, and result in different amounts of improvement for different individuals on the retest, this method is not appropriate. There is also a problem if the subjects simply remember their previous answers, as might occur if the retest was given almost immediately. Tests that are not appreciably affected by repetition (such as measures of sensory discrimination) are the best candidates for this method.

One concern with test-retest reliability is duration of the time intervening between test and retest. The longer the delay before retesting, the lower the correlation will be. For long delays—months or years—the correlation is probably better thought of as a measure of the stability across time of the trait being measured. If the delay is brief—days—then the correlation is probably reflecting reliability of the test.[15]

---

[15]This difference between measuring stability and measuring reliability is illustrated by David Magnusson's (1967) comment that "It is quite natural to consider a measuring tape to be completely reliable despite the fact that it gives different results for an individual's broad-jump performance on different occasions." (p. 107)

Split-half reliability. This takes a slightly different approach. Recall the achievement tests you have taken. They typically have a set of spelling items ranging from easy to difficult, and a set of mathematical items, history items, and so on, each set ranging from easy to difficult. If you were to score the test once based only on the odd-numbered items, and score it a second time based only on the even-numbered items, you would have two tests that should be nearly equivalent. Split-half reliability is measured just that way—by the correlation between scores based on odd- and even-numbered items. If the test is reliable, there should be a high correlation—persons who score high on odd-numbered items should also score high on even-numbered items.

There are two techniques that build on split-half reliability. These techniques examine the "inter-item consistency" more generally. For test items scored as correct/incorrect, the Kuder-Richardson Formula 20 provides a measure that is actually the mean of all the split-half reliabilities you would obtain if you split the test in two every way you could (not just odd versus even). Cronbach's alpha provides a similar measure if the items have answers along a scale, such as a scale from *Strongly Agree* to *Strongly Disagree.*

For the major achievement tests and IQ tests, the test-retest correlations and split-half correlations are typically about $r = .9$. Whatever the tests are measuring, they measure it accurately.

Inter-rater reliability. Another approach to reliability is *inter-rater* reliability. This comes into play when you have several people make ratings from the same data. In this case, you should compute the correlation between the raters' scores on a number of tests to get the inter-rater reliability. If there are more than two raters, you would take the mean of the correlations. Any time the DV is measured by the ratings of several observers, the inter-rater reliability should be reported in the Method section.

Reliability of change scores. It is not uncommon in research to combine measurements in various ways, such as the amount of change from one time to another (the difference between two measurements of the same variable). You need to keep in mind that the reliability of such combined measurements will be less than that of the original measurements. If you will, the *unreliabilities* of the two single measurements are combined. Change scores, such as change from before to after an experimental manipulation of some kind, are probably the most common kind of combined score, but the principle holds for any combination of measurements.

Because combined measurements, such as difference scores, may suffer in reliability, you should carefully consider using them. For example, if you want to compare the change in weight of persons undergoing a weight-loss program to a control group, you could use the change scores. A standard scale to measure weight is highly reliable so the combined score (weight loss or gain) would still be quite reliable. On the other hand, if you compared measurements of attitude toward some social problem before and after some manipulation intended to change the attitude, the two scores (attitudes before and after) are probably not very reliable. Combining them into a change score could make a bad situation worse.

Validity

While reliability can be measured with some precision, *validity* is far more difficult to assess. Validity is concerned with whether we are really measuring what we intend to measure. Two examples: Does an intelligence test really measure intelligence? Are teachers' ratings of their students' aggressiveness (often used in studies concerning aggression and media violence) really reflecting aggressiveness? There are two ways in which a measurement or classification could fail to be valid. One is if it simply measures the wrong thing. The other is if the measurement is confounded—a paper-and-pencil intelligence test, for example, might measure both intelligence *and* reading ability.

We also need to be concerned with whether a test is valid for the persons being tested. An extreme example would be giving someone an IQ test in a language they did not understand, such as English. The test might be quite valid for those who speak English, but clearly not for those who do not.

There are several varieties of validity that have special purposes, and I will address those before examining the most basic issue—does the test measure what we want it to?

Face validity. Face validity is the weakest form of validity, and is concerned with whether a measurement is plausible. For a measurement to have face validity doesn't give it much support, but if a measurement *lacks* face validity, the person proposing it has a clear burden of proof. If I proposed to use body temperature measured by an oral thermometer as a test of intelligence, there is an obvious problem. On its face, this does not seem likely to be valid. But if I used a bathroom scale to measure weight, the face validity is high.

Predictive validity. An important issue for the application of psychological testing is whether a test predicts (correlates with) variables it is meant to *predict in advance*. Two perfect examples are the SAT and ACT. They exist for the sole purpose of predicting college performance. Their correlation with GPA at graduation (and with whether or not people graduate) is therefore a direct measure of their predictive validity.

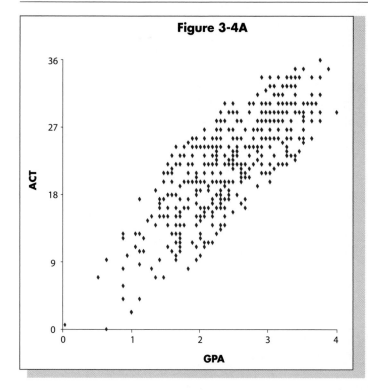

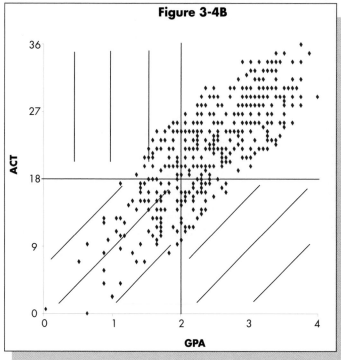

Tests that are used to decide who gets into a training program of any kind (college or vocational) and employee selection tests are almost exclusively concerned with predictive validity. There is, however, a serious caveat about predictive validity. *You cannot assess the predictive validity of a test if you use the test to decide who gets into the training program (or who gets employed).* To make sense of this requires a digression into some statistics, but the graphic presentation in Figure 3-4 should make the matter clear. I once heard a learned educator argue that the SAT should be abandoned because of its poor predictive validity. The correlation of SAT and GPA at graduation is typically about *r* = .3, which is not very good. (In comparison, the Graduate Record Exam (GRE), used in graduate admissions decision for programs from English to Physics, has a correlation with GPA at comple-tion of the graduate degree of about *r* = .1.) But is the argument valid? Probably not.[16]

Consider a diagram like Figure 3-4A, which shows a correlation between SAT and GPA at a hypothetical college of about *r* = .8—a substantial

---

[16] My point is restricted to the argument of poor predictive validity. There is a larger debate about the use of the SAT, ACT, and GRE.

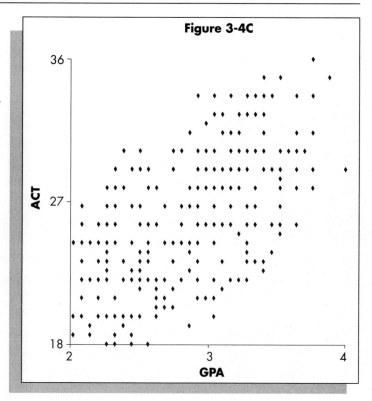

correlation. But note that the diagram includes people who scored so poorly on the SAT that they would be very unlikely to ever be admitted to the college. Those are highlighted in Figure 3-4B with diagonal lines. And it also includes persons whose GPA at graduation is below 2.0 (C on a 4-point scale), but most colleges do not let you graduate with a GPA below that point. Those are highlighted in the same figure with vertical lines. Those two areas represent the people who either did not get admitted or who failed to graduate.[17] Figure 3-4C shows the result—the correlation between SAT and GPA *of those who got in and stayed in*. While this is still a fairly strong correlation ($r = .590$), it is clearly a much weaker correlation. In order to assess the predictive validity of a test, you have to let everyone in regardless of score and not flunk anyone out. On the other hand, the more restrictive the admissions criterion, the lower the correlation between that measure and GPA at graduation. This phenomenon is called *restriction of range*. (Note that it doesn't matter whether you restrict the range of the variables to only high scores, only low scores, or only scores in the middle—the correlation based on the restricted sample will severely underestimate the actual correlation.)

Concurrent validity. This approach to validity is also limited in scope but very useful for its purpose. The issue for concurrent validity is whether a new measure *correlates with* (concurs with) existing measures. Concurrent validity is measured simply by the value of that correlation. Note that a correlation of $r = 1.0$ indicates perfect agreement—the two tests are literally measuring the same thing.[18] The typical correlation between the major achievement and IQ

---

[17] College admissions are never solely on the basis of SAT or ACT, but most schools admit students below these levels only if other factors indicate that they can do the work.

[18] Suppose we measured locations, instead of people, using one thermometer to measure the temperature in degrees Fahrenheit and another in degrees Celsius. They are literally measuring the same thing, and the calculated correlation would differ from 1.0 only due to slight error in reading the thermometer to the nearest degree or fraction.

test is usually about $r = .8$—they correlate with each other almost as well as they correlate with themselves (recall that test-retest reliabilities for these tests are about $r = .9$). But there is a major complication. If the Wechlser Adult Intelligence Scale (WAIS) can predict scores on the Stanford-Binet IQ test, it is measuring essentially the same thing as the Stanford-Binet. *If* the Standford-Binet is really measuring intelligence, then so is the WAIS. To say that the concurrent validity of $r = .8$ validates the WAIS requires the assumption that the Stanford-Binet is valid. That assumption may not be wholly correct.[19]

Concurrent validity can, nevertheless, be valuable. In the area of medical testing, we have tests whose validity is quite well established, such as the HIV tests (also known as AIDS tests, which are actually tests for antibodies to the HIV virus). Their validity has been tested in huge samples for whether the person does or does not develop actual symptoms of AIDS, and they are correct about 99% of the time. If a researcher found a new test for HIV that was faster, cheaper, or easier than the current test, she would want to establish concurrent validity. If the new test matches the classification of subjects based on the old (slower, more expensive, more difficult) test, it should now be preferred.

Construct validity. While predictive and concurrent validity are important, construct validity goes directly to the heart of the matter—does my measurement really reflect the construct I want it to. Does an IQ test really measure the construct of intelligence? For this type of validity there are no easy answers, especially when we are concerned with psychological measurements such as intelligence, attitude, or personality. We can at best estimate construct validity. We cannot at present *measure* it.

How do you establish construct validity? You do science. You establish the validity of your measurement by a whole lot of converging evidence. Thomas Cook and Donald Campbell (1979) address this in detail. I recommend a recent article by Denny Borsboom, Gideon Mellenbergh, and Jaap van Heerden (2004) that provides an interesting review of the concept of validity, the history of attempts to measure it, and some its complications.

Errors in measurement

As noted in discussing the issue of continuous variables, we must always measure to the nearest *something*, whether that is the nearest quarter inch of height or the nearest millisecond of RT. Thus, all measurement contains error.

---

[19] Ulrich Neisser and a panel of others (1996) reviewed what is known about intelligence and intelligence testing. It is not clear that standard IQ tests measure more than academic intelligence—the type of intelligence that helps you do well in school—though they do appear to measure that fairly well. Neisser et al. describe other varieties of intelligence that have been proposed.

But error can arise in other ways, as well. The misreading of an instrument or the misrecording of a datum certainly occur. Care and caution can reduce the frequency of error, but nothing can eliminate it completely.

Given the inevitability of measurement error, it is well to distinguish two general types of error—*constant error* and *variable error*. These have different consequences for interpreting the data from any scientific study.

Constant error is error that is usually in the same direction and by the same amount. Variable error is error that varies in direction and amount. The distinction is easily made by considering a concrete case—shooting at a target. Imagine that you fire three shots from a rifle, aiming for the bulls-eye in a standard target. If you are not experienced in riflery, you will probably exhibit a high level of variable error—your shots will go all over the place, as in Figure 3-5B. This illustrates a high degree of variable error but little constant error—the shots were all over the place, but if you "average" their

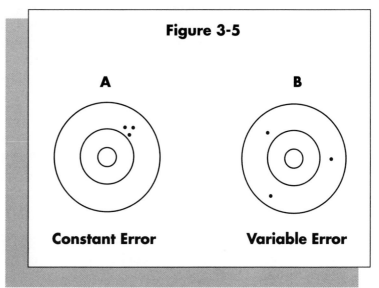

positions, the average is right on the target. On the other hand, suppose that you are an experienced marksman, but the sights of the gun are off, such that if it is aimed exactly at the bulls-eye, it fires above and to the right of the target. In that case, the three shots might look like those in Figure 3-5A.[20] This illustrates a high degree of constant error, but very little variable error—the shots were in the same place, but they were not on target.

Classical test theory (see Magnussen, 1967) has a formula worth considering:

$$t = T + e,$$

where t is the recorded measurement,
T is the "true" score,
and e is error in measurement.

---

[20] I am ignoring, for purposes of this example, the likelihood that an experienced marksman would adjust either their aim or the sights of the rifle.

In test theory, this notes that our measured test score on a subject, such as IQ, reflects a combination of his or her actual IQ and measurement error. "Error" here includes errors in measurement (measuring inaccurately) and errors in recording the measurements (writing the score down incorrectly). But it also includes other things that may give an erroneous reading of the subject's IQ, such as the subject being drowsy versus wide awake, or the subject being upset over a relationship and thus distracted at test time.

In RT research, we take a similar approach. Each trial under a given condition provides an estimate of the subject's "true" RT for that condition. But we know that each trial, or estimate, is confounded by all the things that affect RT—momentary attention, muscular preparedness, and the like—that change slightly from moment to moment. We then take the average of the individual trials as the best estimate of the true RT—certainly a better estimate than we get from any single trial. Note that this use of the average is assuming *variable* error. That is, the things that cause RT to fluctuate from moment to moment will sometimes make it a little slower, and sometimes a little faster. In this case, averaging should largely get rid of the error.

Variable error causes an increase in the "noise" of the data. Variable error thus reduces the consistency of our results and makes any statistical analysis less powerful.

Now consider an experiment to determine whether a new drug increases IQ. We compare the mean IQs of the treated and untreated groups, measuring each subject before and after they receive the drug (or a placebo control). Suppose that the person administering the IQ test makes the same mistake in scoring the exam for each subject, falsely adding five points to each score. Will it affect our conclusions? Not really. This is constant error, and while we will misreport the IQ of our subjects, the *differences* that we are looking for will be the same.[21] If the drug works, the IQs will increase for the treated group and remain about the same for the untreated group. Thus, constant error that occurs for all subjects equally in all conditions will have no effect on our statistical analyses. (A similar situation could occur in an RT experiment if the clock measuring RT began 20 ms late on each trial. Each trial would have a 20 ms error, but the *differences* in average RT across conditions would be the same.)

Operational Definition

Percy Bridgman, a physicist, had a major impact on psychology through his notion of *operationism* (or, if you prefer, *operationalism*). In an effort to

---

[21] As noted elsewhere, in an experiment, we are not typically trying to estimate the population mean.

more precisely define scientific concepts, Bridgman introduced the notion of operational definition of scientific concepts, such as length. "The concept of length involves as much as and no more than the set of operations by which length is determined. In general we mean by any concept nothing more than a set of operations; *the concept is synonymous with the corresponding set of operations*" (Bridgman, 1927, p. 5. Italics in original). An operational definition of a concept is thus a statement of how it was measured. *Length* is defined by the use of a tape measure.

Bridgman's formulation fell on fertile soil in the American psychology of the 1920s, shortly after John B. Watson proposed his Behaviorism as a cure for the problems seemingly unsolvable in a mentalistic psychology (at least one based on introspective data). The hope was that operationism would remove "surplus meaning" from concepts such as hunger or intelligence. The strength of the hunger drive could thus be operationalized as the number of hours of food deprivation. Edward Boring famously applied this to the definition of intelligence: "Intelligence is what [IQ] tests test" (1945, p. 244).[22] On the other side of this coin, if you cannot specify the operations by which a concept was measured then it has little or no meaning. If you talk of "self-esteem" without specifying how it was measured you may be dealing more in metaphysics than in science.

This notion of operational definition has been both a blessing and a curse for psychology. On the blessing side, it simply means that *when we employ a concept such as hunger or intelligence, we should specify how it was measured*. This makes communication clearer. If, in the Method section of a paper, you specify that you used the WAIS to measure intelligence, then the reader knows how you made the measurement. On this level, there is no problem or argument. Indeed, I would argue that such definitions are a serious requirement of any method section. You cannot speak of comparing the effects of two levels of hunger drive on behavior unless you have told the reader how hunger was defined in your experiment.

But there are problems for operationism in the more general sense in which it came to be used in psychology. One problem concerns what we are to make of varying definitions. If I measure length with a yardstick and you measure it with a tape measure, are these the same concept? Well, they are likely to arrive at the same numerical answer, so perhaps so. But what if I define the level of the hunger drive as the number of hours of food deprivation, and you define it as a level of body weight maintained at 75% of the weight under conditions of free feeding. A rat (or human) given nothing to eat for 24 hours and another rat

---

[22] Boring's paper, as well as the Bridgman paper from the same journal, are part of a longer symposium on operationism published in the *Psychological Review*.

given only enough food to maintain 75% of free-feeding weight are doubtless both hungry, but the different operations may lead to different results in an experiment. Which, then, is the "correct" definition? Or are we to declare that there are as many meanings to "hunger" as there are ways of producing it?

Wendell Garner, Harold Hake, and Charles Eriksen (1956) were confronted with a problem in trying to publish their research on perception, in that a journal editor noted that the only way we know a person perceived something is by a discriminatory response. Therefore, the operational definition of a perception is the response that follows it—"the reaction is the perception" (p. 149). We have certainly painted ourselves in a corner, though, if psychologists cannot meaningfully distinguish between a perception and a response! Garner, Hake, and Eriksen noted that Bridgman himself did not seem to endorse the idea that every operation defines a separate concept, and quoted him: "Operational definitions, in spite of their precision, are in application without significance unless the situations to which they are applied are sufficiently developed so that at least two methods are known of getting to the terminus" (1945, p. 248). To pursue the example of length, it seems to me that we are on firmer ground if you use a tape-measure to find the length of a table, I use a yardstick, and we get the same answer than if we instead claim that we have each measured separate, incommensurable concepts. Garner, Hake, and Eriksen proposed a solution to this conundrum that they called "converging operations." In essence, they argued that you must have more than one experimental operation that produces a similar effect. In that case, the various operations converge on a single concept—the concept is not established necessarily by any one operation, but their mutual agreement establishes the usefulness of the concept.

There is also a difficulty with trying too hard to remove surplus meaning— at least in the beginning of a scientific investigation. Joel Michell (1990) noted that "an approach to science that does not let us think beyond that which can be currently observed prevents us from understanding" (p. 27) nature's often-hidden ways of working. Sometimes we have to permit ourselves to deal with messy variables, especially when little is known of the area. As an example, the study of personality has now fairly convincingly shown that there are five dimensions of personality and that they can be measured with suitable instruments—personality tests (for example, the Lippa Big Five—see Lippa, 1991). But the history of the study of personality is a mess. Poorly defined terms, difficulties of measurement, and lack of conceptual clarity made operational definition grossly premature. With enough accumulation of evidence and improvement in theory, it eventually became possible to put forward a reasonable set of measurements (even if there is no generally accepted theory of what specifically determines an individual's personality).

Operational definition in the strict sense fails largely because it confuses the act of measurement with the quantity being measured. To many of us, the length of a table is assumed to exist independently of how we measure it.

That said, I again note the importance of telling the reader how you measured your variables. That part of operational definition stands despite the failure of the theoretical baggage.

Performance vs internal states

A final point for this chapter is the distinction between performance and the internal states that we try to infer from performance. Consider studies of learning and memory, for example, *PsychMate 3.4: Levels of Processing and the Self-Reference Effect* and *PsychMate 2.6: Organization in Memory as an Aid to Recall.* In such studies, our interest is in the formation of memory. But we cannot measure memory (or any other internal state, such as attention or problem solving) directly. Instead, we must infer it from behavior.

A classical example of this distinction between performance (or behavior) and learning comes in the study of motor performance. In the 1940s and 1950s, a number of theoretical issues in learning were addressed using the pursuit rotor

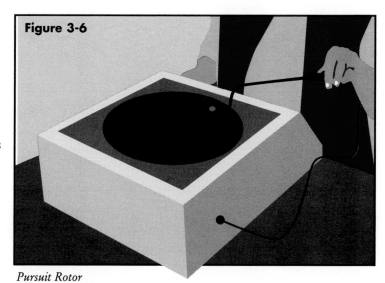

Figure 3-6

Pursuit Rotor

invented by Wilhelmina Koerth (1922). The pursuit rotor (shown in Figure 3-6) consists of a turntable with a dime-sized target embedded in its surface. The target travels in a circle of about 10 inches in diameter. The task is to keep the tip of a stylus on the target as it spins around, typically at 60 rpm. The DV is percent time on target. To aid learning, a buzzer sounds when the subject is on target. Suppose I have you work at this task for 10 minutes, then rest for 5 minutes, then resume. The result would be like the data in Figure 3-7. Performance would improve over the initial practice, but then improve again after the break. That improvement in performance following rest without

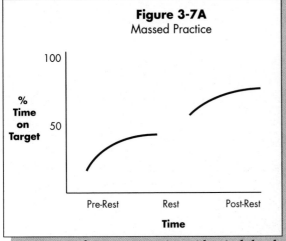

Performance across time with a single break.

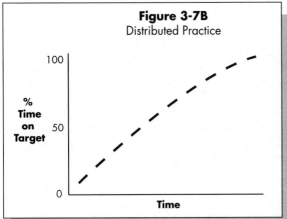

Performance across time with frequent breaks.

practice is called *reminiscence*. Can we conclude, then, that *learning* improved during the rest break? *Performance* clearly did improve, and the improvement in performance during the initial practice is almost certainly due to learning. But surely no learning is taking place during the rest break! As it turns out, the reminiscence is due to recovery from muscular fatigue. During initial practice, the amount of learning is actually masked—learning is leading to improved performance, but fatigue is limiting performance. After the break, the learning that took place during the initial practice is now seen. This interpretation is backed by the finding that if you distribute the initial practice over time—say, 10 periods of one minute each with a one-minute break in between—there is no reminiscence.

The essential point here is that performance may be affected by many factors other than the ones we are trying to measure. In many ways, the history of experimental psychology over the last 50 years or so has been a history of this attempt to infer internal structure and function from performance. An excellent example of this is the measure-ment of the speed of rotation of a mental image, as in *PsychMate 1.3: Rotation of Mental Images.* In that replication of studies by Cooper and Shepard (1973) and Shepard and Metzler (1971), the performance directly measured was RT to determine whether a letter was normal or a mirror image or whether two figures could be rotated to match or were mirror images. But the measures of RT were for the purpose of determining some-thing about the nature of the underlying, internal, (currently) unobservable process of manipulating a mental image.

Chapter 4

Research I

In this chapter, I begin a discussion of a variety of topics related to the enterprise of research. First, I treat the process of reviewing what is already known about an area—the literature survey. Then the ethical treatment of human and non-human subjects is examined.

The Literature Survey

An important part of the job of research is to find out what is already known about an area. Hardly anyone starts a line of research that has not been anticipated to at least some degree in previous work. (If you have never done so, I strongly recommend that you take a look at any recent issue of one of the research journals in psychology and examine the number of references for each article. They seldom number fewer than 20 and often run into the hundreds.) In this section, I review the types of publications and the kinds of information you might get from them, the bibliographical sources to use in searching for information on a topic, and the types of articles that appear in the scientific literature. The next section concerns some tactics or strategies for reading the material you find.

Types of publications

Before examining the methods of searching the psychological literature, it is worth noting the types of publications that are common. Journal articles, edited volumes, and monographs are the three main sources. *Journal articles* constitute the main literature in psychology. These are reports of experiments or other studies. The types of journal articles are discussed below. It is relatively rare for a report of research in psychology to be of book length, and even the most prolific of psychologists seldom publish in book form, except for edited volumes. The process by which articles are submitted to journals and reviewed for publication is detailed in Chapter 8.

Edited volumes are highly similar to journal articles. In a sense, an edited volume is a single-issue special journal. Edited volumes sometimes are based on presentations made at a conference on some issue. Some are festschrifts, often on the retirement of a major scientist.[1] Others occur because a publisher and

---

[1] *Festschrift* is a German word meaning a celebratory (festive) writing. The word is now accepted as an English word.

psychologist decide together that an edited volume on a given topic would be timely. One major difference between articles in an edited volume and those in a journal is that articles in an edited volume usually do not undergo the scrutiny of independent peer review that is typical in journals.

Monographs are books on a single topic. The entire book is written by the same author (or set of authors). Monographs are relatively uncommon as a means of communication in psychology—indeed, in the sciences generally— though they are quite common in other disciplines, such as history and literary criticism. I do not denigrate monographs. I merely note their relative rarity in psychology.

Magazines and newspapers are not usually good resources for your survey of the literature—though an article may pique your interest and suggest a topic for further study. A serious difficulty with magazine and newspaper articles is that they are usually written by journalists who are not experts in the subject matter, and hence are often less than adequately accurate. (There are science journalists who are quite good, of course. Gina Kolata and Daniel Goleman of *The New York Times* and Susan Begley of *The Wall Street Journal* are among them.)

Another serious problem with magazine and newspaper articles is that they usually do not include references to the journals where the research they are writing about was published. At best, you get the names of the researchers, and then must track down the article yourself, using the author search in PsycInfo, PubMed, or some other bibliographical source.

A difference worth noting between journals and magazines is that journals have *continuous pagination* through a volume. If the first issue of a volume contains pages 1 through 227, then issue two begins with page 228. For that reason, you need only cite the year, volume, and page number. Magazines begin each issue with page 1, so you must cite the issue by month or by specific date (if it is published weekly or daily). *Scientific American* is technically a magazine with page numbers starting at 1 for each issue. It is so widely cited for its scientific content, however, that it is often cited incorrectly, with authors failing to specify the month. I once looked up an article on memory by the page number only to find myself in the middle of an article on particle physics! I had to go issue-by-issue through the volume until I finally found my article in the June issue.

Where do you find the literature?

Psychologists are lucky in that the literature in psychology has been carefully indexed since the 1890s. The *Psychological Abstracts* began publication in 1887, and printed the abstracts for articles in virtually all of the relevant journals. Though your library may have the back issues of the *Abstracts* filed away somewhere, they were superseded some years ago by the online catalogue of the psychological literature called *PsycInfo*. *PsycInfo* can be searched by key words (subjects), author names, and even journals. It contains the abstracts of the articles, full bibliographical information, and, in some instances, online access to the full text of the article. You can check off the articles you are interested in and have the bibliographical information and abstract e-mailed to you. Your librarians can show you how to access *PsycInfo*. The old *Psychological Abstracts* are probably still on the shelf somewhere, and should be consulted if you are looking for articles before the 1960s. *PsycInfo* indexes some, but not all, of the earlier literature.

A second major source is the National Library of Medicine (www.nlm.nih.gov/pubmed), which is housed at the National Institutes of Health. *PubMed* is the principal search engine, providing subject and author searches for the world's literature on medicine. It also covers a number of psychology journals and is excellent for subjects involving clinical psychology and other areas that relate to medicine. However, for straight psychology searches, *PsycInfo* is best. *PubMed* replaces the older, print-based *Index Medicus*. *PubMed* also permits you to check off the articles and have the bibliographical information and abstract e-mailed to you.

Finally, the largest compendium of scientific literature is the *Science Citation Index (SCI)* and its companion, the *Social Science Citation Index (SSCI)*. These compile not only the subject and author information but also an extraordinary feature—the *citation index*. The citation index lists all of the articles that have referenced a target article that you look up. For example, if you have located an early article that is foundational for a field (e.g., George Sperling's, 1961, article on visual sensory memory—see *PsychMate 1.7: Iconic Memory*), you can be fairly certain that anyone writing about that area later will refer to that classic paper. To find those articles, look in the citation index of the *SSCI* under Sperling, with the journal title, volume, and page numbers, and you will find a list of articles that refer to Sperling's original article. You will find that many of the references are quite peripheral, but almost every article seriously addressing the phenomena of iconic memory will be there. (Note that the *SSCI* is most often useful for the psychological literature. The computer-based search will alert you if there are additional references in the *SCI*.) Unfortunately, the *SCI* and *SSCI* are extremely expensive, and most colleges cannot afford them. A trip to a nearby research university that has them may be well worth the time and trouble.

Two other computerized databases that are sometimes of use are the *Education Resources Information Center (ERIC)* and the *Education Index*.

If you are researching areas of psychology that overlap with education, these can be quite valuable.

When you have located articles of interest, you will probably find that your library has only a portion of them. There are tens of thousands of journals in the sciences, and only the largest research universities will have them in hard copy. Interlibrary loan is the usual answer. Ask your librarian how to request copies of articles through interlibrary loan. You can also check to see whether the author has a website with the article posted online. It is becoming more common for authors to post them on a website in PDF format, which prints a copy of the original layout of the journal article. You can usually find the author's website using an Internet search engine. If necessary, go to the author's institution's website first—the bibliographical information you find in *PubMed* or *PsycInfo* will list the institutional affiliation of the author(s). Some journals also make the full text of articles available.

Types of articles

Not all journal articles are the same. Some report individual experiments, while others summarize research projects that encompass many individual studies. I describe the general classes of articles in this section.

Review articles are the most helpful if you are beginning research in a new area. These articles review the existing literature in a given area. An excellent place to look for these is in the *Annual Review of Psychology*, a yearly publication of review articles. Of course, there might not be a recent review of the area you are interested in, or the review may be too broad or narrow to help much, but a good review article can save you enormous amounts of time since it will list most of the relevant articles. In a sense, a review article is an article consisting solely of a literature survey.

Empirical articles are the meat and potatoes of the scientific literature. Here, original research is reported. These articles usually include a brief review of the literature (though these sometimes approach the length and thoroughness of a review article). But their main focus is the reporting of the results of new studies—experiments, correlational studies, and the like.

Theoretical articles, such as many of the articles in the *Psychological Review*, are intended to put together the results of many empirical studies in a fashion that produces a "coherent structure of understanding." These report on larger research projects rather than specific bits of experimentation. A theoretical article will, of necessity, include a review of some of the empirical research and sometimes also include new studies.

Meta-analyses are an increasingly common form of article. A meta-analysis is a type of review article, but, in addition to compiling the literature, it attempts to combine the empirical findings of a number of similar studies statistically. In some instances, a meta-analysis based on a few dozen studies can reveal patterns in the data that were too weak to be statistically meaningful in any one of the studies by itself. A good example of a meta-analysis is the study by Cynthia Symons and Blair Johnson (1997) on the self-reference effect, which is discussed in *PsychMate 3.4: Levels of Processing and the Self-Reference Effect*. In addition to strong support for the self-reference effect they were able to show that it is slightly weaker among college students than non-college subjects—a finding that does not easily arise from any single study.

Reading an Empirical Article

It might seem a bit strange for me to offer a section about how to read an article—after all, you do know how to read. But a journal article, especially an empirical one, should be approached strategically. If you refer to Appendix B on writing in American Psychological Association (APA) style that details the parts of an article, you will see some hints there of the remarks to follow.

The *Abstract* is the most important part of an article in many ways. In doing a literature survey, you will read many abstracts, but fewer articles. In many instances, the Abstract will give you enough information to satisfy you that the article is not really pertinent to your line of research, so you can save the trouble of reading the article. But even if the Abstract convinces you that you need to read the article, it can serve as an advance organizer—you have a guide as you read the denser material of the article itself.[2]

The very beginning of the *Introduction* should serve to set the theoretical orientation of the article—what are they up to? How closely you read the literature review that makes up most of the typical Introduction depends on how well you are acquainted with the previous research. The first few articles you read in a new area probably will require a careful reading of their literature survey, but after you have read a few articles in similar areas you will find that some new ones are mostly covering familiar ground and you can skim them for now. You may need to return to a more careful reading later, of course.

The end of the Introduction (or beginning of the *Method* section) should tell you in fairly plain language what the experiment was—the IVs, DVs, and the basic methodology. If it does, then you can usually skip the Method section. It provides the highly specific details of the experiment that you may not need unless you are experimenting in similar ways. Note that many

---

[2] If you doubt the efficacy of organization as an aid to memory, see *PsychMate 2.6: Organization in Memory as an Aid to Recall*. The effects are not subtle.

journals print the Method section in a smaller font. Their assumption is that few persons need to read the level of detail that would permit them to do a literal replication of the study.[3] If you are setting out to actually replicate a study or build on it in your own research, you probably *do* need to read the Method section in detail.

Similarly, the first paragraph or so of the *Discussion* will often give a plain statement of the outcome—what were the principal relationships between variables that were discovered? If it does, then you can probably skip the *Results* section, where the details of the statistical analyses are presented. The Results section is also often set in a smaller font—again, many readers need the overall story that the study tells but do not need the full detail.

Two final thoughts on reading the literature.

First, you must read critically—recall Granit's comment about the "critical" review of the evidence. Despite the best efforts of reviewers, you must finally make your own judgment in regard to the quality and worth of the articles you read. Second, you must try to learn what is known without letting that put blinders on you. To paraphrase John Ziman (1968) you must "[learn] the consensus, without turning it into an orthodoxy" (p. 69).[4]

Ethical Issues in the Treatment of Research Subjects

I have divided treatment of ethical issues into two sections. Here, I discuss the ethical treatment of research subjects. In Chapter 7, I discuss ethical issues in regard to the treatment of data and publication of research.

Before beginning the technical discussion of issues and methods in psychological research, you should become aware of the ethical issues involved in that research. Psychological research affects people's lives. The subjects who participate are directly affected, and the results obtained may indirectly affect many others, including fellow scientists who are relying on the integrity of others' results. The APA publishes an extensive *Ethics Code*. The latest revision was published in 2002. Most of that code is concerned with ethics in professional psychology—psychological testing, counseling, and treatment and does not concern us here. The topics below are covered in the *Ethics Code* in Section 8 on *Research and Publication*. The entire code is available for free download from their web site at www.apa.org/ethics. There is also a guide to

---

[3] See Chapter 7 for a discussion of issues related to replication.
[4] See the discussion of "paradigms" in chapter 2.

ethical treatment of non-human animals in research, available at www.apa.prg/science/anguide.html. A couple of other web sites have information concerning Institutional Review Boards and researchers. The site for the United States Food and Drug Administration is www.fda.gov/oc/ohrt/irbs/default.htm. The site for the United States Department of Health and Human Services is ohrp.osophs.dhhs.go/irb/irb_quidebook.htm.

The first serious legal protections for research subjects were formulated only at the end of World War II. With the liberation of the concentration camps, the Allies began to discover the enormity of the Nazi terror. In addition to the 15 million or so people who died in the camps of cold, disease, starvation, and murder, there were thousands (at least) who were subjected to "experiments" by the Nazi doctors and (literally) mad scientists. These included exposing naked people to freezing winter weather to measure how long it took them to freeze. Joseph Mengele, the Butcher of Auschwitz, was especially interested in using twins to provide experimental controls so pairs of twins who entered the concentration camp at Auschwitz were kept alive (for a while) to permit him to test various poisons and toxins. The Nazi party officials who had been involved in the concentration camps in general, and these "experiments" in particular, were tried by the Allies at Nuremburg, Germany, shortly after the end of the war. Though there existed no body of international law that applied to such cases, the tribunal in essence wrote its own. Among the strongest statements of the Nuremburg Code was that people cannot be the subject of experiments without their consent. The Nuremburg Code is published in *Trials of War Criminals* and is easily available on the Internet. A second important document in the effort to prevent such crimes is the Helsinki Agreement, adopted by the member states of the United Nations in a meeting at Helsinki, Finland, in 1964, is *Recommendations Guiding Physicians in Biomedical Research Involving Human Subjects.*

Though the horrors of the concentration camps are well known, we should not make the mistake of assuming that only the Nazis were capable of ignoring common human decency. The United States Public Health Service, a branch of the U.S. government, began a study in 1932 in which a group of 400 poor, mostly illiterate, black men in Alabama who had syphilis and 200 non-syphilitic controls were followed and periodically examined to plot the course of untreated syphilis. They were told that they were receiving treatment (which included a painful spinal tap) for "bad blood." Lest you imagine that this was some weird, clandestine study, you should know that reports of the study were routinely published in the medical literature—e.g., Pesare, Bauer, and Gleeson (1950) and Rivers, Schuman, Simpson, and Olansky (1953). The latter principally presents the personal recollections of Eunice Rivers, a nurse involved in the study, who adds the "personal interest" story of the men helping free her car from mud on poor country roads as she was transporting them to town for their "treatments." During World War II, a number of the men in the study were drafted into the Army. The researchers intervened to have them exempted because they knew that if the men were drafted their syphilis would be treated. The last stage of syphilis is usually not reached for several decades after the initial infection. In this tertiary (third stage) syphilis, the spirochete that causes the disease invades the nervous system producing damage to the brain and spinal cord, which results first in a characteristic shuffling gate, then further motor and cognitive damage, ending in dementia and death. The study was only ended when it became a major item of national news after Jean Heller of the Associated Press published an article in the *Washington Star* on July 25, 1972. Twenty-eight of the subjects had died of syphilis. Another 100 died of complications related to syphilis. Forty of their wives and 19 of their newborn children were also infected. But for the public outcry that occurred when the story finally broke, the study probably would not have ended until all the subjects were all dead. None of the so-called "scientists" who took part in the study was ever disciplined. A cure for syphilis (a simple injection of penicillin) was widely available in 1943, and the natural course of the disease was already well known when the study began.[5] In the 1990's, the US Congress voted reparations for the remaining victims, and in a White House ceremony on May 16, 1997, President Clinton apologized to the victims and their families. Five survivors and representatives of three others were present. Here is an excerpt from his remarks.

> So today America does remember the hundreds of men used in research without their knowledge and consent. We remember them and their family members. Men who were poor and African American, without resources and with few alternatives, they believed they had found hope when they were offered free medical care by the United States Public Health Service. They were betrayed.

> Medical people are supposed to help when we need care, but even once a cure was discovered, they were denied help, and they were lied to by their government. Our government is supposed to protect the rights of its citizens; their rights were trampled upon. Forty years, hundreds of men betrayed, along with their wives and children, along with the community in Macon County, Alabama, the City of Tuskegee, the fine university there, and the larger African American community.

---

[5] A more complete history of the Tuskegee syphilis study is *Bad Blood: The Tuskegee Syphilis Experiment,* by James H. Jones (expanded edition, New York: Free Press, 1993).

The United States government did something that was wrong — deeply, profoundly, morally wrong. It was an outrage to our commitment to integrity and equality for all our citizens.

To the survivors, to the wives and family members, the children and the grandchildren, I say what you know: No power on Earth can give you back the lives lost, the pain suffered, the years of internal torment and anguish. What was done cannot be undone. But we can end the silence. We can stop turning our heads away. We can look at you in the eye and finally say on behalf of the American people, what the United States government did was shameful, and I am sorry. (Applause.)

The American people are sorry — for the loss, for the years of hurt. You did nothing wrong, but you were grievously wronged. I apologize and I am sorry that this apology has been so long in coming. (Applause.)

It is worth noting that, even ignoring the ethics of the Nazi "experiments" and the Tuskegee Study, nothing of any scientific value was obtained from any of them.

The Institutional Review Board

The National Research Act of 1974 requires all organizations that deal with human research to establish Institutional Review Boards (IRBs) to review proposed research for ethical concerns. Guidelines for protection of human subjects were drawn up in the Belmont Report of 1978, and the federal laws governing IRBs were passed in 1981.

An important concept in evaluating the ethics of a proposed study is that of "minimal risk." Minimal risk is defined as a level of risk no greater than that of everyday activities. Most psychological research involves no more than minimal risk. No study can be said to be without *any* risk—there is always the possibility that a subject will fall down walking across the floor of the laboratory, hit her head on a table and die. But that possibility is the same as if she were walking across the floor of her dorm room or apartment.

Note that ordinarily the IRB is asked to pass judgment only on the ethics of an experiment. They do not review the proposed studies for their scientific value. However, *if the proposed study involves more than minimal risk or involves deception*, the IRB must then consider whether the potential benefits are sufficient to justify the deception. A poorly-designed study that won't hurt anyone is bad science but not bad ethics. If there is a chance of harm, benefits must be weighed against risks. Note that risk is not prohibited. Competent adults, properly informed, can certainly agree to be subjects in research that has some level of risk beyond that of daily life.

Informed Consent

At the very heart of any idea of ethics in research with human subjects is that of *informed consent*. A researcher has the absolute responsibility to determine that subjects are capable of consent. In most settings, consent is not a problem, but in dealing with persons who are subject to orders by others, extraordinary caution must be exercised. Those populations include soldiers, prisoners (of which more is discussed later in this chapter), students, and employees among others. Subjects must consent to be in a research study, but that consent only counts if it is informed. What is needed to make consent informed? The APA *Ethics code* lists eight areas about which the subjects must be informed.

1. the purpose, duration, and procedures of the study

2. the right to refuse to participate and the right to withdraw at any time after participation has begun

3. foreseeable consequences of refusal or withdrawal

4. any factors that might influence the prospective subject's decision, such as discomfort or risks

5. any possible benefits of the research—whether to the subject or more generally

6. any possible limits to confidentiality

7. any incentives for participating, such as class credit or money

8. names of people to contact to ask questions

In addition, subjects must be given the opportunity to ask questions about the study.

A note on the use of prisoners as research subjects. Based on discussions with friends who have been in studies as prisoners, I argue that they cannot provide the level of informed consent necessary to be used as subjects in research. Archival research using records of prison populations can certainly be unobjectionable (provided other concerns of anonymity, etc. are met). But *no ethically acceptable data can be gathered from prisoners.* Why? First, you as a researcher will not have control over the selection of a "random" sample. The warden will not give you that control—he or she will edit your subject list (sometimes for perfectly legitimate reasons of security). More importantly, you cannot guarantee a prisoner the right to refuse to participate. If a correctional officer is present (which will be the case if you test a group of prisoners), then from the prisoners' point of view they have been ordered to participate. Even if you make it clear to the prisoners that they are not required to participate, *they have no reason to believe you and every reason not to*. To refuse to participate in front of a guard would render them vulnerable to the view of the staff that they are "uncooperative," thus possibly lessening chances for parole or other privileges. Even if you arrange for them to avoid detection by the guard, they know that your data sheets are subject to seizure while you are inside the prison.

Persons convicted of felony crimes are, quite properly, deprived of many civil liberties. It is that deprivation of liberty that is the principal component of imprisonment, though the daily realities of prison life certainly add to the unpleasantness of that punishment. But freedom from experimentation is not a civil liberty, *it is an absolute right*. The laws "invented" at Nuremburg are now part of the United Nation's Declaration of Human Rights, which its member nations have pledged to respect. (Granted, some of those countries fail to respect that commitment, but the commitment itself makes it harder for them to carry out atrocities, at least when the abuses are opposed by public campaigns such as those of Amnesty International).

Consent by minors. In the case of minor children (under the age of 18), the consent of the parents or legal guardian is required. The consent of the child is also required, but it is acknowledged that the child alone cannot give informed consent. The consent obtained from the child must be at an age-appropriate level. It should be clear that not all of the elements of consent listed above are going to be understood by children of different ages. With an infant, the consent would be given solely by the parents. For a six-year-old, you would need the child's "consent," but might not be able to explain the study clearly enough for that to be full, adult consent. For an adolescent, the consent from the child would probably be as full and complete as the consent from the parents. These rules also apply to adults with limited capacity for consent, such as the mentally retarded—a guardian's consent would be necessary along with consent from the person following an appropriate level of explanation.

Improper inducement. It is unethical to offer excessive pay or other inducements if they are likely to be coercive. Note that an offer to pay a college student $6 per hour for being a subject would not be an excessive inducement, but the same offer to a prisoner who has no other means of making money may lead that person to feel that they cannot afford to refuse.

Exceptions. There are a few exceptions to the need for formal, written, informed consent. One exception involves anonymous questionnaires, where a person's willingness to answer the questions is taken as consent. (This does not, however, imply that all survey research is automatically exempt. Most is, but it still requires IRB approval.) Another is for the study of "normal educational practices." In other words, if I as a faculty member want to try out two different methods of teaching a subject, I do not require informed consent. In organizational settings, such as businesses, studies of factors related to organizational effectiveness are exempt, as long as confidentiality is maintained and there is no threat to the subjects' employment.

An interesting exemption to informed consent was added relatively recently by the U.S. Food and Drug Administration (1998). This involves the experimental testing of emergency room procedures used on persons too severely injured to be able to provide consent and when there is simply not enough time to attempt to get consent from family. The purpose of the exceptions is to allow "research on life-threatening conditions for which available treatment options are unproven or unsatisfactory...while establishing additional protections to provide for safe and ethical studies." The rule is available at www.fda.gov/oc/ohrt/irbs/except.html. These experiments, of which there have been very few, require FDA approval. Part of the reason to permit this research without informed consent is that many emergency procedures in common use have never been tested for efficacy. Absent serious evidence that the common practice actually works, one can hardly argue that others cannot be tried.

A concern in regard to consent that has arisen recently concerns the use of chart reviews in medical research. Traditionally, these have not required the consent of each individual patient whose medical records ("chart") were examined by a researcher in order to record information, as long as it remained unidentifiable. In 1996, the Department of Health and Human Services issued new medical privacy rules as the Health Insurance Portability and Accountability Act (HIPAA), which was designed to address concerns about medical information sharing for purposes of treatment, payment, and quality-assurance audit. However, they also apply more broadly, and it is not yet completely clear how they affect chart reviews beyond the obvious need for more stringent review by and IRB. Katherine Uraneck (2001) reviewed the basic issues. The Act itself can be obtained at the website of the Department— www.hhs.gov.

Deception

The use of deception in experiments is forbidden by the APA Ethics Code with some exceptions. The principal problem with deception is that it violates the assumption of informed consent. If you fail to tell a subject about a substantive aspect of the research, then you have deprived them of the ability to make an informed decision about participation. Deception is permitted if there is simply no other way to do the research, *and* there is "significant scientific, educational, or applied value." No deception is permitted if it would be "reasonably expected to cause physical pain or severe emotional distress."

When deception is permitted, the debriefing of subjects becomes even more important. The use of deception must be explained during the debriefing. If it is not possible to debrief the subjects at the end of the experiment (for example, if that would permit information about the deception to get to other subjects), then debriefing must be done as soon as data collection is finished. In addition, at the time of debriefing, because deception was used, the researcher must offer the subjects the opportunity to withdraw their data.

Debriefing

It is an ethical requirement that subjects be informed as soon as possible of the "nature, results, and conclusions" of the study. If it turns out that subjects misunderstood the nature of the study, the debriefing gives an opportunity to correct that misunderstanding. If the debriefing suggests that the subject may in some way have been harmed, the researcher is required to take action to minimize the harm.

Control Groups and Placebos

To determine whether a treatment is effective, we must have a comparison—a control group. (See Chapter 1 on the use of control groups.) A special issue arises in regard to research on medical treatments. In most cases, the control group of interest is NOT an untreated group, but rather a group receiving the standard treatment (see Kenneth Rothman & Karin Michels, 1994). For an obvious example, suppose that you devised a new treatment for appendicitis. An untreated control group would be unethical since we know the result of untreated appendicitis—a horrible, painful death. What is really needed for most tests of medical treatments is a demonstration that the new treatment is better than the existing treatment.

This clearly does not apply if there is no existing treatment. In that case, a true placebo control would be justified to provide a measure of how well patients do without the treatment. "Placebo" comes from the Latin "to please," and is simply a sham treatment. If the treated group gets a pill, the placebo control group gets a similar pill but with no drug in it. In the evaluation of surgical procedures, placebos sometimes include making a surgical cut, but not performing the actual surgery, so that the patients do not know that they received no treatment. The issue of the use of placebo controls is complex and beyond the scope of this text. A general discussion of the nature of placebos and theoretical accounts of their actions is given by Steve Stewart-Williams (2004).

For reasons apparently to do with the Food and Drug Administration (FDA) regulations for approving new drugs, several pharmaceutical companies are now using true placebo controls in the evaluation of their drugs. Amy Marcus (2004) recounts the rather bitter debate concerning this practice.

When a new treatment is shown to be more effective than existing treatments, there is an ethical obligation to then provide that new treatment to subjects in the control group. Indeed, clinical trials are sometimes actually halted when a new treatment proves especially effective so that the control patients can immediately receive the superior treatment. It is standard procedure in such medical trials to make estimates of the number of subjects needed to get a statistically significant result showing one treatment superior to another. If a treatment turns out to be especially good, a statistically significant result may be obtained before the full study is finished, prompting the researchers to end the clinical experiment early. In one study of the efficacy of a combination of heart medications (Pitt, et al., 1999), not only was the experiment stopped, but *The New England Journal of Medicine* took the step of publishing the article on its web site over a month before it was scheduled to appear in the print version. On the other side of this, a clinical trial can be stopped if problems such as unanticipated side-effects occur.

Use of Non-Human Animals in Research

While this textbook is principally concerned with research on human subjects, much of psychological research involves non-human species. More complete information is available at www.apa.prg/science/anguide.html. The points below summarize the APA *Ethics Code* on the humane care and use of animals.

Federal, state, and local laws should be followed for the acquisition, care, use, and disposal of animals. Persons conducting research with animal subjects have the obligation to know the regulations (generally and for the specific species they work with) and to make sure that those regulations are followed by all personnel. Reasonable efforts are required to minimize discomfort, illness, and pain. Pain, stress, or privation are permitted only if the scientific, educational, or applied purposes are sufficiently important, and no alternatives are available. Surgeries are required to use appropriate anesthetics and analgesia. When an animal is sacrificed, it is to be done in a humane manner.

Chapter 5

Experimentation I

An experiment usually consists in making an event occur under known conditions where as many extraneous influences as possible are eliminated and close observation is possible so that relationships between phenomena can be revealed.

(Beveridge, 1957, p. 13)

The aim of this chapter is to introduce a number of issues in regard to experimentation (as well as correlational research). The outcome of an experiment does not merely reflect on the adequacy of the underlying theory. It also depends on the myriad of details of just how the experiment was conducted (the "auxiliaries" discussed in Chapter 3).

This chapter begins with a brief admonition concerning keeping a record of your methodology. Next, there is a formal treatment of the basic research designs—more complex designs are reserved for Chapter 6. The validity of experiments and threats to their validity are presented next. Finally, there is a discussion of experimental subjects and the relationships between them, the experiment and the experimenter.

Keeping a record of your methodology

An important practical point about conducting research cannot be emphasized too much. *Keep a record of your research!* As you plan an experiment and conduct it, you will make many decisions that affect the outcome. Some will be obvious; others less so. You will need to make decisions on such things as constructing word lists for a memory experiment or determining the order of presentation of stimuli. At the time, these will seem to you to be things that you won't soon forget. But if we, as psychologists, know much of anything with certainty about the mind, it is the terrible fragility of memory—though we were not the first to note it.[1]

---

[1] A great deal has been written about problems of memory. The student of psychology can scarcely have avoided it. The vagaries of eye-witness testimony are well-known to psychologists though less well known to the courts and the jurors who listen to eye-witness testimony (Kenneth Deffenbacher & Elizabeth Loftus, 1982).

In regard to the vagaries of memory, I cannot resist a couple of quotes. Richard F. Burton, a 19th-century explorer, was famed for descriptions of his journeys through eastern Africa and his travels, disguised as a Muslim, to the Islamic holy cities of Mecca and Al-Medinah during the annual pilgrimage, or *Hajj*. In 1860, he made a trip to Salt Lake City, Utah. His *The City of the Saints* recounts the journey by wagon from St. Louis to Salt Lake City and then on to San Francisco at a time when travel was primitive to a terrible degree and attack by Indians was a real possibility.[2] In his preface, he remarks on the difficulties of keeping good records from which to later write about his travels and recommends the "Patent Improved Metallic Pocket-books" for the traveler, having used them to write "in sight of the objects which attracted my attention." He quotes Samuel Johnson, an 18th-century poet, essayist, and lexicographer on the difficulty of relying on memory.[3] Johnson was writing about his travels to the New Hebrides Islands to the west of Scotland in 1773, which Burton described as "somewhat of a feat in the locomotive line" (Burton, 1861/1963, p. *xxxix*): "An observer deeply impressed by any remarkable spectacle does not suppose that the traces will soon vanish from his mind, and having commonly no great convenience for writing, defers the description to a time of more leisure and better accommodation. He who has not made the experiment, or is not accustomed to require rigorous accuracy from himself, will scarcely believe how much a few hours take from certainty of knowledge and distinctness of imagery; how the succession of objects will be broken, how separate parts will be confused, and how many particular features and discriminations will be found compressed and conglobated with one gross and general idea" (Burton, 1861/1963, p. xl).[4] Burton then added, "Brave words, somewhat pompous and diffused, yet worthy to be written in letters of gold" (1861/1963, p. xl). While Johnson wrote of memory for travels, the same is certainly true of the details of an experiment. When we are wrapped up in it, we feel that we could not forget or misremember a detail, but soon enough we can and do.

Larry Squire (1995, p. 197) quoted Charles Darwin (1876) on the even greater problem of what we might term differential forgetting. "I had during many years followed a golden rule, namely, that whenever a published fact, a new observation or thought, came across me which was opposed to my general results, to make a memorandum of it without fail and at once; for I had found by experience that such facts and thoughts were far more apt to escape from the memory than others."

---

[2] To Burton's obvious disappointment, they were not attacked.

[3] In Johnson's *Dictionary* of 1755, he famously defined a network as "anything reticulated and decussated, with interstices at the intersections." He apparently wanted to be sure it got used.

[4] Johnson's *Dictionary* defines Conglobate (adj.) as "Moulded into a ball; consolidated."

The same problems plague data. As we record data, especially if by hand onto data sheets, then transferring the data to computer files, we too often assume that the organization of the data, so clear to us at the time, will remain so. It won't. In haste, we abbreviate and later can't remember what we meant. In assigning names to variables, we label things in ways that at the time are as clear as a rain-washed sky after the sun emerges. A few months later, when we think of an additional analysis, we find that the clouds have returned. I use "we" here quite deliberately. Ask your professors—most can recount near-horror stories of trying to recover the meaning of data (or the details of methodology) after the lapse of some time.

The remedy to the problems of memory is to keep copious notes made *at the time* ("in sight of the objects," if you will). A laboratory notebook should be part of your equipment. Note that in computerized experimentation, the program that controls the experiment will itself be a record of the details of the methodology, but that record can become obscured as well. Even though the details are preserved, they can be difficult to decipher later.

Experimental Designs

The goal of science is to understand phenomena, whether they are the physical and chemical phenomena of the inanimate world or the physiological, cognitive, and behavioral phenomena of complex living organisms. In order to understand a phenomenon, we must have reliable evidence about the relationships between variables. We need reliable evidence about the phenomenon itself so we are certain of what we are trying to explain. We also need reliable evidence to let us test hypotheses about the nature of the phenomenon.

A basic goal in experimental research is to discover whether some experimental treatment had an effect. A familiar example is research to discover whether some medical treatment improves the recovery of the patient. If it does, then the treatment had an effect. In general, a "treatment," is anything we do to a person (or rat) in our study. Put another way, each "treatment" represents one level of an independent variable (IV). An "observation" is a measurement of the dependent variable (DV). For example, we could seek to determine by experimentation whether a particular method of studying (IV) improves retention of the material studied (DV). Or, we could seek to determine whether people respond more quickly (DV = reaction time) to an expected stimulus than to an unexpected one (IV= probability of a stimulus). Both of these examples illustrate research with a single independent variable. I present those simple research designs first. Nineteenth-century experimental science often followed this "rule of one variable"— hold all conditions equal except for one that is systematically varied.[5] The resulting experiments can determine the effect that different levels of an independent variable have on a dependent variable. More complex designs with several independent variables are more often used in psychological research, however, and they are considered in detail later in this chapter.

At this point, it is useful to introduce a symbolic notation for simple experimental designs. I will use the letter T to stand for "treatment" (with each treatment being a level of an IV) and the letter O to stand for "observation" (a measurement of a DV). The dimension of time is represented by position from left to right. This notation is modified slightly from Donald Campbell and Julian Stanley (1963), and the series of designs discussed below closely follows their presentation. I use their names for these research designs. Most of the examples are my own, but the basic scheme is taken from Campbell and Stanley's classic book, *Experimental and Quasi-Experimental Designs for Research*.

Keep in mind as you read the descriptions of the various research designs that their purpose is to eliminate alternative explanations. The special goal of the designs detailed below is to eliminate experimental *confounds* or *confounding variables*. Confounds are things that co-vary with, or correlate with, the IV you are attempting to manipulate. As a simple example, suppose you wanted to compare the effects of caffeine on RT. You measure RT before and after the "treatment"—giving the subject a dose of caffeine or giving them a placebo. But suppose that the subjects who get the caffeine are, on average, quite a bit older than those who do not. Any differences in RT that you want to attribute to the presence (or absence) of caffeine are *confounded with* age, making interpretation of your data equivocal at best. Note that RT increases somewhat with age. So if caffeine improved RT, that improvement might be hidden by the slowing in RT due to age. On the other hand, if the no-caffeine control group was the older group, the effect of the caffeine might be exaggerated. Confounds can produce a spurious difference. They can also mask, exaggerate or diminish a real difference.

Pre-Experimental Designs

Campbell and Stanley use the term "pre-experimental" to describe some research designs that fail to adequately control for the sources of internal

---

[5]As Robert Sessions Woodworth (1938) noted, this rule applies only to the IV. We often can usefully measure several DVs—in RT experiments, we usually analyze both RT and error rates. In the first edition of his *Experimental Psychology*, Woodworth barely noted the factorial designs. Ronald Fisher's (1925) *Statistical Methods for Research Workers*, which first presented in one place the methods of analyzing factorial experiments, was not yet well known to psychologists.

invalidity. Why not just leave out the designs that do not work and teach you the ones that do? The answer is that the successful experimental designs are successful precisely because they correct the errors of the poor designs. Therefore, unless you understand those poor designs, you will not really know why the successful experimental designs work.

Diagnostic testing. The first "research design" I want to consider was not included in Campbell and Stanley's presentation but is added here for the sake of completeness. Diagnostic testing does not represent a research design as such but is certainly a powerful and widely used tool, especially in technological applications. If I wish to know whether there is an electrical current flowing through a wire, I take a reading with a volt meter. A physician, who suspects that a patient has suffered a heart attack, performs a diagnostic blood test. The meter reading or test result is a diagnostic test. Note that diagnostic testing works in the cases described precisely because a thorough scientific understanding of electricity (or of cardiac physiology) has reduced the tests to pure technology. Diagnostic testing is adequate in technological or engineering application precisely because there is no longer any scientific discovery involved. Unfortunately, this method of obtaining information has, by itself, little benefit for science. Only when information about heart attacks is combined with other variables (age, smoking habits, and cholesterol levels) do we move into scientific discovery.

The one-shot case study. The most direct test of whether a treatment has an effect is surely to apply the treatment and observe the result. The one-shot case study can be represented in the following way:

$$\boxed{T \quad O}$$

T represents the application of some "treatment," which is followed by an observation (O) that is the measurement of some dependent variable.

Suppose that in Pascal's experiment discussed in Chapter 1, Perier had taken a barometer to the top of the Puy-de-Dôme, and there measured the height of the column of mercury. What would that tell us? It should be clear that it would tell us the height of a column of mercury at that location at that time. But that fact would mean precious little.

In the psychological domain, suppose that I administer a drug to a group of subjects and then measure their reaction times. Can I conclude that the drug changed their reaction times? Because I have no idea what their reaction time would have been if they had not taken the drug, I have no basis for deciding whether the drug affected reaction times.

There is one situation in which this design could be informative, and that is when there is an implicit control group: To test the efficacy of appendectomy in the treatment of appendicitis, we do not need an untreated control group because we already know that the outcome of untreated appendicitis is invariably death.

You observe best a difference between events, not simply an event.

(Boring, 1952, p. 252)

This research design is sometimes used naively, especially in some areas of social science research. Researchers observe that persons who abuse their children were often the victims of child abuse. Therefore, they want to conclude that being abused as a child is predictive of abusing children as an adult. But this finding is hard to interpret without an explicit measure of the incidence of child abuse among people who were not abused as children. Unless we know the base rate of the phenomenon in the general population, we have no basis for a conclusion. Since this is a correlational study, we cannot conclude that having been abused causes the adult behavior of abusing, even if the incidence of being abused is higher among child abusers. The problem is that other factors (such as social class) may be the true causal variables. Even if we control statistically for some possible alternatives, we cannot know that we have eliminated all of them.

The static-group comparison. "You are not ready to make a scientific statement until you have a comparison to present." (Boring, 1954, p. 578).

The next two research designs, although still pre-experimental, offer comparisons. The first, called the static-group comparison, adds an untreated control group (labeled T_0) to compare with that of the treated group.

The static-group comparison design is represented in notation as:

$$T_0\ O$$
$$T_1\ O$$

T_0 represents the untreated control group—if you will, the null (0) treatment. T_1 represents the treated group. There may, of course, be more than two levels of the independent variable. For example, if there were two different treatments in addition to the untreated control group, you could just add T_2, etc.

Campbell and Stanley give as an example of this design a comparison of freshmen to seniors on some dimension (for example, whether classes get harder—and GPAs lower—from freshman to senior year). Here, the treatment is attending college. Even if we randomly select the two samples, however, we still cannot assume that they are equivalent. In this example, the senior class does not contain the individuals who dropped out of school, while the freshman class still contains some person who will drop out before they become seniors. Assuming that many people who withdraw from school do so because of low grades, it is almost certain that the average senior GPA will be higher than the average freshman GPA.[6]

One improvement that can be made on this design is to add statistical control of possible confounds. Suppose you did a study on post-surgical shivering—a real problem for patients not under general anesthesia as operating rooms are usually kept fairly cool. You compare the body temperatures of surgical patients at the time of arrival in the recovery room. The question is how a group given a new type of blanket that keeps patients warmer (T_1) would compare to a group given the standard blanket (T_0).[7] If it can be shown that the two groups were nearly identical in age, weight, and length of surgery—all factors that could cause differences in body temperature regulations and shivering—then a least some possible confounds can be eliminated as alternative explanations.[8]

The one-group, pretest-posttest design.

Another improvement over TO (the one-group, posttest only design) is to include a pretest on the same DV. Though still pre-experimental, this design also makes a comparison. Symbolically, this is represented as

If we want to determine whether exposure to certain arguments changes people's attitudes about something, we might first test their attitudes, then expose them to the treatment, then test them again. If their attitude has changed, we would like to credit that to the treatment. But therein lies a problem. The first observation (measurement) may have acted as a treatment itself. That is, the very exposure to the attitude survey may have sensitized the subjects to the issue. They may change their answers to items on the attitude measure because of the pretest (with or without changes due to the treatment). Basically, this design can only establish that the treated group changed. It cannot establish that the treatment is what caused the change. In addition to change caused by the pretest itself, we might have to worry about change produced by other factors. If we measure attitudes toward some minority group and then retest two days later, a change in attitude may reflect not our

---

[6] This is a *cross-sectional* study using people at two different developmental stages. The design would be strengthened if a *longitudinal* study were used, in which you get the GPAs of freshmen, and then get the GPAs of those still in school in their senior year.

[7] Note that the "null" treatment here is the standard treatment, rather than no blanket.

[8] But note the difficulty of embracing the null hypothesis of no difference.

treatment, but things people have read in the newspapers or seen on television (i.e., events external to the experiment).

Note that those external events could make our treatment look more effective than it is, make it appear to be effective when it is not, or counteract the effect of the treatment.

Like the diagnostic test, this design can actually be quite informative, but only when many aspects of the research situation are very well understood. It is only when there is an implicit control group whose score is known with a high level of precision that this design is adequate. (The implicit control group is mentioned above in regard to the one-shot case study. Consider the following situation. As reported by the press (Peter Kendall, 1994), Paul Krebaum, a chemist for the Molex Corporation in Lisle, Illinois, who worked with a class of chemical compounds called thiols, solved a long-standing problem—how to get rid of the odor of skunk spray. Skunk spray is both extremely malodorous and notoriously difficult to get rid of. The usual recommendation used to be washing with tomato juice, but that was more of an old wives' tale than a workable solution. Most animals have evolved a considerable aversion to the smell of thiols, which are responsible for the odors of decomposing flesh and fecal matter. Skunks have evolved a thiol spray as a defense against predators. Krebaum knew from his laboratory work that a simple solution of hydrogen peroxide and baking soda would neutralize the smell of thiols .[9] A colleague had a cat that got sprayed by a skunk, and he mentioned it to Krebaum, who suggested he try the formula he used for getting rid of thiol smells in his laboratory. It worked. When tested, the odor was immediately gone. In this case the first O was the pre-treatment observation that the cat stank. The second O was the post-treatment observation that the cat no longer stank. In this case, the lack of an explicit control group is not necessary, but only because we already know that skunk odor does not suddenly vanish and that an untreated control group (or cat) would stink for a long time!

Final comments on the pre-experimental designs.

Pre-experimental designs are often used in social-policy research (often because experimental designs are not possible), and you should know why they are difficult to interpret. It really will not do to just assume that people making policy arguments are using their evidence in logically meaningful ways. They should. But with humans being as they are, even people who know better may sometimes trust their data further than they should. A thorough knowledge of research design in psychology will not make you expert in all areas of research,

---

[9] In case you ever need it, the recipe is 1 quart of 3% hydrogen peroxide, 1/4 cup of baking soda, and 1 teaspoon of liquid soap. Keep fresh water at hand, in case you get any of the mixture in the eyes.

but it will give you some knowledge of many areas. Although no one is proof against mistakes, I hope that it is transparently obvious that being one of the people who (sometimes) knows the difference is worthwhile.

True Experimental Designs

As discussed briefly in the opening chapters, the secret to true experimentation in psychology is random assignment of subjects to conditions of an experiment. In the next chapter, I present a detailed account of how randomization is accomplished. The main reason to use randomization is to assure that the groups being compared differ only in the treatment (level of the IV) to which they were exposed.

The Pretest-Posttest Control Group Design.

The pretest-posttest design discussed above makes a strong assumption—namely that the observational measures are not reactive. That is, it assumes that taking the first observation does not affect the second observation. Any changes from first to second observation are, therefore, the result of the treatment. In some cases this assumption is justified. But how should we proceed if we are not sure?

We achieve adequate control only when we add an untreated control group. This is the pretest-posttest control group design. In this design, we pretest each group on the DV. We then treat one group (T1) leaving the control group untreated (T0). Afterwards, we retest each group. If we observe a bigger change in the treated group, we can legitimately conclude that it was caused by the treatment.

In the notation used earlier, this design is represented as

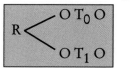

where the R indicates random assignment of the subjects to the two conditions.

This design was alluded to earlier in the discussion of the development of control group designs and the inadequacy of earlier experimental designs in this regard, especially in training experiments. "The classical experiments on transfer [of training] without a control group are open to the criticism that you cannot tell how much practice in skill *A* affects skill *B* unless you have tested *B* before the practice, and then this initial testing of *B* may itself have acted as practice on B to vitiate the result. You can measure this special practice effect of the initial testing on a control group, however, and then accept as significant the difference between groups" (Boring, 1954, p. 584). An example of this would be to take a group of people who have never before played basketball and test the effect of watching a motivational film on free-throw shooting. The pretest consists of 100 free-throws with the score being the percentage of baskets made. The subjects then watch the motivational film and return to the gym to shoot 100 more free-throws. I submit that they would do better the second time around even if the film had no effect whatsoever. One hundred "test" trials might well constitute 100 practice trials! But the comparison to the untreated group would reveal how much the free-throw shooting changed simply due to the pretest. Any change beyond the improvement of the untreated group is presumably due to the motivational film. Figure 5-1 reflects

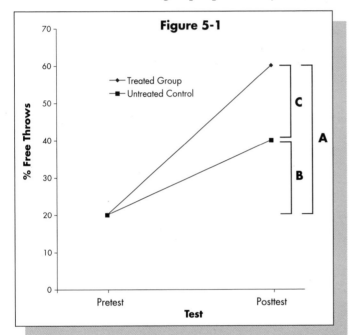

Figure 5-1

such a study. Both the untreated control group and the group watching the motivational film increased from before pretest to posttest. In Figure 5-1, *A* reflects the change in the treated group, and *B* reflects the change in the untreated control group, presumably due to the practice involved in the pretest. *C* would then reflect the change in the treated group that was *due to the treatment.*

As an example, suppose that barometric pressure did not change with altitude but did change with other changes in the weather. In this case, Perier may have found changes in the length of the column of mercury as he went up and down the Puy-de-Dôme, but the changes would have been unrelated to altitude. Only because he had the readings taken at the base of the mountain over the same time period could he rule this out.

One way to improve the pretest, posttest control group design is to explicitly match the subjects along dimensions known to be relevant. To return to an example already mentioned in Chapter 3, if you were interested in testing two different methods of teaching reading, you could just randomly assign the available subjects to one or the other of the two treatments. (Note that an untreated control is irrelevant here. We know that few people learn to read if not taught.) But random assignment does not guarantee equality of the two groups. You could fairly easily guarantee, however, that the two groups were essentially equal along at least one important dimension—reading readiness.

Reading readiness refers to the degree to which a child is prepared to learn to read. There are standardized tests for reading readiness. Those tests measure such things as how well the child knows the alphabet, whether he or she can recognize a few simple words, and the like. To ensure that the groups are equal on this important variable, you would give the test of reading readiness to the whole pool of subjects. You would then take the two highest-scoring subjects, assign one of them to a method of learning reading randomly (a coin toss would do), then assign the other child to the other group. This would be repeated with the 3rd and 4th highest-scoring subjects, and so on. Note that you would still have random assignment of subjects to groups, but with an assurance that the two groups will be nearly identical in reading-readiness scores.

The Solomon four-group design. While the pretest-posttest control group design achieves adequate control over the possibility of reactivity to the first observation, it does not rule out the possibility that the *first measure may interact with the treatment* by either increasing or decreasing its effectiveness. In experiments where the initial testing may have acted as a "treatment," Solomon (1949) recommends the use of the four-group design. In addition to the two groups of the pretest-posttest control-group design, the four-group design adds two additional groups of subjects who do not receive the pretest. The two additional groups differ in whether or not they receive the treatment. The two traditional pretest-posttest groups permit the standard comparison of change from pretest to posttest, but the two added groups permit us to determine whether the change from the first to the second observation was due to "contamination" from the first observation. If the same treatment effect is found both with and without the pretest, we are justified in concluding that the pretest itself had no effect on posttest scores.

The Solomon four-group design is represented in notation as follows:

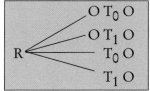

Solomon (1949) gave as an example a pretest on spelling that emphasized words with *ie* and *ei*. If the treatment were a spelling lesson, the students might be inclined to pay more attention to it if they had the pretest—in essence, the pretest showed them the need to carefully study the lesson. Note that the problem is not one of simple reactivity. Testing the students on one set of spelling items will not change their score on the posttest if the posttest uses different words (though equated for difficulty and familiarity). But the pretest might change *how well the treatment works*. If we now find an improvement in spelling for the treated group but no improvement for the control, we would like to claim that the improvement is solely a result of our treatment. In the standard two-group design that claim is equivocal. But if the same pattern of results occurs in the two groups not given the pretest, we can be sure that the posttest results were not influenced by the pretest. We can then justify using the difference between pretest and posttest scores for the treated group as a measure of the effect of the treatment.

The Solomon four group design permits a rich set of comparisons, which are not detailed further here. The interested reader should consult Solomon (1949) and Solomon & Michael Lessac (1968). The latter detail the use of the four-group design in developmental studies involving either enrichment or deprivation of some experience as the treatment. Campbell and Stanley (1963) discuss briefly the appropriate statistical analysis for this design. The Solomon four group design is mentioned more often in textbooks such as this one than in the research literature. It is probably underutilized, perhaps because it doubles the number of subjects needed for the research. Despite its expense and the required sophistication needed to use the design properly, it remains the best approach to use when there is a risk that the observations themselves are reactive. One use of the design in published research is in a study by Anthony Spirito, James Overholser, Sally Ashworth, John Morgan, and Carolyn Benedict-Drew (1988) on the efficacy of a suicide awareness curriculum for high school students. In the study, the use of the design clearly revealed the reactive nature of the pretest. They used a pretest of attitudes concerning suicide, followed by a suicide-prevention program or no-treatment control, and then a posttest. While the suicide-prevention program did have some effect on attitudes, comparison to a treated group that did NOT have the pretest showed that most of the change in the posttest attitudes was due to the pretest!

How important a consideration is the interaction between a pretest and the treatment? In studies of training and development, it can be a very real concern. However, in well-explored areas of research, one can sometimes reasonably well rule out such complex effects on the basis of previous research and may not need this design.

Extension of the control group designs to multiple levels of the IV.

I need to note that all of the designs discussed previously that employ control groups may have more than the two levels of the IV. First, there may not be a null treatment (T0)—as noted, ethical considerations may require that the control group be the standard treatment, rather than no treatment. Second, the designs can extend to several levels of the IV. In the examples above, I compared T0 to T1. But suppose that the treatment were a dosage of a drug. We might be interested in determining the effect of varying dosages. Using a previous example, I might compare dosages of 0, 50, and 100 mg of caffeine. Or I might want even more levels of the dosage (see the discussion in Chapter 6 on determining the number of levels of such a variable). Finally, there may be more than one IV. The latter designs are examined in some detail in the next chapter.

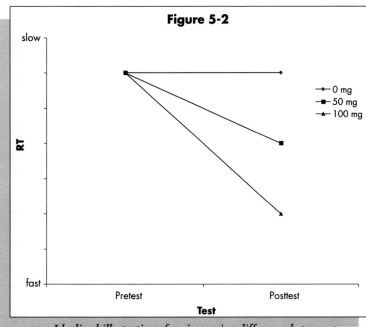

Idealized illustration of an increasing difference between pre- and posttest RTs with increasing dosage level.

Validity of an experiment

Recall that the question of the validity of a measurement concerns whether the measurement actually measures what it purports to measure (e.g., whether an IQ test really measures intelligence). The validity of an argument concerns whether the premises compel the conclusion. We can also ask whether an experiment is valid, but here we must distinguish three varieties of validity. An experiment is *externally valid* if the result generalizes to (is true of) some population beyond just the particular subjects used (the sample). For example, does a result obtained using college students as subjects apply to the general population? An experiment is *internally valid* if the differences between treatment groups on the DV are really produced by differences in the IVs and not by some unknown, uncontrolled factor (an extraneous or confounding variable).[10] Finally, an experiment is *ecologically valid* if the experiment generalizes beyond the laboratory to real world situations.

External Validity

In almost all experiments, we test a rather small group of subjects chosen so that they will (hopefully) be representative of the population from which they came (see Chapter 7 for more on representativeness). Note that we really do

---

[10] A confounding variable is sometimes referred to simply as a "confound."

not care about the behavior of our specific subjects, per se. Rather, it is what they tell us about people in general that is of interest. That is the issue for external validity—do our particular subjects tell us something about some more inclusive group.

We typically hope that the findings of our psychological experiments will generalize to all humans, or even generalize across species. But we seldom have the ability to get a random sample of the general population, which is the best way to assure external validity. In most real world research, we must content ourselves with what is called a "convenience" sample—the people we have available to us. A majority of psychological research on humans uses the persons available to most psychologists—college students. But how representative are college students of the general population? They are likely to be, on average, a bit smarter than the unselected population, certainly better educated, of higher average socio-economic status, and so on.[11] Eric Jaffe (2005) reviewed the issues in regard to the use of college students as subjects.

A methodological issue arises here. Is the intent of our research to predict the value of some DV for different groups, or to predict the proportions of people holding certain views? In the case of survey research, we are usually interested in exactly that. The whole point of public opinion polls prior to an election is to predict the outcome—what percentage is likely to vote for candidate X? In this case, representativeness of the sample is of enormous importance (see Chapter 6 for some examples). But in many experiments, such as most of those in *PsychMate*, our interest is not in predicting, say, the mean RT for the population of all persons rotating a mental image. Rather, we are interested in the *pattern* of differences in RT across different levels of the IVs. In those cases, we are interested in group comparisons, not predictions of population means, so we are safe so long as our sample follows the same pattern. In the study of basic mental processes, the use of college students is likely to lead to better overall scoring (faster RTs, fewer errors), but the same general pattern. In studies of individual differences, such as attitudes, abilities, and the like, this is much more of a problem.

I need to address briefly another type of generalization, namely generalization across species. Does what we learn from the behavior of one species tell us something about others? This is the essential question for the area of *comparative psychology*. The unsophisticated answer is that results sometimes generalize across species, and sometimes don't. And it should be of no surprise that generalization is typically greater across related species.

B. F. Skinner (1938) defended his use of the white rat as virtually the sole species he studied by noting that "it is reasonable, at least in the beginning, to

---

[11] The "unselected" population refers to the entire population, including college students.

restrict oneself to a single, representative species" (p. 47) Hence he thought he could justify his title, *The Behavior of Organisms*, despite the fact that the book is mainly about the bar-pressing behavior of white rats. The failure of that assumption eventually became overwhelmingly clear (Shettleworth, 1972). But there are also some interesting generalizations. John Garcia and Robert Koelling's (1966) work on learned taste aversion showed that rats will learn to avoid food with a novel taste if they become sick after eating it, but they will not learn to avoid food with a novel taste if eating it is followed by electric shock. Their work suggested that rats are biologically prepared to learn some associations (such as taste and sickness) more easily than others.[12] That result was strengthened enormously when it was shown to generalize to quail (Wilcoxon, Dragoin, & Kral, 1971), snakes (Burghardt, Wilcoxon, & Czaplicki, 1973), and humans (Carrell, Cannon, Best, & Stone, 1986). (In humans, taste-avoidance that occurs in many cancer patients undergoing chemotherapy or radiation therapy is due to the same mechanism and is frequently accompanied by severe weight loss.)

Ecological validity

> Lists of nonsense syllables, numbers, or unrelated words, so much used in studies of learning and retention, certainly give an air of artificiality to the laboratory experiments. Are these laboratory performances anything more than stunts or games with no real bearing upon what human beings do in daily life?
>
> Robert Sessions Woodworth (1938), p. 69.

The issue of ecological validity concerns whether the results of experiments conducted in relatively artificial laboratory settings generalize to the wider world. The sciences have benefited enormously from bringing phenomena into the laboratory for study. Producing a phenomenon on demand, when you are best prepared to observe and manipulate it, leads to far greater precision in any science. But it runs the danger of divorcing the phenomenon from its usual context. A good example is the study of memory. When Ebbinghaus (1885/1913) set himself the task of comparing recall after varying amounts of time, he noted the problem, inherent in memorizing prose or poetry, that one passage might be inherently easier than another. To avoid that problem, he

---

[12] This finding has been used by ranchers to control predation of sheep by coyotes and wolves. They set out poisoned carcasses of sheep that the predators eat. After becoming ill, they tend to avoid animals with a similar smell (Gustavson, Kelly, Sweeney, & Garcia, 1976).

memorized lists of consonant-vowel-consonant trigrams[13] that are essentially devoid of meaning. But consider that we never actually tried to memorize most of what we remember. When was the last time you set yourself the task of memorizing a list of nonsense syllables? The danger here is that the laboratory task is so artificial as to tell us little about how memory works in the real world.[14] Note that this is always a balancing act—if we try to study memory only in the "real" context of daily life we would have so many confounds that our results would likely be meaningless.

The degree to which this is a problem likely varies enormously for different areas of psychology. Studies of perception have given us enormous insight into how we gain knowledge of the world, even though the knowledge we gain in everyday life is often social and laboratory studies isolate perception from social contexts. Garcia and Koelling's (1966) work on taste aversion cited above used various drugs to induce sickness in rats after they ate a novel food. Had they been forced to rely on non-experimental observation, it is doubtful that this discovery would ever have been made. On the other hand, studies of social interaction may tell us little if subjects know they are being observed, and their behavior recorded. If you know that someone is observing to see whether you will aid a stranger under some circumstance, you may show far more pro-social behavior than you would if left to yourself.

Some researchers aim to set up their experiments in ways that give them laboratory control but still retain good ecological validity. William Brewer and James Treyens' (1981) study of recall for the contents of an

Figure 5-3

"Office" used in Brewer & Treyens (1981).

office serves as a good example. Their subjects came to what was apparently a graduate student office to complete an experiment as a requirement for an introductory psychology course. The assistant left each subject alone in his "office" (seen in Figure 5-3) for 30 seconds, purportedly to see if the laboratory was ready. He then returned and asked each subject to come next door to the lab. There, the subject was asked to recall the contents of the office. While waiting, the subjects probably looked around the office, as one would do in a strange room. But they probably did not make any effort to memorize the contents. Hence, their recall

---

[13] A CVC trigram is a set of three letters, such as DAQ, that do not form a word. They are sometimes called *nonsense syllables*.

[14] Frederic Bartlett (1932) gave a detailed critique of the shortcomings he saw in Ebbinghaus' methods and, like Brewer and Treyens, proposed some methods of retaining experimental control while avoiding the artificiality of CVC trigrams. His study of the recall of a Native American folk tale, "The War of the Ghosts," is one of the most famous studies in psychology.

would be based on something like real-world observation, rather than deliberate memorization.[15]

Campbell and Stanley (1963) also note the threat to external validity if the same treatment has different effects, depending on whether it is given in the context of an experiment or not. The point is that you might react differently to the same treatment in a natural setting than when you know you are being observed as part of an experiment.

All of that said, how did Woodworth answer his question?

He noted similar criticism by Frederick Bartlett (1932), who famously sought to study memory for materials of more intrinsic interest than nonsense syllables, for example, stories. But he also fought back. "In spite of the criticism the ordinary memory experiment is justified by its results. The charge of unreality is less serious than it seems....Such problems occur all the time in daily life....A sequence of numbers in a street address, letters in the designation of a radio station, or syllables in a word is essentially a nonsense list....The same general findings are obtained with ... numbers and words as well as nonsense syllables. The curve of forgetting shows the same general character with various types of material" (p. 69). It is worth noting that in this day of multiple passwords and PINs, we memorize quite a few things that are near equivalents of nonsense syllables.

There is an inevitable tension between laboratory and "field" studies. Each has limits. One task for the experimental scientist is to devise ways of bringing experimental control to bear while keeping the tasks as much like the "real" world as possible.

Internal Validity

In any experiment, we are ultimately concerned with whether the effects observed (such as differences in responding under different experimental conditions) were actually caused by the different experimental conditions. If they were, then the experiment is internally valid. If not, then the experiment is invalid. If some extraneous variable that we did not properly control is affecting the data, the experiment is said to be *confounded*, and, as noted previously, such an extraneous variable is sometimes called a confound. How might an experiment be invalid? How might it be confounded? A number of types of extraneous or confounding variables have been identified that can threaten the internal validity of an experiment. These are discussed below.

---

[15] One finding of the study was that many subjects recalled the books on the bookshelf of the office despite the fact that there were none! This provides an excellent demonstration of the effect of everyday knowledge (what Bartlett called *schemas*) on memory, and illustrates the reconstructive nature of memory.

The following classification of sources of experimental invalidity comes in part from that of Campbell and Stanley (1963). Others come from a discussion by Theodore Xenephon Barber (1976) of *Pitfalls in Human Research*—a book that should be part of the intellectual equipment of any psychological scientist. Other sources of invalidity that they discuss are scattered in other parts of this text. Both books are highly recommended. Some of these sources of internal invalidity can be ruled out by employing the proper control groups and through random assignment of subjects to treatments. Others, especially those identified by Barber, are trickier. But keep in mind the fact reiterated throughout this text—no single experiment can absolutely rule out all extraneous variables. Replication (see Chapter 7 for a discussion of various forms of replication) is necessary to establish any empirical finding.

History. History refers to the events that happened to our subjects other than the experimental treatment. One thing that happened differently to different groups of subjects was our treatment manipulation. But were there other differences? For example, consider a study of teenagers' attitudes toward suicide before and after they attend an in-school suicide prevention program. We compare the changes in their attitudes to those of students at a school where no such program was in place (but we gave the questionnaires just the same). We find that there are significantly greater attitude changes in the experimental group than in the untreated controls. But suppose that a student committed suicide in one of the schools during that time. We could no longer assume that the differences between the groups were due to our treatment. The dramatic and terrible incident of the suicide of a fellow student would surely have some effect on attitudes toward suicide.

Problems of history are especially likely in long-term experiments and in experiments of a decidedly social nature. A single-session experiment on attention is unlikely to have a problem of history, but a pretest, posttest design with several months separating the two tests may be contaminated by events in the news that can either act directly on the posttest or interact with the treatment to change the posttest scores.

Maturation. The problem of maturation is similar to that of history, except that it reflects changes due to the passage of time itself, rather than specific events. Examples include subjects growing older or, on a shorter time scale, growing sleepier or hungrier. Examples: [1] Maturation is a particular problem with studies of learning using infants as subjects because the subjects are changing so rapidly in terms of size, motor skills, perceptual acuity, and brain organization. A two-month study conducted on infants will see remarkable changes in what they can do even if no treatment of any kind is applied. [2] In studies of practice, especially with motor skills, fatigue (mental or muscular) may set in, reducing performance. In this case, the level of performance may not indicate the true amount of learning.

Instrumentation. Instrumentation refers to a threat to internal validity based on changes in the calibration of instruments, including human instruments. If you used a photometer to measure the intensities of lights presented in a psychophysical measurement of the absolute threshold for light, changes in the instrument (e.g., a buildup of dirt that reduces the light getting into the photometer) would change the apparent results of your study.

The restandardization of IQ tests and other psychological "instruments" is needed from time to time because the tests get out-of-date. Word meanings can change subtly, as words that were once common become rarer and vice versa. In the restandardization of the Minnesota Multiphasic Personality Inventory (J. N. Butcher, W. G. Dahlstrom, J. R. Graham, A. Tellegen, & B. Kaemmer, 1989), one item that was dropped was "I like to play spin-the-bottle."[16] Have you ever played spin-the-bottle?

Experimenters typically get better at conducting a specific study with practice. They may simply become "smoother" at leading the subjects through a series of tasks, thus perhaps eliciting greater effort from their subjects. Providing practice before formal data collection starts is one way to handle this problem. That is, simply treat the first few subjects as practice for the experimenter and delete the subjects' data.

Note that instrumentation changes are less of a problem if the subjects receiving the different treatments are tested in alternation. If you test the entire control group, then test the entire treated group, any changes in your own conduct would affect the latter more than the former. If every other subject was in the control or treatment group, then changes in instrumentation would be likely to affect the two groups about equally.

Statistical Regression. Regression refers to a statistical phenomenon in which groups that score extremely high (or low) on some variable will usually be closer to the mean when retested. This occurs because extreme scores are sometimes the result of a combination of circumstances that is unlikely to be repeated on later testing. For example, suppose that I test a new method of teaching reading by taking a group of students who scored extremely poorly on a test of reading skills. After exposing them to my new method of teaching reading, I retest them and find that their scores have increased. My new method is triumphant! But wait. The scores would have increased even if I had done nothing. Here's why: some of the students who scored poorly (and thus were included in the study) did so because of extraneous factors (they had a fight

---

[16] See J. N. Butcher, et al. (1989) for the revised edition. The early studies for the first edition are reprinted in W. G. Dahlstrom & L. E. Dahlstrom, L. E. (1980).

with their parents, they stayed up late the night before, etc.). Those subjects will probably not have the same thing happen again when we retest them, and their scores will improve. Of course, some of the original poor scorers did poorly because they cannot read very well. They will not be expected to improve on retesting, but improvement by part of the group will raise the overall average.

Regression was first described by Francis Galton (1885), who plotted scatter diagrams of the heights of children and their mid-parent heights.[17] He noticed that extremely tall parents usually had children who were taller than average, but the children were not as much above average as their parents. Extremely tall children usually had parents who were taller than average, but the parents were not as much above average as they were! The mystery is clarified when you consider that a person who is extremely tall probably had both the genetic disposition to be tall and an environment in which that "genetic tallness" could express itself. That *combination* of genes and environment is unlikely to be present for both generations.

Persons with extreme scores will "regress" toward the mean because the circumstances that produce extreme scores are unlikely to be repeated (either for the individual or across generations). To rule out statistical regression as a confound requires an appropriate control group. In essence, this problem can be solved by using the change from pretest to posttest in the untreated control group as a measure of the amount of regression. Any additional change in the treated group could then be assumed to be the result of the treatment. For the example above of a regression effect in a study of reading (where the subjects were chosen on the basis of poor reading scores on the pretest), consider Figure 5-4. Here, *A* represents the improvement in reading scores for the group receiving the new method of instruction, which looks like a lot of improvement. But when you examine the untreated group, you note that their scores improved almost as much (indicated by *B*).

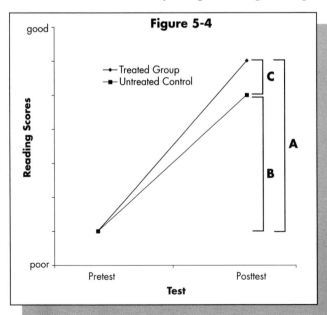

Figure 5-4

[17] The "mid-parent" height is the average of the father's and mother's heights. The usual symbol for the Pearson Product-Moment Correlation is *r* from *r*egression. Galton had described the phenomenon earlier, but called it *reversion*.

Only the difference indicated by C can honestly be attributed to the new reading instruction.

Selection bias. Selection bias occurs when the selection or assignment of subjects to groups results in non-equivalent groups. In general, random selection and random assignment can be counted on to avoid systematic selection bias. More is said about this in the discussion of randomization in Chapter 6.

Experimental Mortality. "Mortality" may be an overly-dramatic word for this since we seldom actually kill our subjects. What is meant by mortality here is drop-out rates. Subjects may drop out of our study for many reasons, but the danger is that the people
who drop out may differ in some systematic way from those who do not drop out. So even if we start with comparable, representative samples, the subjects still in the study at its conclusion may not be a represen-tative sample. Some examples will help to clarify.

Suppose that you perform a test concerning the effect of stress on performance. You randomly assign subjects to a low-stress or high-stress condition, where the level of stress in manipulated by the speed with which subjects must perform some task. If random assignment has done its duty, the two groups should be reasonably well matched in all ways at the beginning. But suppose that some people cannot tolerate stress well. About equal numbers of such subjects were assigned to each condition, but the low-tolerance subjects will only drop out of the high-stress condition. If you find little difference in performance between the two stress levels, it may be because stress has little effect on the task OR it could be that the low-tolerance subjects in the high-stress condition dropped out, and the two groups are no longer equivalent in their response to stress.

Mortality can be a problem in a correlational study, as well. To return to a previous example, suppose that you want to compare freshman grades to senior grades at your college or university. You select a sample of each class and find that grades are, on average, higher for seniors than for freshmen. Can you conclude that people improve in some fundamental way (they become smarter, or learn to study better, or get better at taking tests) from their first to last years in college? No. Not everyone who begins the freshman year survives to the end, and it is precisely the poorest students who are most likely to drop out of school. To conclude that there was a real change, we would need to compare senior grades to freshman grades for the same sample. (One other possible explanation that could explain the facts is that senior courses are easier. I leave it to you to decide how likely it is that this counter-argument is true.)

Note that this same problem exists in almost any study comparing high school dropouts to high school graduates. Studies routinely find that salaries are higher among graduates than dropouts, and school boards search for ways to keep students in school on the assumption that those who stay in school will benefit economically (and in other ways) from that education. The differences in salaries, however, may not reflect the value of the education as much as the generally lower opportunity, ambition, or intelligence of those who dropped out.

The following sources of internal invalidity are from Barber (1976). These represent somewhat different problems and distort the data in different ways. Nevertheless, they are important issues for research with human subjects.

Misrecording of data. A number of investigators (including Kennedy, 1952; Rhine, 1974; Silverman, 1977) have reported that experimenters not only misrecord data but, more importantly, tend to misrecord the data in the direction of the expected effect. In his research on extra-sensory perception (ESP), Rhine (1974) made it a general rule that data must be recorded by someone who did not know which stimulus was presented. Note that the issue here is not deliberate fudging of the data (though that undoubtedly sometime occurs—the ethical issues are treated in Chapter 7).

Kennedy (1952) concluded that "human beings ... are not trustworthy recording devices" (p. 515). This point has already been made in the beginning of this chapter though in the context of remembering the details of the experiment. Fortunately, the advent of computerized data recording reduces this effect.

Note that in some studies the data must be repeatedly handled by the experimenters. In many studies, the data are coded originally on data sheets by the experimenter then entered into a computer for further analysis. Even if no systematic misrecording occurs, every handling of the data will increase the opportunity for misrecording. The issue of systematic versus random errors in measurement was discussed in Chapter 3.

Personal Attributes. "An experimenter's sex, age, race, prestige, anxiety, friendliness, dominance, etc. *may* at times affect how subjects perform in [an] experiment" (Barber, 1976, p. 52, emphasis in original). The point is that the personal attributes of the experimenter may change the subjects' behavior in unpredictable ways. Some experimenters are friendlier than others, thus putting the subject more at ease. Others may be so unfriendly that the subject deliberately tries to give results counter to those they think the experimenter wants. Joseph Masling (1966) gave this phenomenon its official name—the "screw-you effect." "Psychologists have many motives for conducting research, and Ss have many motives for complying with research requirements" (Masling, p. 96).[18]

Somewhat quaintly, Barber (1976) notes that "An unmarried male experimenter typically conducts the experiment somewhat differently when his subject is a pretty, single woman than when his subject is a male" (p. 54). But his point is well taken. Experimenters may respond differently to different subjects, and subjects may respond differently in kind. If there are sex interaction effects, what appear to be differences in how males and females behave in an experiment may be due to the way they were treated rather than to intrinsic differences between males and females.

A difficult problem may arise if a racist subject encounters an experimenter of a different race (or vice versa).

This problem of experimenter characteristics is worse when there is a lot of interaction between the experimenter and the subject, such as in conducting an interview. In computerized experiments, the effects are presumably muted. (Note that in the *PsychMate* experiments there is no experimenter.)

In much research, where the task to be performed is well understood by the subject, the attributes of the experimenter probably play only a minor role. If the effect is largely on the subjects' motivation, there is likely little harm done beyond possibly increasing variability by having some unmotivated subjects. That can be offset by increased sample size.

Some researchers use pre-recorded instructions in an effort to reduce the effects of personal attributes, but those may introduce their own artificiality.

What should be encouraged (and trained) is a friendly but business-like approach to all subjects. What we need for our experiments are subjects who are well-motivated and properly oriented to the task. However, experiments are social encounters between humans, and the characteristics of those humans will matter.

Barber (1976) reviewed a number of studies in this regard, and there have been many since. One problem is that we do not know in a predictive sense what sorts of characteristics might matter, for what sorts of subjects they might matter, or for what tasks they might matter. Barber notes that because this is true, replication and cross-validation of studies remain extremely important.

Unintentional Expectancies. Experimenters typically expect (or at least want) a certain outcome. A serious concern for experiments using humans (or even non-human animals) as subjects is whether experimenters who know the expected outcome of an experiment might unwittingly bias the subjects'

---

[18] In the older psychological literature, it was common to use the abbreviations *S* for subject, *O* for observer (in perceptual experiments), and *E* for experimenter. These are no longer standard usage.

responses so as to affect the outcome of the experiment. That could produce an effect where there otherwise would have been none, exaggerate a real effect, or reduce the strength of a real effect. In any case, it would produce a misleading, confounded result.

Whatever the means by which the experimenter unintentionally communicates the expectation, the subject might try to produce the expected result. Subjects are generally motivated to give you the results you want, especially if paid. They usually see "doing their job" as producing what you want—which is just what one ordinarily hires an employee to do. In some experiments, they can easily do so. (More rarely, we hope, they will intentionally give you the opposite result—the "screw you" effect.)

Despite a great deal written on this subject, there is relatively little evidence that experimenter's biases unintentionally affect subjects' responding. Many studies have purported to demonstrate it, but Barber (1976) argues that most are actually the result of loose procedures, misrecording, or outright fudging of the data. While the possibility of such effects in any specific experiment cannot be ruled out, increased automation of stimulus presentation and response collection probably reduce the chances of this considerably. Robert Rosenthal and Donald Rubin (1978) reviewed research on unintentional expectancy effects at length. Barber's was among the replies to their lead article in *The Behavioral and Brain Sciences*. Barber (1976) discusses two of Rosenthal's experiments in detail, showing that the results were more likely to be due to incorrect data analyses than unintentional expectancies.

Some Final Comments on Personal Attributes and Unintentional Expectancies. Experiments to try to demonstrate the subtle (or not-so-subtle) effects of the personal attributes or unintentional expectancies of experimenters have typically used experimental tasks that require a high degree of face-to-face interaction between the experimenter and the subject. Many of the studies of these effects used Robert Rosenthal's person-perception task in which the subject is shown a series of photographs of faces and must rate them on a scale indicating whether they have recently been experiencing success (high ratings) or failure (low ratings). The actual faces used were shown by preliminary studies to be neutral—they were not easily rated as experiencing either success or failure. This task, of course, presents a fairly ambiguous situation for the subject and involves a constant interchange between the experimenter and the subject, maximizing the possibility that "body language" or other unwitting communication from the experimenter may affect the subjects' responses. A task of this kind is certainly the best starting point for studies of experimenter effects since it maximizes the possibility that they can occur—if subjects think you want low ratings, they can easily give them to you. (It is worth noting that with current technology this experiment could easily be automated so that the experimenter does little more than lead the subject to the computer, thus presumably minimizing the experimenter's impact on the subject.)

In many other experimental paradigms it is much harder for subjects to influence the results. In reaction time studies, for example, the only way a subject could alter the results (give faster RTs to condition A than to condition B) would be to slow their overall responding sufficiently to permit that additional decision. Since the instruction is to respond as quickly as possible, the only way to reverse a difference between conditions would be to slow responding to what should have been the faster condition. In that case, the data would be so messy that anyone experienced in RT studies would probably realize that the subject was simply not performing the task as instructed. In a complex experiment (such as the factorial experiments in *PsychMate*), it is unlikely that a subject could accomplish this without adding a high level of both variability and error to the data.

In some circumstances, it may be worthwhile to explicitly warn subjects that they are simply to perform the task to the best of their abilities and not concern themselves with the expected outcome. In a situation where subjects might be tempted to try to figure out what you want and can easily bias their results, it is best to tell them not to try to figure out what is "really" going on, and to just respond as they have been instructed. That raises the issue of *demand characteristics*.

Demand characteristics. Though not the first to note the phenomenon, Martin Orne (1962) did more than anyone else to bring the issue of demand characteristics to the attention of psychologists. "The subject's performance in an experiment might almost be conceptualized as problem-solving behavior; that is, at some level he [*sic*] sees it as his task to ascertain the true purpose of the experiment and respond in a manner which will support the hypothesis being tested. Viewed in this light, the totality of cues which convey an experimental hypothesis to the subject become significant determiners of the subject's behavior" (p. 779). Orne called that "totality of cues" the *demand characteristics of the experiment*. He noted that a substantial source of those cues lie in the experimental situation itself. The basic problem is that the subject may be responding to the demand characteristics of the experiment, rather than to the level of the IV to which they are exposed.[19]

---

[19] The interested student should consult Orne's original article, as well as more recent commentaries by John Kihlstrom (2002) and Ralph Rosnow (2002), offered on the 40th anniversary of Orne's paper. Orne's paper is reprinted in that collection along with the new articles.

A point worth considering is that even if your demeanor as the experimenter does not affect the *pattern* of data, it still may affect the *quality* of the data. If subjects are motivated and clearly understand the instructions, you will have less error in measurement—their performance in the experiment will more nearly match their true ability. Noisy data require larger sample sizes to get the same effect. What you want subjects to do is follow instructions and work hard. As long as they do that, they will give you good data (i.e., valid data). But if your manner suggests to your subjects that you are not really taking this seriously, they will tend to slop their way through the tasks. If the experimenter acts professionally, subjects will perceive that they are participating in something worthwhile (whether they are or not). By and large, subjects (especially paid subjects) want to do a good job. The work ethic is not, in fact, dead.

If you must leave the subjects in ignorance of the hypothesis, *tell them so.* And tell them why. You can/should tell them that no deception is being practiced—they know exactly what is taking place in the experiment. Then tell them that you want them simply to respond to the best of their ability and not worry about trying to figure out what is *really* going on. (Unfortunately, many people teaching Introductory Psychology spend lots of time discussing social-psychological experiments that involve deception, such as studies of obedience and of bystander apathy, leaving their students with the false impression that most psychological experiments are "really" about something other than what the subjects are told.)

Subjects will try to give us the data they think we want. Some even see that as their task. It is the task of the experimenter to make sure the experiment does not permit the subjects to do so and discourages them from trying.

Chapter 6

Experimentation II

In Chapter 5, we were concerned with the validity of experiments and discussed a series of research designs leading up to the pretest-posttest control group design as an example of a true experiment. I begin this chapter with the development of more complex experimental designs. Details of randomization and counterbalancing are then considered followed by a series other issues.

Recall the pretest-posttest control group design (and its extension into the Solomon four-group design). This true experimental design is intended to deal with the various threats to internal validity in ways that make the interpretation of the results relatively straightforward. Reactivity of measures and other threats to internal validity are dealt with by having an appropriate control group (or groups). This design is just about the simplest of what are called *factorial* designs. Factorial designs are those in which there is more than one IV. In the pretest, posttest control group design, the IV's are treatment versus control and before versus after. This design is referred to as a 2 x 2 ("two by two") design, indicating that each IV has two levels.

Factorial designs are common in psychological research. Indeed, they probably make up the bulk of psychological research. Before beginning a detailed consideration of the factorial design, however, we need to return to a point first mentioned in Chapter 3 regarding the various ways of describing variables.

Between-subjects versus within-subjects designs

An issue of concern in many experiments is whether to use a between-subjects design or a *within-subjects* (or repeated-measures) design.[1] If each subject experiences only a single level of an IV, then the variable was manipulated between subjects. On the other hand, if each subject experiences all levels of the IV, it was manipulated within subjects.

In many instances, practical considerations limit us to one design or the other. When we study variables inherent in the subject, such as their sex or religion, we are pretty much stuck with between-subjects designs. Of course, in these instances, we are also doing correlational research with its inherent problems in determining causality. But even when we have the ability to assign

---

[1] "Within-subjects" and "repeated-measures" mean the same thing—each subject is measured repeatedly. I will use them interchangeably because they are used interchangeably in the literature.

subjects to levels of an IV, and thus have an experimental design, it may make little sense to test a person under more than one level. As an example, suppose we want to compare two methods of teaching reading. We could either assign subjects to one of the two methods randomly or match them on the basis of a reading readiness score and then randomly assign one of each pair to one method, with the other individually therefore assigned to the other method (see Chapter 5). But it would make no sense at all to teach each subject by both methods. Whatever they learned by the first method would still be known and would hopelessly confound any measure of learning by the second method.

The essential rule of thumb for deciding whether a repeated-measures design can be used is whether the effect of each treatment can be reversed. If it can, then repeated measures may be appropriate. The issue can be summed up by an old joke: A lady walking past a man lying drunk in the gutter remarked, in disgust, "Sir, you are drunk!" Opening one eye, the drunk replied, "Yes, madam, and you're ugly. And tomorrow, I shall be sober." A sober person can become drunk, and a drunk one can become sober. Because the condition is reversible, we could use a repeated-measures design. Suppose, as another example, that we performed an experiment to determine the effect time of day has on reaction time. We could use a between-subjects design and test each person either in the morning or at night. We could improve our experiment by testing each person under both conditions. The improvement would come from (1) having perfectly matched pairs of subjects, and from (2) having twice as many subjects in each condition. If we had 20 subjects available to test and tested each in only one condition, we would have 10 subjects per condition. If we used repeated measures, we would have 20. (We would also need to counterbalance the order of testing, with half of our subjects tested first in the morning and half tested first at night.)

In some research situations, such as the multiple-trial RT designs that make up the majority of the experiments in *PsychMate*, a repeated-measures design is almost a necessity. Consider the experiment on comparing sentences to pictures in *PsychMate 2.4: Sentence-Picture Comparison*. Subjects decide whether a sentence (such as "The plus is above the star.") is true or false in regard to the "picture" of a plus above a star or a star above a plus. One variable is whether the sentence was true or false. If we presented this as a between-groups variable, such that each person got only true sentences and the other got only false sentences, the subjects would not need to make any choice and we would get extremely fast, perfectly accurate RTs that would tell us nothing! Similarly, in the experiment on lexical decisions in *PsychMate 2.1: Lexical Decisions* (in which subjects decide whether a string of letters is a word or not), the non-word condition is absolutely required in order to make the task work, even though RT to the non-words is largely meaningless—we are really interested in the comparison of RT to pairs of related or unrelated words.

Note, though, that in some situations we have a choice between the between-subjects design and the within-subjects design (such as comparing memorization in the morning versus at night). That choice brings with it a potential problem—do we get the same results with both designs? Unfortunately, the answer is "Not always." Consider an experiment by Behar and Adams (1966). They compared RTs to different stimulus intensities and found that RT decreased with increases in stimulus intensity when they used a within-subjects design, but not for a between-subjects design.

In an experiment on eye-blink conditioning, Robert Grice and John Hunter (1964) found that a loud stimulus produced a greater rate of conditioned responses than a soft tone but only if the subject experienced both.[2] In the between-subjects comparison, in which the subject heard either a soft tone *or* a loud one, there was virtually no difference in response rates for loud and soft tones. Grice (1966) reviewed these and other examples. More recently, Alvin Wang and Margaret Thomas (2000) reviewed their research on mnemonics (memory techniques), in which they varied the time interval before recall. When subjects always experienced either a brief or a long recall period, there was an advantage for the mnemonic only for short delays. Other studies, such as Mark McDaniel and Michael Pressley (1984) had subjects recall at both short and long delays and found that the mnemonic was effective at long delays.

Why do these two techniques sometimes yield different results? In all likelihood, being exposed to all of the conditions of the experiment (i.e., all of the levels of the IV) changes the subjects' strategies.

It is often difficult to perform both versions of the experiment to identify these differences. But in some instances we can do so rather easily. To return to an earlier example, suppose that we were interested in the effects of time of day on some kind of psychological variable, such as reaction time. We might test each subject twice—once early in the morning and once late at night. (Because there might be a practice effect, we would want to randomly assign half of our subjects to be tested first in the morning and half tested first at night.[3]) In this case, we can analyze the data using only the first test. This

---

[2] In classical conditioning of the eye-blink reflex, a brief puff of air to the open eye (the unconditioned stimulus—UCS) causes a reflexive blink (the unconditioned response—UCR). When the puff of air is preceded repeatedly by a buzzer (the conditioned stimulus—CS), the buzzer will elicit an eye-blink without the puff of air. The eye-blink to the buzzer is a conditioned response (CR).

[3] It would also be useful to give the subjects lots of practice before the two tests so that no further practice effects would occur.

would be a between-subjects comparison. Then we could analyze the data from both tests—again comparing memory scores for morning versus night. But in this latter analysis, we would have a within-subjects comparison. For any experiment of this variety, it should be clear that we would always want to do both analyses to check for different results depending on whether a variable is manipulated within or between subjects.

Mixed designs.

Though we need not dwell on it, it is possible, and frequently either necessary or desirable, to combine between- and within-subjects IVs. Indeed, the first factorial design I discussed was the pretest-posttest control group design, in which the comparison of pretest to posttest is within subjects, while treatment group versus control group is a between-subjects IV.

Research Designs with Multiple Independent Variables

Experiments that use a single IV can definitely be valuable. Examples from *PsychMate* include the experiments on rotation of mental images and on recall versus recognition. The former replicates the studies that were largely responsible for the resurgence of imagery as a legitimate area of study. The latter replicates a study that helped clarify why recognition usually leads to better retrieval than recall.[4] But psychological phenomena are often quite complex, and more complex research designs are frequently needed. That added complexity usually comes in the form of a factorial design—that is, an experiment (or correlational study) with more than one independent variable.

What do factorial experiments reveal that single-factor studies cannot? For one thing, they permit the testing of two IVs in one experiment. The tests of each IV alone are called the *main effects*. If there are differences in the mean DV across the levels of an IV, there is said to be a main effect of that IV. Factorial designs also permit the discovery of *interactions*. An interaction occurs when the effect of one IV on the DV *depends upon the level of the other IV*.

Consider the following: At present, there is quite a bit of press concerning the "epidemic" of obesity in the USA. Obesity is related to higher rates of diabetes, strokes, and heart attacks. Diabetes increases the risk of kidney failure, blindness, and a number of other ills. In light of this, who is healthier—

---

4 See *PsychMate 1.3: Rotation of Mental Images* and *PsychMate 2.7: Recall, Recognition, and Encoding Specificity.*

a person who can eat what she wants and never gain a pound or the person who puts on weight by merely walking past a chocolate cake? Clearly, a person whose metabolism is such that they do not easily store body fat is less likely to become obese and avoid all the problems associated with obesity. But our remote ancestors, prior to the invention of agriculture, seldom encountered large quantities of fat or sugar and were probably often hungry and undernourished, especially in winter and early spring. In that environment, the person who can easily store fat actually has an advantage—when they do encounter higher quantities of fat or sugar, they can gorge themselves, thereby avoiding malnourishment. They, therefore, would be healthier and likely to have more offspring, thus gradually spreading this advantage through the population.

Note that whether the ability to easily store fat is good or bad *depends upon the situation*. In the remote past of our species when fat and sugar were seldom available, it conferred a distinct advantage. In our current situation of an abundance of fat and sugar, the same ability to easily store fat is a disadvantage. Whether your body stores fat easily or not may be an advantage or a health risk—depending on your circumstances. That is an interaction. It is the *combination* of variables that matters.

I have already illustrated situations in which interactions are important, in the discussion of the pretest-posttest control group design. At its most basic, this is a 2 x 2 design with repeated measures on the before-and-after factor. Consider an experiment to determine whether a weight loss program really works. We could randomly assign subjects to either a weight loss program or a control condition. We weigh each subject before the experiment begins, and then weigh each subject again after some appropriate period of time. Figure 6-1 shows an ideal outcome— both groups weigh the same before the experiment begins, the control group does not lose weight, but the group enrolled in the weight loss program does. The effect of before vs. after *depends upon* whether the person was or was not in a weight loss program. That is an interaction.

Another example of an interactions was illustrated in Chapter 5 in the discussion of controlling for

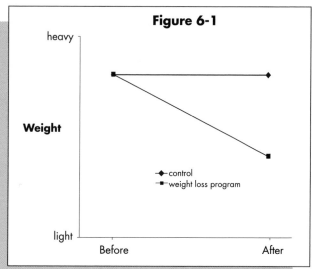

Idealized data from an experiment on effectiveness of a weight loss program.

regression to the mean (see Figure 5-3 in Chapter 5). In the example given, students who scored poorly on a reading test were taught reading by a new method. The worry, though, is that their scores would improve simply as a result of regression to the mean. But an untreated group would also show regression. So we can use the control group to measure the amount of change due to regression. Any *additional* change in the group receiving the new method would presumably be due to the new method of reading. In Figure 5-3 of Chapter 5, I show a possible outcome. The line marked B indicates the amount of change due to regression in the untreated group, while C shows the improvement due to the new method of teaching. In this case, most of the improvement is due to regression.

Something to notice in these examples—an interaction occurs when the lines of the graph are not parallel. Many of the experiments in *PsychMate* are concerned with interactions, and those can serve as examples of the importance of interactions and factorial designs.

In *PsychMate 1.6: Selective Attention and Response Competition*, the issue was the measurement of the size of the focus of the "zoom lens" of attention. Subjects respond as quickly as possible to indicate whether a target letter is an "S" or an "H." On some trials, there are letters flanking the central target letter, and those can either be repetitions of the target letter (*congruent noise*) or the opposite letter (such as an "H" surrounded by "S"s—*incompatible noise*. Incompatible noise causes a considerable slowing of RT relative to the no-noise and compatible-noise conditions due to response competition. Barbara Eriksen and Charles Eriksen (1974) used that known effect to study how well subjects can focus visual attention and *ignore* the incompatible flankers. They found that if the flankers were moved away about one half of one degree of visual angle, the slowing in RT due to incompatible flankers disappeared, suggesting that subjects could restrict visual attention to an area about one degree across. Figure 6-2 shows typical data from the *PsychMate* version of that experiment.[5] Note that the lines are not equidistant—there is an interaction.

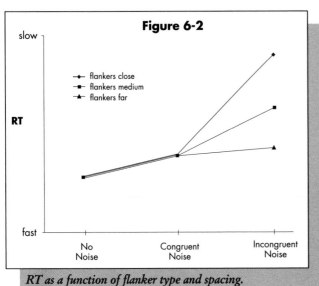

Figure 6-2

slow

-◆- flankers close
-■- flankers medium
-▲- flankers far

RT

fast

No Noise   Congruent Noise   Incongruent Noise

RT as a function of flanker type and spacing.

---

[5] The neutral noise condition is omitted to simplify.

A slightly different take on the issue of interaction is seen in the replication of Saul Sternberg's (1966) experiment in the *PsychMate 2.2: Scanning Short-Term Memory.* Sternberg predicted that if we search the contents of short-term memory serially (one item at a time) rather than in parallel (all items at once), we would expect that RT would increase with the number of items in the memory set that must be searched. That prediction was confirmed. He further predicted that if the search is self-terminating (terminated when a match is found), then the slope of the line relating RT to memory set size should be one half as much for positive probes (that match an item in the memory set) as for negative probes. Because the two lines were almost precisely parallel, Sternberg concluded that we must be performing an exhaustive search in which we keep searching even when a match occurs. Sternberg went on to develop a model of the search of short-term memory that makes it clear that an exhaustive search can actually be faster. Figure 6-3 shows typical data from the *PsychMate* version of this experiment. Here, it is the *lack* of an interaction that is theoretically interesting.

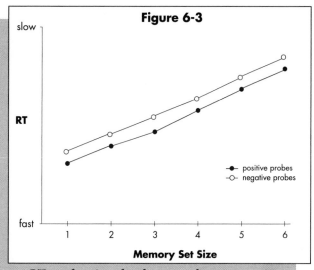

Figure 6-3

RT as a function of probe type and memory set size.

Sternberg's (1969) additive factors logic for attempting to experimentally tease apart the stages of cognitive processing relies heavily on the notion of interaction. This logic is presented in *PsychMate 2.10: Additive Factors Methodology.* In brief, if two experimental manipulations affect the same stage of processing, they should produce an interaction. If they affect different stages, the effect should be additive with no interaction.

I will illustrate this with an example that is very different from the domain of Sternberg's experiment but that makes the same point. If you have ever tried to read while in a moving car (hopefully as a passenger, and not as a driver), you know that the vibration of the car makes reading more difficult. It is also harder to read under low illumination. But both amount of vibration and amount of illumination affect the same stage in reading—the input to the eye. So, even if each has some effect on its own, the combination should produce an even further deterioration in reading. Such a result is shown in Figure 6-4A. In this graph, *A* represents the slight extra difficulty in reading caused by

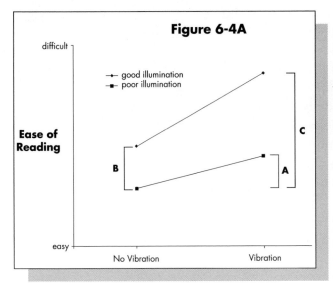

Figure 6-4A

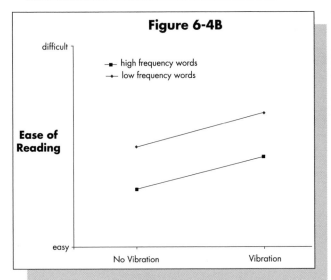

Figure 6-4B

vibration, *B* represents the slight increase in difficulty due to poor illumination, while *C* represents the further deterioration in reading due to the *combination* of vibration and poor illumination. The fact that both vibration and illumination affect the same stage of input to the eye is reflected in their interaction.

Figure 6-4B illustrates the other possibility—that two variables affect different stages of processing and, therefore, do NOT interact. One variable is again the level of vibration, which causes an increase in difficulty of reading. The other variable is the frequency with which the words appear in English—*low-frequency* (rare) words are generally harder to read than *high-frequency* (common) words. But *there is no interaction* because vibration affects the input of the information to the eye, while word frequency affects the stage of finding the meaning of the word in the mental lexicon.

I take my last example of an interaction from the area of cognitive neuroscience. In *PsychMate 2.4: Sentence-Picture Comparison*, Figure 2.4.3 shows the results of an fMRI study of the process of comparing a simple picture (a star above a plus) and a sentence, such as "The star is not below the plus." Erik Reichle, Patricia Carpenter, and Marcel Just (2000) compared two different strategies for performing the task. One was a verbal strategy in which subjects tried to match their own description of the picture to the sentence. In the visual-spatial strategy, subjects were instructed to "form a mental image of the objects in the sentence and their arrangement" (p. 268), prior to seeing the picture. They examined activation of brain locations underlying verbalization (Broca's area) and spatial processing of sensory information (superior parietal lobe). They found that subjects using the verbal strategy showed increased activity in

Broca's area, but not in the superior parietal region. Subjects using the visual-spatial strategy showed the opposite result—increased activation in the superior parietal lobe but no change in activation of Broca's area. In this example, the change in activation recorded by the fMRI was the result of an interaction of the instructions (verbal versus visual-spatial) and the brain locations.[6]

Blocking Factors

In addition to using factorial designs to include factors of theoretical interest, we can also use them to allow for control variables. In this case, we add a control variable to the experiment as an additional IV. In discussing between-groups versus within-groups designs at the beginning of this chapter, I gave an example of examining RT as a function of time of day. If we did the comparison of RT in early morning to late at night, we could include a second variable that is a control variable of order. Compare the following hypothetical results. Figure 6-5A is the result when we simply compare recall in morning versus night. As drawn, this shows no difference. But if we considered the effect of morning versus night separately for those measured first in the morning and those measured first at night, we might find a different result. Figure 6-5B shows the hypothetical results of such a factorial design. Note that for those who were tested first in the morning, RT was higher for morning than night, with the opposite effect for those first tested

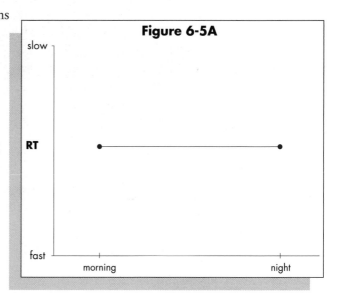

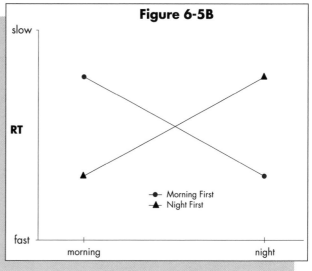

---

[6] This also demonstrates a *double dissociation*, with one task affecting one region of the brain and not another. The opposite is true of the other task. Gazzaniga, Ivry, and Mangun (2002) discuss the logic of double dissociations as evidence of separation of functions in different regions of the brain.

at night. If we found such a result, we might suspect that we are simply seeing practice effects—the first session of measuring RT led to improvement in the second. We should probably then redo the experiment with extensive practice prior to testing to get beyond any improvement from practice on the RT task. Any time that order effects might be present in an experiment, you can add order as an explicit IV in your analysis and test for the possibility of an interaction between order and the variable of real interest.

Other variables can also be used as blocking variables. It is often useful, if you have tested enough subjects, to include sex as a blocking variable in analyzing the data. Sex differences would show up as interactions between the variables of direct interest and sex. While sex differences in some cognitive abilities are well-documented, they are also not well understood. Diane Halpern (2000) offers an especially thorough review of such differences and their possible causes, both social and biological.

Randomization

In the discussion of the true experimental designs, much was made of randomization, and the topic deserves some elaboration. Randomization occurs in two general modes—random selection and random assignment. Both rely on the use of tables of random numbers, or random number generators within computer programs. This will be discussed further after a discussion of how to do random selection and random assignment.

Random selection of a sample of subjects from a population.

In statistics, a distinction is made between a *population* and a *sample*. A population includes all of the people (or dogs or rocks) of interest. For a psychologist devising an IQ test, that might be all adults (within some geographical region such as the USA). For a political pollster trying to predict the outcome of an election, the population is all likely voters. But we can never measure the IQ of all people, or question all likely voters on their preferences— there are just too many of them.[7] We must, therefore, rely on a sample, or subset of the population. The most important quality of a sample is that it must be *representative*. That is, the sample must be like the population in all relevant ways. (See *PsychMate 3.6: Survey Research* for a fuller treatment of random selection and of other issues in regard to surveys. A good recent treatment is one by Jon Krosnick, 1999.)

---

[7] On election day, of course, we do get the opinions of the population of all people who vote. That's what an election is. So remember—if you don't vote, you don't count!

How do we obtain a representative sample? A straightforward way is to use a random sample. A random sample is one in which every member of the population of interest has an equal chance of being selected for the sample. Suppose you wanted a random sample of students at your university. If you could obtain a list of all students currently enrolled, you could simply number them, and then use a random number generator to produce a list of numbers in the range from 1 to the total number enrolled. You could then contact each person whose number was selected and obtain a random sample. There are two things to note: First, a random sample does not guarantee that you have a representative sample. It does guarantee that there is no *systematic* bias in the selection process. You might accidentally over-sample smart people, or females, or dog lovers. Depending on the purpose of your sample, those deviations from representativeness may or may not be important. Statistically, the larger the random sample, the smaller the deviation from representativeness. Second, in real research situations such as standardizing an IQ test or predicting the outcome of an election, it is nearly impossible to get a true random sample.

Now a cautionary tale: The 1936 presidential election was between Alf Landon, the Republican candidate, and the Democratic candidate Franklin D. Roosevelt, who was running for re-election for the first time. The *Literary Digest*, a popular magazine of the day, conducted a poll to try to predict the outcome of the election in advance. This was in the earliest days of political opinion polling, and the techniques for accurate polling were not well understood. They got a random sample of 100,000 people from telephone directories and automobile registrations.[8] They sent each person a postcard, asking them to indicate their preference and return the card. About 20,000 did so. (They could have stopped there, since a poll with a 20% rate of return is probably useless.) The persons who returned their poll overwhelmingly favored Landon, and they confidently predicted a Republican victory. Roosevelt carried the Electoral College vote in all but two states, making the 1936 election the most lop-sided in U.S. history until that time. Why were they so spectacularly wrong? The year 1936 was at the height of the Great Depression. Automobiles and telephones were both fairly new technologies, and then, as now, new technologies were expensive and were first purchased by the relatively wealthy. Therefore, the polling generally favored the Republican Party. They simply guaranteed themselves an unrepresentative sample! Note that the Gallup poll and other major political polls typically use a sample of

---

[8] Unlisted numbers did not then exist, so that was not a problem.

about 1,500 people, and have an excellent record at predicting the outcome of presidential elections.[9]

How do the modern polls manage accurate predictions with only 1,500 people? They make a serious effort to get a representative sample. They use computer-generated phone numbers, which results in lots of calls to numbers not in use, but also makes sure unlisted numbers are not exempted. They also use stratified random sampling to make sure their samples are representative along dimensions that are known to affect voter preference, such as party preference, sex, ethnicity, and geographical location. (See *PsychMate 3.6: Survey Research* for a fuller explanation.) The important lesson here is that a large sample is better than a small sample *if and only if it is representative* In addition to *PsychMate 3.6: Survey Research,* the interested student should also consult Arlene Fink's (1995) excellent overview of the techniques of sampling for surveys. (It is one of a set of short, highly informative books on survey research published as the *Survey Kit* by SAGE.)

In truth, we seldom manage to base experiments on random samples. Instead, we use what are called "convenience samples." Most research in psychology is done on college campuses, and college students are the subjects in most of our experiments. Are they truly representative? Probably not. For one thing, the average IQ is slightly higher for college students than for the unselected population. On the other hand, when we conduct experimental research, we are seldom trying to predict something about the population, such as what percent of voters will favor each candidate. Instead, we are trying to determine a set of relationships among variables, and those typically hold fairly well at the level of individuals. (This is demonstrated in many of the *PsychMate* experiments in the analyses that show individual subjects' data.)

---

[9] There are two exceptions. Polls suggested that Harry Truman would be defeated by Thomas Dewey in 1948. A famous photograph shows Truman, sporting a coprophagous grin, holding up the *Chicago Tribune* with its banner headline "Dewey Defeats Truman" At that time, however, polling was slower than at present. Analysts then and now agree that Truman turned a close election around in the last week or so. Had the election been held a week earlier, Dewey might well have won. In 2000, we witnessed the debacle of the network news organizations calling the election in Florida first for George Bush, then for Al Gore, and then back to Bush. But their own exit polls were simply too close to make a legitimate call—the election was won by a tiny margin. The error was not in the polls, but in the absurd rush to report "news" before they knew what had really happened. (Of course, there was more to come in that disputed Florida election, which made "hanging chads" a part of the national vocabulary.)

Random assignment of subjects to levels of a between-subjects IV

A more common practical problem for experimental research comes not from random selection, but rather from the need to assign subjects to levels of the independent variable(s) (IVs). This is usually easily accomplished using random assignment. Suppose that you were investigating the role of practice in skill acquisition, and you need to compare the performance of subjects who have received one of three levels of training prior to testing. A simple procedure would be to randomly select a level as each subject comes to the laboratory for testing. Drawing one of three tokens from a bag, tossing a die (1 or 2 assigns the subject to level A, 3 or 4 to B, 5 or 6 to C), or running a random number generator set to choose in the range of 1 through 3 would all work. But note a problem: If you randomly choose the condition as each subject comes to the lab, you could end up assigning most of the subjects to one condition and hardly any to another. If you tested nine subjects, and, by chance, the first five were assigned to level A, levels B and C would be underrepresented. You could get around this by "reserving" three subjects for each condition, but there would still be a problem if you tested all of the level A subjects first. (See the discussion on Instrumentation in Chapter 5).

But note also that true randomness is really less important than that subjects not be assigned systematically, so just testing every third person under each condition would probably suffice—subjects 1, 4, 7 etc. are assigned to level A; 2, 5, 8 etc. to B; and so on.

Ordering of levels of a within-subjects IV

In within-subjects (repeated-measures) designs, each subject is tested under each level of the IV(s). It would be possible to simply assign the order of the levels randomly for each subject. If there were four orders, we could write them down on cards, shuffle the cards, and then use that order for the first subject, then shuffle again and use the new order for the next subject, etc. (A computer program can also randomize the order—equivalent to shuffling a deck.) But this would not be the best way to handle the problem. Instead of random assignment, this is best dealt with by counterbalancing.

Counterbalancing. In repeated-measures designs in which each subject is tested once under each level of the independent variable(s), you need to control for *order effects.* As an example, suppose that you were interested in whether caffeine affects the speed of cognitive processing. You could compare performance of subjects on some cognitive task either shortly after ingesting caffeine, or when they have not consumed any caffeine for several hours. But a possible confound arises. If you test all subjects without caffeine first, then give them caffeine and retest them, there may be lingering effects of the no-caffeine test—for example, it might have served as practice for the second test. Thus the second test, under the influence of caffeine, may be affected by the previous test. A straightforward way to handle this problem is *counterbalancing*. That is achieved by testing half of the subjects without caffeine first, and then with caffeine. The other half are tested in the reverse order—with caffeine first, then without. To have complete counterbalancing, you would need to have an even number of subjects since two subjects are needed to complete the counterbalancing. *Complete counterbalancing* occurs when every possible ordering of the levels of the IV is tested.[10]

The counterbalancing of two levels of an IV is illustrated in the following table, where A and B denote two levels of an independent variable, such as with or without caffeine.

	Condition		
Subject Number	First	Second	
1	A	B	
2	B	A	
3	A	B	
4	B	A	etc.

If there are three levels of the IV, as would occur if you test three different dosages of caffeine—say, 0, 50, and 100 milligrams (a cup of coffee contains about 100 mg of caffeine)—you would need to counterbalance those three levels. The table below shows the complete counterbalancing with the three levels of the IV designated A, B, and C.

	Condition			
Subject Number	First	Second	Third	
1	A	B	C	
2	A	C	B	
3	B	A	C	
4	B	C	A	
5	C	A	B	
6	C	B	A	
7	A	B	C	etc.

---

[10] There is another solution in some cases—simply have subjects practice the task to asymptote (i.e. until they show no further improvement), and then test them under the various experimental conditions. If they are truly at asymptote, then further "practice" will not matter.

Note that Subject 7 gets the same ordering as Subject 1. Complete counterbalancing of three levels of the IV thus requires testing multiples of six subjects since there are six possible orderings.

If there were four levels of the IV (such as four levels of dosage of caffeine—0, 50, 100, and 150 mg), a total of 24 subjects would be required to have a complete counterbalancing (each of the six orders needed for three levels, times four). The number grows rapidly. With five levels of the IV, 120 subjects would be needed. For six levels, 720 subjects would be needed for a complete counterbalancing.

Clearly, complete counterbalancing becomes a near impossibility beyond four levels of the IV. What is needed, then, is some way to reduce the number of subjects needed, while still maintaining a reasonable level of counter-balancing. The usual approach is to use a *Latin square design*. (Geoffrey Keppell, 1982, gives a more complete account, including discussions of statistical analysis.)

Construction of a Latin square design for five levels of a DV is illustrated first. A Latin square consists of a J x J matrix of numbers, where J is the number of levels of the IV, such that each number occurs once in each row and once in each column. One example is

1	2	3	4	5
2	3	4	5	1
3	4	5	1	2
4	5	1	2	3
5	1	2	3	4

To use the Latin square, you would now need to randomly assign the levels of the IV (designated with letters) to the numbers. I used a table of random numbers to produce the following assignment, by assigning 0 or 1 in the table to designate condition A, 2 or 3 for B, etc. The first digit in the random number table was a 6 (C), the next a 0 (A), the next was a 5, but C was already used. The next was a 3 (B), the next a 9 (E), leaving only D. So, the first line of my Latin square would consist of

1(C)	2(A)	3(B)	4(E)	5(D)	(Subject 1)

I then complete the square

2(A)	3(B)	4(E)	5(D)	1(C)	(Subject 2)
3(B)	4(E)	5(D)	1(C)	2(A)	(etc.)
4(E)	5(D)	1(C)	2(A)	3(B)	
5(D)	1(E)	2(B)	3(A)	4(C)	

Subject 1 would then get the five treatments in the order C, A, B, E, D. Subject 2 would get treatments in the order A, B, E, D, C, and so on through the first five subjects. For the second set of five subjects, I would make a new Latin square by again randomly assigning letters to the positions. This process would be repeated as often as needed. The only constraint is that the number of subjects would need to be a multiple of 5.

Notice that the Latin square does not provide complete counterbalancing. It does, however, produce a reasonable approximation. Random assignment of conditions to the positions of the Latin square at least assures that there is no systematic bias—at least over several repetitions with new assignments.

There is one improvement that can be made to the Latin square. That is to use a *digram-balanced* Latin square. In a digram-balanced Latin square, *each treatment is followed by each of the other treatments an equal number of times.* Here is an example:

1	2	3	4
2	4	1	3
3	1	4	2
4	3	2	1

Note that 1 is followed equally often by 2, 3, and 4, and is the last treatment once.

W. A. Wagenaar (1969) gives perhaps the most complete treatment of digram-balanced Latin squares, including instructions for building them. He also gives examples of digram-balanced Latin squares through a 20 x 20 square. One limitation that Wagenaar notes is that digram-balanced Latin squares are only possible for even numbers of levels of the IV.[11]

Geoffrey Keppell (1982) gives a more complete account of the use of Latin squares, including using them to control "junk" variables, such as the assignment of treatment conditions if several different experimenters are used. Ronald Fisher and Frank Yates (1963) provide an extensive set of examples of Latin squares.

---

[11] An almost digram-balanced Latin square can be produced for odd numbers of levels if each subject is tested twice under each condition, with the assignment of levels controlled by two Latin squares, one of which is the reverse of the other. Consider these two Latin squares:

1	2	3		3	2	1
2	3	1		1	3	2
3	1	2		2	1	3

If subject one is tested in the order 1 2 3 3 2 1, subject two in the order 2 3 1 1 3 2, and subject three in the order 3 1 2 2 1 3, then 1 is followed by 2 and 3 twice each, 2 is followed by 1 and 3 twice each, and 3 is followed by 1 and 2 twice each. Each level is followed by itself once—1 1, 2 2, and 3 3 occur once each. Each level is the last once.

A cautionary note. Edwin G. Boring, a noted scholar of the history of psychology and a major methodologist, writing on experimental control noted of counterbalancing (he was speaking of experiments on training, but the point applies generally), "when these orders are combined, it is hoped that practice effects due to priority will cancel out, but, of course, you cannot be sure. *Counterbalancing is not constancy*" (1954, p. 125, emphasis added). *Neither is randomization*, I might add. Why not? The basic problem is one of *asymmetrical transfer*. By transfer, I mean any effect that exposure to one level of the IV has on the response to another. If I test RT under two conditions, with a block of trials for each condition, the first block of trials may show a practice effect. That is, RT might be faster for the second block because of the practice from the first block. If the practice effect is the same for each condition, then counterbalancing would remove any order effects—while RT would be faster for the second block for each subject, half of the subjects would gain a little for condition A and half would gain a little for condition B, and everything would be alright—the transfer is symmetrical.[12] But suppose that I compare mean RT for a two-choice task versus mean RT for a four-choice task. Half of my subjects do the two-choice version first, and half do the four-choice version first. Those doing the two-choice version first would have to switch to the four-choice strategy on the second block, giving me the "correct" finding of faster two-choice RT than four-choice. But suppose that subjects doing the four-choice task first then simply treated the second block of trials as also being a four-choice task—that is, they prepared themselves to respond to any of the four stimuli, even though only two are now being used. Those subjects might show no difference between two- and four-choice RT. Thus, half of my subjects would show the true difference and half would show no difference. If I then average these two groups of subjects, I would find a smaller difference than I should. That is asymmetrical transfer. (Note that this problem is not restricted to an IV with two levels. The possibilities for asymmetries increase enormously with more levels of the IV—there may be asymmetrical transfer between A and B, but not between A and C or B and C.)

What can be done about this problem? Probably the best solution is to add *order* of testing as a blocking variable in the statistical analysis. If order of testing interacts with the effect of number of choices, you would have to conclude that asymmetrical transfer occurred and was a serious confound. You might then turn to a between-subjects design to measure the difference. That design is much less powerful because it does not control for all of the many

---

[12] Again, if you are not interested in practice effects themselves, you could simply have the subjects practice the tasks to asymptote before beginning data collection. Any practice effects would therefore be removed.

variables that can affect RT other than number of choices. However, it effectively solves the problem of asymmetrical transfer.

Random ordering of trials.

In many research paradigms in psychology (including most of those in *PsychMate*), each subject is tested many times in each condition (i.e., level of the IV). Each *trial* in the experiment consists of a single test under one condition, and then the several trials under each condition are averaged to produce a single score for that condition. Reaction-time research almost always takes this form. In this case, we typically present the trials in a random order. You can conceptualize this process easily. Suppose that you are testing a subject in an experiment with two repeated-measures IVs with three levels of each. There are thus nine types of trials. Suppose further that you present each type of trial 10 times. There are thus 90 trials. To provide a random ordering of these 90 trials, you could write each trial type on 10 cards, then shuffle the deck of 90 trials, and then present the trials to the subject in that order. For the next subject, just re-shuffle the deck for a new random order. The ordering of trials in the various *PsychMate* experiments that use multiple trials of each trial type is done using a computerized version of that procedure. (There is a further discussion of random number generators later in this chapter.)

In Chapter 3, the idea of the "true" score from classical test theory was mentioned. In reaction-time research, the RT on each trial of a given type is regarded as an independent estimate of the true score but is distorted by error. The "error" could be due to momentary inattention, variation in muscular preparedness to make a response, or the fact that the same trial type has occurred several times in a row (see the next paragraph). But if the errors are random from trial to trial, the average of the RTs for a given condition should yield a number very close to the "true" score for that subject for that condition.

An issue arises for this approach in that random ordering of trials can produce relatively long "runs" of the same stimulus (or of stimuli calling for the same response). In doing the RT experiments in *PsychMate*, you have likely noticed this. Garner, Hake, and Eriksen (1956) noted that "modified random sequences are used [in experiments] which prevent long runs, since most subjects do not believe that long runs can occur by change and thus are unwilling to use them" (p. 153). Subjects tend to respond to one of these long runs in one of two ways, each of which reflects the *gambler's fallacy* (see "The Logic of Gambling" in Lionel Ruby's 1954 book, *The Art of Making Sense*, for an excellent presentation of this common misinterpretation of probability). If a subject has made a response of "1" six times in a row, she may begin to think that a response of "2" is overdue. If the next trial does call for a response of

"2", she will be fast and accurate, but if it again calls for a "1", she is likely to be slow and the probability of an error will be high. Another subject who has made a response of "1" six times in a row may make the opposite mistake and begin to *expect* to respond "1." He would then be fast and accurate if the next trial did call for a response of "1," but slow and error-prone if it called for a "2!" Fortunately, this will not occur very often, and over a large number of trials will have little effect on mean RT.[13]

A note on randomization. Most statistics textbooks have a table of random numbers at the back of the book, along with the tables of values of various test statistics. Many of those are taken from a book issued by the RAND Corporation (a private research group) in 1955, titled *A Million Random Digits with 100,000 Normal Deviates.*[14] That book made available a very long list of random digits that researchers could use in various ways, such as those detailed above, at a time when few researchers had access to computerized random-number generators. The concept of randomization is not new. Devices essentially equivalent to modern dice have been found that date back to 2750 BCE (see Deborah Bennett's 1998 book *Randomness* for this history). But the ability to produce random series of digits quickly and easily is quite new, having to await the advent of modern computers. Note a technical caveat: So-called random number generators produce what is called a *pseudo-random* series of digits because they actually produce the same set of digits each time. If used naïvely, that would be the equivalent of starting at the same place each time in a random number table. To make the lists more acceptable, the programs use a random number *seed*. The seed is a number chosen arbitrarily, by applying a series of operations on numbers that are currently available to the computer. For example, you could *concatenate* (string together) the digits of the date (for example, 3/26/09 would become 32609), then multiple by the current time in hours (if it were 6:23 pm, then on a 24-hour clock, 6 pm becomes 18), then divide by the current minute (in this example, 23), then round to a whole number. For our example, the number would equal 25520. The trick is to then run the random number generator 25520 times (or whatever the seed), and then start using the digits from that point. In essence, this chooses a random (or at least highly arbitrary) starting point for the random

---

[13] Prior to computerized experimentation, when randomization was necessarily done "by hand" using random-number tables, it was common to swap a few trials in the list whenever a run of more than 4 or 5 occurred, which avoids this problem. While that solution could still be used, it is difficult to program. On the other hand, prior to computerized experimentation, it was not usually possible to produce a new random order for each subject.

[14] The thought of 100,000 normal deviates may seem a little strange—who are these normal deviates? It actually refers to randomly chosen digits that come from a normal distribution, rather then a rectangular distribution in which all values occur equally often, which is what generates the usual random numbers.

number table. See Bennett (1998) for a good, basic discussion of random number generators.

Random number generators typically give a set of numbers between 0 and 1 to some large number of decimal points. But if you are randomly assigning subjects to levels of a DV, you almost always want a list of random digits between 1 and the number of levels. A simple formula converts those numbers to any range desired, and is incorporated in most random number generators.

A final note about the randomization of the order of trials. Randomness is generally the best way to ensure that the subject cannot predict what the next trial will be. True randomness, however, is far less important than that the order be arbitrary and unpredictable.

Other Issues in the Conduct of Experiments

In the several sections that follow, I detail several practical points concerning experimentation. These do not all apply to all experiments.

Deletion of data

An issue that becomes of practical importance in many experiments concerns when you can reasonably omit the data from a subject from the final analysis. Sometimes a subject performs in ways that suggest that they were not following the instructions. Now clearly, if the subject is simply not doing the experiment, it is reasonable to delete their data. The difficulty is that one must do so with scrupulous honesty. You obviously should NOT delete data simply because a subjects' performance does not meet your theoretical expectations. That would be a deliberate fudging of the data, and a violation of the ethical principles discussed in Chapter 7 concerning the treatment of data. If you omit every subject whose pattern of responses is different than predicted, you can manufacture any result you want—it just would not be the truth. I address the accepted methods here in some detail.

In an RT task with many trials, if a subject has a high error rate, it probably indicates that she either did not understand the instructions or that she was trying so hard to have fast RTs that she was guessing on many trials. Since guessing is definitely NOT what you want the subject to do, you would clearly be justified in deleting her data. A principle that is very helpful in this regard is to *set out the criteria for rejecting data ahead of time.* In RT research, many experimenters set a criterion of errors on no more than 10% of trials. Note that by using a criterion of no more than 10% errors *set in advance*, you would delete the data if there were more than 10% errors *no matter whether the data matched your prediction or not.* I cannot give you a precise criterion, however.

I suggest 10% here, but if the task were particularly difficult, a higher criterion—say, 20%—might be better. Whatever the criterion, state it in your Method section. Note that the Subjects section *must* report the number of subjects whose data were eliminated and the criterion. You occasionally see a statement such as "Data from 3 subjects were deleted due to error rates in excess of 10%."

Unfortunately, it is not always possible to specify all of the criteria for deletion in advance. With people being as they are, you will occasionally have someone come up with a new way to mess up your experiment. If your experiment lasts over several sessions, or if it is impossible to know the pattern of the subject's results before you make a decision, you are in pretty good shape. If someone's behavior suggests that they are not following the instructions, you can safely delete their data after one session, or otherwise before you know their final results. That way, you cannot be causing a bias based on deleting data that contradict your expectations. But in some cases, you cannot avoid knowing the pattern of the subject's results at the time you must decide whether to delete their data. Perhaps the best solution in that case is to discuss the issue with a disinterested colleague—describe the subject's behavior and see if they agree that it suggests that they were not following the instructions.

The vast majority of subjects will provide you with good data—even if they contradict your expectations. A small minority seem unable or unwilling to follow simple instructions. Many years ago, when I was in graduate school, I tested a subject in an RT experiment. During the practice session, he frequently had RTs below 100 ms. Needless to say, he also had an error rate of about 50% on those trials. I repeatedly told him not to guess, but to wait until he saw the stimulus. He assured me that he was following those instructions. If you have ever been a subject in an RT experiment, such as many of those in *PsychMate*, you will realize the silliness of claiming that you are making a response to a stimulus in less than 100 ms. I dismissed the subject after the first session, since he clearly was not following the instructions. A few days later, I encountered a fellow graduate student who was looking rather worried. On asking the source of his problems, he told me that he had just tested a subject whose performance was dreadful, and whom he was sure was not following the instructions. However, he had the dilemma that he also knew the results of the subject's performance, which contradicted his hypothesis. He was thus in the position of wanting to delete the data, but unsure that he could do so legitimately. On a hunch, I asked the subject's name. It was the same guy who had jeopardized my test results. I advised my colleague to delete the data with a clear conscience. A few days later, I saw a sign-up sheet for experiments on a departmental bulletin board and saw that the same person had signed up for another experiment. Written beside his name was a warning, "Don't use this guy!" So at least three of us had found the subject unable to follow simple instructions. I guess my point is that you will occasionally encounter people who are playing in some game other than the one you are in. Delete the data with a clear conscience. (But report it in the Subjects section!)

In single-trial RT research, a slightly different problem occurs. RT varies from trial to trial quite a bit, even in the same experimental condition. The level of preparedness varies from trial to trial, and there are inevitable lapses in attention. The result is that the distribution of RTs is usually extremely positively skewed as shown in Figure 6-6.

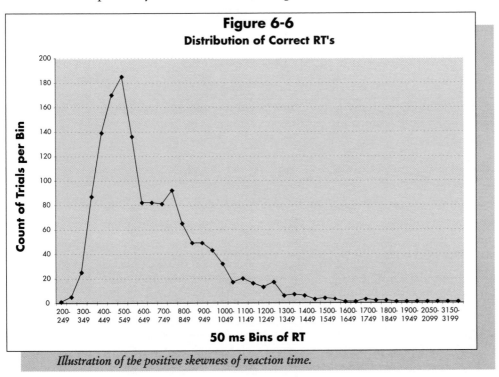

Illustration of the positive skewness of reaction time.

The few trials in the outer edge of that skewness are almost certainly a result of momentary inattention to the task—in an experiment with RTs averaging 400-500 ms, a trial with an RT of 3000 ms is almost certainly a botched trial. Such trials can legitimately be dropped from the analysis—they reflect noise, not signal. The problem is how to recognize such *outliers*. Omitting outliers will, of course, change the mean RTs. But if the outliers are from trials in which the subject was distracted, or otherwise not really doing the task, the mean RT without them will better reflect the "true" RT for that condition. Several methods are used to avoid this problem. One is to use the median RT, instead of the mean. You may recall from your statistics course that extreme scores have a greater effect on the mean than on the median. Another approach is to set a criterion for *truncation* of RT. That means simply omitting any trials where the RT exceeds some criterion. A common criterion is to omit trials on which the RT is more than three standard deviations above that subject's mean for that condition. Rolf Ulrich and Jeff Miller (1994) give a detailed analysis of the effects of various methods of truncation. Mark van Selst and Pierre Jolicoeur (1994) also address the issue.

Although truncation of RTs to eliminate outliers is certainly justified, in practice, it seems to make relatively little difference. If outliers are due to momentary lapses of attention or similar problems, they should occur relatively equally across types of trials, adding a small amount of statistical noise to the data but not affecting the pattern of difference in mean RTs, which is usually what matters.

The Extreme-Groups Design

If you are investigating a relationship between variables and little has been previously published on the specific issue, you might want to begin by simply finding out whether there *is* a relationship. (This is exploratory research.) An accurate description of the nature of that relationship will then come from further research. Of course, if there is no relationship, then further research is not needed.

If you can assume that the relationship between the IV and the DV is unidirectional (the value of the DV trends only upward (or only downward) as the IV increases), you should probably use an extreme-groups design. Examples of a function that fit this description include almost any study of the effects of practice—performance improves with practice and eventually reaching a plateau but never declines. Another example can be seen in *PsychMate 1.3: Rotation of Mental Images,* where there is an increase in RT with an increased amount of rotation (using absolute angle of rotation).[15]

The extreme-groups design simply means that you start with relatively extreme values of the IV. An example is Pascal's experiment, discussed in Chapter 1, in which the effect of air pressure on the Toreccelian vacuum was maximized by comparisons at the base and top of a 3,000-foot mountain. Instead of trying to find an effect by climbing up a step-ladder (in which case

---

[15] Not all functions are like this, however. The relationship between arousal and performance, mentioned in Chapter 2 as the Yerkes-Dodson law, is an inverted-U—performance improves as arousal increases up to a point, but too much arousal causes performance to deteriorate. In this case, extremely high and low levels of arousal *both* lead to poor performance.

the effect would likely be too small to have been detected), Pascal maximized the IV and had the vacuum measured at the highest point he had available.

In a correlational study, Christiane Capron and Michel Duyme (1989) examined the difference in mean IQ of adopted children born to biological parents with either high- or low-socio-economic status (SES) and raised by adoptive parents with either high- or low-SES.[16] The high-SES parents were typically physicians, lawyers, and college faculty with education beyond a bachelor's degree. Their low-SES parents were mainly unskilled laborers with only six to eight years of schooling. They deliberately looked at only very high and very low SES parents, so as to maximize the likelihood of finding significant differences. [17]

The point here is really pretty simple—if the intent of your research is to find out whether there is any relationship, do not look for small, subtle effects that may be too small to detect. Instead, maximize the range of the IV that you use. If you use extreme groups and the difference is not significant, there probably is either no relationship, or the relationship is too small to matter. (Again, note the problem if you have a curvilinear relationship, in which a straight line is a poor fit to the data.)

Determining the Shape of Functional Relationship

Scientific investigation is almost always concerned with discovering relationships between variables. It is often the case that, in the beginning of a scientific investigation, we have only rather vague predictions about the relationships between variables. Once we have established that there is a relationship between two variables, we need to know more precisely what the relationship *is*. In the case of the relationship between two nominal variables, there may be little else to know beyond the direction and degree of the relationship. There is a relationship between handedness and sex, but we have characterized the relationship fairly completely when we know the direction (males are more likely to be left-handed than females) and the degree (approximately 10% of males and 5% of females are left-handed) of the relationship.

Things are more complex when we consider the case of two ordered variables that are more-or-less continuous. Consider the case of a relationship between two ordered, quantitative variables, such as RT and the number of

---

[16] Socio-economic status is usually a combination of educational level, income level, and job status.

[17] They found a mean difference favoring children of high-SES biological parents by about 16 points, and a mean difference favoring children of high-SES adoptive parents of 12 points. The research thus suggests that both environment and genetics are important in determining IQ.

items in short-term memory to which a stimulus must be compared. (See *PsychMate 2.2: Scanning Short-Term Memory*) In this case, we can be even more precise about the nature of the relationship. In Sternberg's (1966) original data, the relationship between RT and the memory set size is RT = 396 ms + 38 ms * MSS.[18]

Another way of saying that two variables are related is to say that one variable is a function of another—in Sternberg's case, RT is a function of the size of the memory set. For the experiment on rotation of mental images, RT is a function of the degree of rotation. The *serial position effect* (see Chapter 2) is a statement that the probability of recall is a function of the position of the item in the studied list.[19] But note that this language implies a causal direction—RT does not cause the memory set size, rather memory set size causes RT.

In the case of functions between ordered variables that are more-or-less continuous, there is a further question to be answered. Not only must we state the direction and degree of relationship, but we must also state the *shape* of the function.

How many levels of the IV do we need? This depends very much on the complexity of the function. If you know that the function is linear, you need only two points to be able to describe the relationship since two points on a line provide all the information you need to calculate the formula for the line. But as the function becomes more complex, more points will be needed to specify the relationship. If there is a single inflection point, or change of direction of the function—for example, in the serial position curve—you would need at least three points. This is called a quadratic trend. If there are two inflections, at least four points would be needed. This is a cubic trend. Higher-order trends are also possible, but fortunately they are rare in psychological experimentation. Figure 6-8 illustrates linear, quadratic, and cubic trends, as well as the higher-order trend with three inflections—a quartic trend.

The general rule, then, is that you need at least two more levels of the IV than the number of possible inflections in the function. You cannot even hope to detect a quadratic trend with only two data points, or to detect a quartic trend with only three points. But more points than this minimum are probably

---

[18] Note that this is a *linear* function, or one that is well-described by a straight line. Recall that the formula for a straight line is Y = a + bX (you may have seen it as the equivalent formula Y = mX + b). Here, *a* is the *intercept*, or the value of Y when X is zero, and *b* is the *slope*, or the change in Y for a given change in X. For Sternberg's formula, 396 ms is the theoretical RT if you had no comparisons to make, and is comprised of the time needed to identify the stimulus and to make a response, omitting the time needed to make the comparisons. In his data, each comparison added 38 ms, so the slope of the line is 38 ms per item added in the memory set.

[19] Though in this case, the relationship is *curvilinear*—recall is best at the beginning and end of the list, and poorer in the middle.

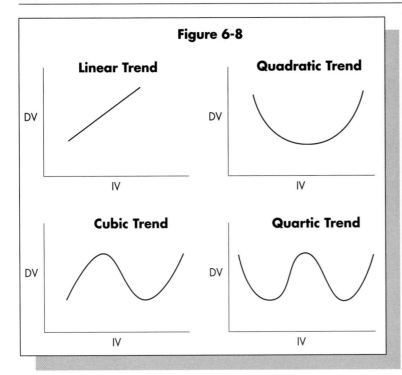

Figure 6-8

Linear Trend

DV

IV

Quadratic Trend

DV

IV

Cubic Trend

DV

IV

Quartic Trend

DV

IV

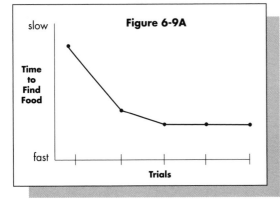

Figure 6-9A

slow

Time
to
Find
Food

fast

Trials

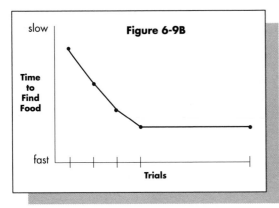

Figure 6-9B

slow

Time
to
Find
Food

fast

Trials

needed to get a good idea of the exact nature of the curve. Another consideration is the *spacing* of the levels of the IV. Consider an experiment on maze-learning in rats. If a hungry rat is placed in a maze in the same starting point each time, and there is always food in the same goal point, the rat will become faster and faster at reaching the food. But performance can only improve up to a point. That point is reached when the rat runs as quickly as it can with no errors—it just can't get any faster, thus the curve flattens out at some point. Figure 6-9A shows hypothetical data for such a study, with five equally-spaced points along the quadratic curve. But note that the fourth point is largely wasted. Figure 6-9B shows a more optimal assignment of levels of the IV, with the points closer together where the curve is changing the fastest. Of course, the optimal placement of the points (levels of the IV) may only be possible after preliminary testing.

A caveat: When trying to learn the shape of a truly continuous function, we can only test a limited number of points along the line, then infer the rest. We can never be absolutely certain how the function behaves *between* the points we tested. Figure 6-10A shows the typical curve relating mean rate of growth to age for females. The rate of growth is very high at birth, and then it gradually slows to a fairly steady rate during late childhood. At about age 12, there is a pronounced *growth spurt*, and then the curve drops to zero at about age 15—most women have reached full adult height by that age.[20] If we tested our subjects every three years (starting at birth as year 0), the growth spurt would appear in our data (Figure 6-10B). But if we tested the growth rate of our subjects every five years we would completely miss the growth spurt (Figure 6-10C).

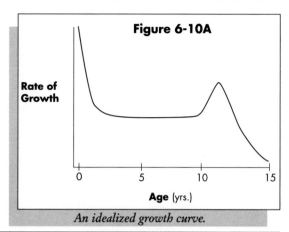

An idealized growth curve.

Curve fitting. Various computer programs are available that estimate the best-fitting curved line through a non-linear function—a task that is truly daunting without the number-crunching power of a computer. They also provide a measure of the degree of fit. A quadratic trend, for example, might be best fit by either a power function or an exponential function.

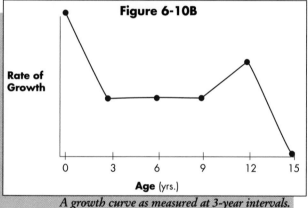

A growth curve as measured at 3-year intervals.

As an example, performance of almost any task improves with practice, providing a quadratic trend. That curve has usually been taken to be best fitted by a power function (see Gordon Logan, 2002), though Andrew Heathcote, Scott Brown, and D. J. K. Mewhort (2000) suggest that it is better fit by an exponential function.

Backing Up Your Data: Cautionary Tales

In Chapter 5, I emphasized the need to carefully (and clearly!) record your methodology because details that seem obvious and unforgettable often turn out to

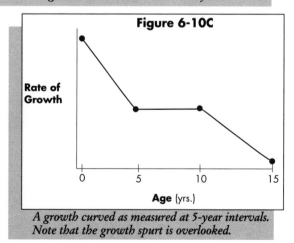

A growth curved as measured at 5-year intervals. Note that the growth spurt is overlooked.

be quite forgettable. In addition to that caution, another is in order—back up your data frequently and to multiple locations.

Given the enormous amount of time you invest in collecting data for any kind of psychological research, you simply cannot afford to have a failure of a

---

[20] *St. James' Research Methods textbook*

computer hard drive or some other misfortune ruin your study. Hard luck can happen, and do not assume it can not happen to you.

As a graduate student, I was acquainted with a woman who was completing her doctoral dissertation. The small town where she lived was leveled by a tornado. A number of people died, and many people lost their homes, so the loss of her dissertation data was hardly the worst of the situation. Nevertheless, she had to start from scratch on her study. The data sheets that she had carefully stored at home were scattered to the winds.

Some years ago the building housing the school of business at a large university burned to the ground. All of the faculty members had been admonished to carefully back up their computer files to floppy disks (this was a few years ago!). Most had done so. Unfortunately, most of them had left the backup disks in their offices alongside their computers. Oh, well.

If you have your data stored electronically, make backup copies to flash drives, to network drives, or however you can. If you have data sheets, where you have recorded data on paper, make copies frequently. In either case, store a copy of the data somewhere other than where the main copy is stored.

Chapter 7

Research II

No isolated experiment, however significant in itself, can suffice for the experimental demonstration of any natural phenomenon; for the "one chance in a million" will undoubtedly occur, with no less and no more than its appropriate frequency, however surprised we should be that it happened to us.

Fisher, 1935/1960, pp. 14-15.

An idea you occasionally encounter in the older literature of science is that of the *experimentum crucis*, or crucial experiment. The idea was that if a theory predicts a certain result, and that result is obtained, then the theory is verified. The discussion of the logic of science and hypothesis testing in Chapter 2 should have made it clear that a crucial experiment is more myth than reality. After two chapters devoted to the ins and outs of experimentation, this chapter returns to a discussion of *research*. By research, I mean the accumulation of evidence across many different studies that gradually refines theorizing and leads to well-developed models of how the world works.

In this chapter, I take up several topics that are concerned more with the research program than with individual experiments. These include the importance of replication and the use of marker variables, the distinction between confirmatory and exploratory research, and the ethics of handling data.

First, I present two quotes that sustain the theme of research versus experimentation. Donald Campbell and Julian Stanley (1966), in their influential book on *Experimental and Quasi-Experimental Designs for Research* noted that "continuous, multiple experimentation is more typical of science than once-and-for-all definitive experiments" (p. 3).

O. Kempthorne (1976) similarly remarked that "a single experiment is only one step, a very important one for the particular experimenter, in the long, sustaining effort of humanity to build a validated model of the world" (p. 32).

Replication

> A phenomenon is experimentally demonstra-
> ble when we know how to conduct an
> experiment that will rarely fail to give us a
> statistically significant result.
>
> Ronald Fisher (1935/1960, p. 14)

Replication is an important part of the scientific enterprise. As my graduate school mentor, Charles W. Eriksen (frequent personal communication), remarked, "No experimental result is carved in stone." Well, someone may have carved one somewhere, but they shouldn't. Eriksen's point is entirely valid—any single experiment may simply be wrong. This is especially true when we must rely on a sample of subjects—sampling error can occur.

Even with multiple replications that probability is never reduced to zero, but it can become so small as to be ignored. There are experimental results that virtually never fail to replicate so we can have very high reliance on them. (The experiments in *PsychMate* were chosen precisely because they usually work.)

It is worth noting a few different types of replication. This classification is due to David Lykken (1968). First, there is what he called *literal replication*. In a literal replication, the experimenter repeats the original experiment as exactly as possible. This sort of replication is most often carried out by the original experimenter, and I recommend it to any experimenter. Lykken notes that "asking the original [experimenter] to simply run more subjects would perhaps be about as close as we could come to attaining literal replication...." (p. 155). This variety of replication, if successful, verifies the original result. Unfortunately, if the original result was due to some error in the design of the experiment, or some other of the "auxiliaries," then a literal replication may simply repeat the error.[1]

Closely related to direct replication is Lykken's (1968) second variety of replication—*operational replication*. Here, the experimenter seeks to duplicate the original sampling procedures and experimental conditions but may vary the details. If you were to read another researcher's Method section and repeat the experiment the best you could, there would be slight differences. Your

---

[1] In physiological research, you sometimes see an experimental result from one subject repeated on another. The experiment on each subject, then, is treated as a replication. What we would call "subjects" are then referred to as "replicates." This approach is most often used in situations where the variability from subject to subject is near zero and no statistical analysis based on a sample is really needed.

equipment might not be exactly the same, for example, or you might use different word lists in a memory experiment, though the words were chosen in a similar manner. If an operational replication fails, the original Method section may not have noted all of the essential conditions for replication. What Lykken called the "experimental recipe" may have omitted some such condition. His example was the investigation of Clever Hans, a horse that was claimed to be able to do addition and subtraction, among other wonders. Early replications were successful, but later, when the experimenters made sure that Hans' owner did not know the answer to the question asked of him, Hans could not answer. Lykken notes that the original "recipe" did not specify that the owner must know the answer. The failure of the replication showed that the "recipe" was wrong.[2]

A successful operational replication has a similar problem to that of a direct replication. If, for example, the experimental result does not generalize beyond the type of subject originally used (i.e., lacks *external validity*—see Chapter 3), then a successful operational replication that used the same type of subject would be misleading.

Lykken's third type of replication, *constructive replication*, is the most important. Constructive replication occurs when you deliberately *avoid* trying to do the same experiment as the previous researcher. "To obtain an ideal constructive replication, one would provide a competent investigator with *nothing more than* a clear statement of the empirical "fact" which the first author would claim to have established...and then let the replicator formulate his [*sic*] own methods of sampling, measurement, and data analysis" (1958, p. 156, emphasis in the original). An assignment that I use in my own Research Methods course asks each student to set up an experiment to verify the finding of W. E. Hick (1952) and Ray Hyman (1953) that RT increases as the log(base2) of the number of choices among stimuli or responses increases. But I do not specify the stimuli or responses. (The stimuli must be presented on a computer screen since part of the point of the exercise is learning to set up experiments using E-Prime—the programming environment underlying *PsychMate*. Similarly, the responses are limited to the computer keyboard.) Some students

---

[2] See Joseph Jastrow (1935). *Der kluge Hans* (Clever Hans) became a well-known marvel around 1904, being estimated to have the mental capacity of an 11-year-old child. Shown a list of numbered words and asked a relevant question, he would paw the ground a number of times to indicate his selection. Shown 1=scissors, 2=nail, and 3=magnet, and asked, "Which is magnetic?" he would paw the ground thrice. Two psychologists, Carl Stumpf and his student, Oskar Pfungst, discovered that the horse's owner, Herr von Osten, was unwittingly signaling Hans to paw by learning forward. Von Osten would straighten up slightly when the correct answer was reached, and Hans had (quite cleverly!) learned to stop pawing on that signal. Once this was discovered, Pfungst could make Hans give any answer at will, as Hans would follow the same signal from Pfungst.

use letters as stimuli; some use pictures. Some ask for responses on the numeric keypad; some use letter keys. They test each other as subjects, and the results are usually a remarkable affirmation of the Hick/Hyman law (see *PsychMate 5.1: Reaction Time Procedures*). This provides a constructive replication of that law—the Hick/Hyman Law rarely fails to give us a statistically significant result.

The difference between operational and constructive replication is captured nicely in Lykken's statement that "just as a reliable but invalid test can be said to measure something, but not what it claimed to measure, so an experiment that replicates operationally but not constructively could be said to have demonstrated something, but not the relationship between meaningful constructs, generalizable to some broad reference population, which the author originally claimed to have established" (1958, p. 156).

Another example of constructive replication was discussed in Chapter 5, in the section on external validity. The demonstration by Garcia and Koehling (1966) of one-trial learning of taste avoidance following sickness replicates across diverse species, including rats, quail, snakes, and humans.

A clear example of the failure to produce a replicable phenomenon is research on the paranormal. The existence of paranormal phenomena, such as clairvoyance and telekinesis, remains in real doubt, but that doubt would vanish if someone could find a "recipe" that would reliably produce the phenomenon for different investigators. For a good discussion, see James Alcock (1981). In the years since he wrote his 1981 work, *Parapsychology: Science or Magic*, the situation has not changed.

Marker Variables

A useful notion in the conduct of research (as opposed to individual experiments), and related to the notion of replication, is that of a *marker variable*. There are two slightly different uses of this term. One use refers to replicating part of one experiment within a second experiment intended to extend the basic finding. If a basic effect is well-documented and easily reproduced, it can be included as part of other experiments as a check on their reliability. In designing a study that is intended to extend a previous result, you should make it a habit to include a relevant subset of the conditions from the previous study. If those replicate in the new experiment, that gives you a good indication that the results of the new conditions you have added are valid as well. If they fail to replicate, you can place little reliance on the data from the new conditions.

A second, slightly different use of the term marker variable refers to replicating a condition within an experiment and is illustrated in *PsychMate 1.6: Selective Attention and Response Competition.* Again, the point of the marker variable is to include conditions for which the results are nearly certain—to provide a check on the other data. In that experiment, subjects must identify whether a central target letter is an "S" or an "H." On most trials there are other letters flanking the target, and the point of the study is to see how different flankers affect RT (the specifics are not relevant here). As a control, there are trials on which there are no flankers. A second IV is the distance from the target to the flankers. That experiment is set up so that the trials with no flankers are also divided into three levels, reflecting the distance from the target to the (nonexistent) flankers. That is equivalent to randomly dividing the no-flanker trials into three groups. This serves as a marker variable because those three conditions are the same, and thus their mean RTs should differ only due to chance factors. If you were to find that those three RTs are significantly different, then you can be pretty sure that something is wrong, and the rest of the data are suspect as well. In practice, the mean RTs of those three conditions rarely differ by more than 10 ms.

Exploratory vs. Confirmatory Research

Along the way to making "validated models of the world," to use Kempthorne's (1976) fine phrase, we do research in one of two general modes. Sometimes we are simply trying to find out what happens when we manipulate these IVs. We have no prediction to make so the result does not confirm (or disconfirm) anything. At the beginning of any research enterprise, when we have only the bare bones of hypotheses, we are usually operating in this *exploratory* mode. But if our exploratory research begins to show us what the important variables are and how they relate to one another, we can begin to make predictions. Those predictions may be point predictions from mathematical models/theories or predictions of overall patterns from qualitative models/theories. Research to test those specific predictions shifts us to the *confirmatory* mode of research.

Data that suggest a hypothesis do not constitute a test of it. In exploring a rich data set, you are almost guaranteed to find some "statistically significant" relationships. After all, if your statistical confidence level is 0.05, you can expect one spurious "significant" finding for every 20 analyses. If a result was not predicted in advance, but arises from a post-mortem "fishing expedition," it should not be trusted without confirmation.

Similarly, if you conduct an experiment and the results are different than expected, but in a way that suggests a different explanation for the phenomenon under study, those data must now be treated as exploratory, not confirmatory.

There is an added importance to this distinction that affects the issue of the statistical power of an experiment. In the statistical analysis of an experiment, we calculate the probability of getting a relationship (in many cases, a difference between means) as strong as we found if the hypothesis of no relationship is true. If that probability ("p value") is low enough (typically, less than .05), we reject the claim of no relationship and assume instead that there is a relationship. But note that "p" values in statistical hypothesis testing are calculated on the assumption that any rejection of the null hypothesis of no relationship between the IV and DV confirms the alternate hypothesis that there is a relationship. It does, but in confirmatory research our research hypothesis is usually more specific than the statistical alternate hypothesis. The value of "p" is the probability of getting *any* variation from the null hypothesis due to sampling or measurement error. If we use the conventional rejection level of .05, we will mistakenly reject the null hypothesis 5% of the time. But in confirmatory research, we are predicting a specific variation from the null hypothesis (i.e., a specific pattern of results). The probability of getting the predicted pattern out of all the possible patterns other than no difference is thus much lower than the stated 5%.

An example may help. Suppose you want to find out whether there is a sex difference in simple RT to a light.[3] You have no basis for even a guess as to the outcome, so this is exploratory research. You test a number of males and females and then compare their mean RTs using a statistical test. Assuming that there is no sex difference in RT (the average male has the same RT as the average female for the whole population), you will get a spurious difference large enough to cause you to make a mistake and declare that there is a sex difference 5% of the time (using the standard level of significance). But you would reject the null hypothesis of no difference *no matter which sex was faster*. Now compare exactly the same study with the addition of a strong theoretical claim that females will be faster (fancifully, peripheral nerve conduction velocities are the same for males and females, but on average females have shorter arms, thus shorter peripheral nerves, thus faster RT).[4] In this case, the null hypothesis will still be rejected 5% of the time. But the

---

[3] *Simple* RT is RT to single stimulus, as opposed to the usual *choice* RT, where you have to decide which stimulus of several occurred. I have no idea whether there is a sex difference, but I doubt it.

[4] Peripheral nerve conduction has a velocity of about 200 m/s. If males' arms are on average 3 inches longer than those of females, this would add less than half a millisecond to the RT

theory would only be (erroneously) supported by those instances in which females were faster. The erroneous results that favor males will not support the research hypothesis. Thus the probability of getting a predicted result that erroneously rejects the null hypothesis (confirmatory) is smaller than the probability of erroneously rejecting the null hypothesis in any direction (exploratory).

The more complex the pattern of means predicted by the theory, the less likely it is that that specific pattern will arise due to errors in sampling or measurement. Consider an experiment like the one in *PsychMate 1.3: Rotation of Mental Images.* Subjects report that they make the decision about whether two figures match by mentally rotating one until they are in the same orientation. If that introspective report is true, then RT should increase as the amount of rotation needed is increased. But suppose RT increased from 0 degrees to 90 degrees and then decreased from 90 to 180 degrees. We would certainly have a relationship, but it would definitely not be the one predicted. Our hypothesis would not only be contradicted if we found no relationship between RT and the amount of rotation, but it would equally be contradicted if the wrong relationship were found. Assume for the moment that there is no relationship. There are many ways that the data spuriously indicate a relationship, and the probability of that occurring is estimated by "p." But only a pattern of a continuous increase in RT would support our hypothesis. The probability of having *that* result arise by chance is much smaller than the putative value of "p."

In factorial designs, the probability of getting a spurious interaction of any kind is .05 (using the conventional level of significance). But the probability of getting a specific interaction predicted in advance is vanishingly small. For example, B. A. Eriksen and C. W. Eriksen (1974) predicted that the increase in RT due to response competition would disappear if the flanking letters were moved outside some presumed area of focal attention. They produced precisely that interaction. That experiment is replicated in *PsychMate 1.6: Selective Attention and Response Competition.*

This same argument applies to multiple experiments, such as Eleanor Rosch's (1975) demonstration of increases in RT for sentence verification and increases in ratings of goodness-of-example that precisely parallel the probability of production of examples of categories. That experiment is replicated in *PsychMate 2.3: Typicality in Categorization.*

Ethics in the Recording, Analysis, and Reporting of Data

> To be persuasive, we must be believable. To be believable, we must be credible. To be credible, we must be truthful.
>
> Edward R. Murrow
> (cited in Spirer & Spirer, 1993, p. 103)

Edward R. Murrow was a famous radio (and later television) news announcer, who broadcast to the U.S. from the London rooftops as bombs fell during the Battle of Britain in 1939. He was speaking of news reporting, not science. But his words fit science as well. Scientific research doesn't really count until it is reported to other scientists. When you write a report of your scientific research, you seek to persuade others. But others will not be persuaded if you lack credibility, and the surest way to ruin your credibility is by misreporting your research. Integrity is as important in science as it is in other human endeavors. Perhaps even more so.

Integrity of the data

There is a cost to the research community of improper collecting and reporting of data. Other people may well rely on your data as the basis of their research. If you make it up, they may waste time and/or grant money on a wild-goose chase that is bound to be expensive given the funds available to most researchers.

Why cheat? Because advancement as a scientist (promotions, grants, prestige) is gained by results. If you want to get ahead as a scientist, you need to make discoveries. There are always individuals willing to cheat. Barber (1976) reviews a number of cases in his chapters on the Investigator Fudging Effect and the Experimenter Fudging Effect. (Barber's work on pitfalls in human research is also discussed in Chapter 5.) More recent cases of data fudging have been revealed, mainly in biomedical research.

Why do people suppose they can get away with cheating? If you simply make up the data, won't you get caught? There are a couple of reasons why fraud is often difficult to detect. One reason is that many scientists work alone. Data collection as well as final data analysis is often performed by one individual, even though that individual may be a member of a larger research team. If such a person chooses to falsify data, they can easily make it nearly impossible to detect.

A second reason is that even if others replicate an experiment, but fail to get the same result, that will not reveal a fraud. Failures to replicate can show that a result (or the replication) was wrong, but that certainly does not indicate fraud. In new areas of inquiry, it is often not known what variables need to be controlled, and erroneous results can occur. Erroneous results can also occur through careless experimental design, with no hint of fraud. The likelihood that someone will decide to replicate a finding increases with the importance of the result, however. So erroneous results in important research areas are usually detected, whether the erroneous result was the result of deliberate fraud or not.[5]

Outright data fabrication certainly occurs, though we hope rarely, but less serious instances of data manipulation are no less unethical. I have in mind here the improper selection and editing of data. While it is proper to delete the data from subjects who obviously were not performing the experimental task as instructed, scientists may sometimes unethically delete data from subjects who do not perform as expected. A researcher may rationalize the decision to exclude data: "We didn't get the effect in the first five subjects, so we'll just treat them as practice." A researcher may also decide to capitalize on chance: "We got the effect in the first five subjects, so we can stop now." Even less subtly, a researcher may simply delete the data from any subjects whose results do not conform to expectations. Selecting only the data that support your hypothesis is fraud. In Chapter 6, I discuss the criteria for (nonfraudulent) deletion of data.

A related problem comes about when it is not clear exactly which data are to be included, and the decision is made only after the researcher knows whether the data agree with the hypothesis. This has especially been the case in studies of alleged psychics, where experimental protocols have often been violated by the subjects. See Percy Diaconis (1978) for a discussion of some cases of this problem. James Randi (1980) noted a similar problem in the studies of Uri Geller (a then-famous Israeli psychic) undertaken by Russell Targ and Harold Puthoff (1974). In essence, Geller was able to decide which attempts at various psychic phenomena "counted." If anything happened that prevented him from practicing deception, he would claim that there were other reasons the failure did not count as such.

A trickier case arises when a researcher conducts an experiment several times, changing the method slightly until he or she achieves only a single positive result. Is it unethical to then report only the one positive result? My

---

[5] Research fraud is detected more often in biomedical research than in psychology. While it might be the case that fraud occurs more often in biomedical research, it probably reflects the greater likelihood of replication, given the importance of, say, a new treatment for cancer.

answer is that it depends. Perhaps the best approach would be to report the positive result, but note that it failed under other circumstances that might indicate boundary conditions for a successful replication. Were I in this position, I would first replicate the experiment that worked to be sure that it was not a fluke.

Reporting of literature

When scientists write the results of research for publication, there is a clear expectation that their review of the literature will cite research that contradicts their views, as well as that which supports them. Though not as damning as outright fraud by faking or selectively editing data, it is clearly an ethical lapse to fail to cite contradictory results in a report of research. Incidentally, if someone else has published such a result and you do not cite it, you can expect them to point it out to you! Failure to cite is only an ethical problem if you knew about the contradictory result and deliberately failed to mention it. If you were unaware of it, then of course, you could not mention it. A thorough review of the literature is the best way to avoid this problem.

Availability of data

The data on which a research report is based are to be made available to other competent professionals for purposes of verification and reanalysis. Exceptions occur if the data cannot be shared without violating confidentiality of subjects, or in the case of proprietary data that may be legally protected. Though not stated in the APA Ethics Code, the usual rule of thumb is that data should be retained for five years.

Reviewers

There is an expectation that persons reviewing articles for publication or grant proposals maintain confidentiality until the review process is complete. The point here is that the article might change substantially in the review process so earlier versions should not be shared.

Duplicate publication

It is a violation of scientific ethics to attempt to republish data already published elsewhere. The point is to prevent people from submitting several articles based on the same data to different journals to "pad" their bibliography. Exceptions are permitted (assuming they are properly acknowledged) if further analyses bring to light new relationships not previously noted. An exception could arise if you do an experiment and report it, but a later experiment suggests a hypothesis that could be tested with data from the first experiment, though you had no reason to make that test at the time. Data from the first experiment could legitimately be treated as confirmatory research.

Publication credit

Only persons substantively involved in a piece of research are to be given authorship credit. Persons who made minor contributions, such as helping test subjects, are acknowledged in the Author Note that follows the References. Most journals list authors by order of the degree of their relative scientific contributions to the article, and the order of authorship should reflect that. (A few journals, such as the *Journal of Physiology (London),* list authors alphabetically and ignore degree of contribution.)

Chapter 8

Scientific Communication in Psychology

Upon the completion of an experiment or series of experiments, the researcher's next step is to communicate the results to other scientists. Such communication is necessary to make the information available to others to guide their own research and thinking. Frankly, it is also the case that scientific reputations are made by *publication*. No matter how brilliant your discoveries might be, they must be communicated to others before you can bask in the glory. For most working scientists, reputation, promotion, and salary are (at least in part) determined by the number and quality of publications. The following section describes some of the details of the process of communicating research results.

Publication of a journal article is the premier means of scientific communication in psychology. *Presentation* of results at scientific meetings, however, is also important.

Presentation

There are two principle forms of presentations of research results at scientific meetings. A number of general and specialized scientific organization host meetings for the purpose of presentation and discussion. Both the Association for Psychological Science and the American Psychological Association hold large annual meetings, as do a number of regional groups such as the Midwest Psychological Association. More specialized groups, such as the Psychonomic Society and the Society for Research in Child Development have their own, usually annual meetings. Presentations at these conferences are usually of two kinds—presentations at poster sessions and papers presented during the various sessions of the conference.

In *poster sessions*, the persons presenting are given bulletin board space—usually about 4 feet by 6 feet—to display their work, which is often in the form of a very brief paper printed large so that people can read it from a few feet away. Poster sessions usually last about two hours with the author remaining with the poster until the session ends. This format permits a large number of presentations simultaneously.

Papers are presented in sessions that typically are about two hours in length. The organizers of the conference try to put papers on similar topics together so that several of the papers of a given session would be of interest to the same persons. Though it varies, a typical format for papers is that each person has 15 minutes to make his or her presentation with five minutes for question-and-answer. A moderator introduces each presenter and keeps track of the time, signaling when the presenter's time is running out. A well-organized moderator keeps the timing fairly tight. This is beneficial if you are attending a meeting where there are several papers you want to hear in separate, overlapping sessions. You will sometimes hear people speak of "reading" a paper at a conference. Many presenters quite literally read their prepared text because, with only 15 minutes to present what is often a fairly complex study, there is little room for an error of timing—you simply aren't permitted to run over by five minutes. Given an hour to make a presentation, one can afford an occasional digression or off-the-top-of-the-head comment. Given only fifteen minutes, one must use every second carefully.

Poster presentation.

When submitting a presentation for a conference, there is usually a choice of asking to present a paper or a poster. Papers are usually regarded as somewhat more prestigious than posters, but other factors can affect the choice. One of the advantages to a poster is that it gives the authors and persons interested in their work a chance to discuss the details—unlike a paper session in which the time for questions is highly limited.

Journal articles

Conference presentations, whether posters or papers, sometimes reflect completed research, but often serve to communicate preliminary results or perhaps one of the several experiments making up a research project. But even if a project has been presented at a conference, publication as a journal article reaches a much wider audience, and makes the research available for as long as copies of the journal are held in libraries. When research that has previously been presented at a conference is published in a journal, the previous presentation is mentioned in the Acknowledgements paragraph of the Author Note.

The process of publication begins when the author(s) submits a manuscript to a journal. A cover letter informs the editor of the submission, and it is accompanied by several copies of the manuscript to be sent to reviewers. Of course, submitters now often use electronic media so that the manuscript is sent via e-mail to the editor and forwarded by the editor to the reviewers. Once accepted, text of an article can be copied by the printer directly from a word-processor file.

When a manuscript is received, it is date-stamped to preserve the date of submission. The editor then sends copies of the manuscript to reviewers for their comments. Typically, three reviewers are used. Some editors have a team of "action editors" to whom they assign manuscripts in specific areas of research. In that case, the action editor selects the reviewers. It is reasonable for authors to suggest reviewers whom they know to be knowledgeable about the area of research, though the choice of reviewers lies with the editor.

Reviewers are usually asked to return their reviews within 30 days. In addition to offering their comments and suggestions, the reviewers are usually asked to indicate whether they think the manuscript should be published. Upon receiving the reviews, the editor writes his or her own review, and then sends the reviews and a decision about publication to the author, as well as to the reviewers, who then see each others' comments. The editor either rejects the manuscript as unworthy of publication, asks for revisions, or accepts the manuscript. Some editors, if the manuscript needs only minor revision, will use the category of "accepted pending revision." In that case, the authors know that the manuscript will be published when they have made the requested changes. It is relatively rare for a manuscript to be accepted without any revision.

Some journals use "blind" review, in which the reviewers do not know the name of the author, and the names of the reviewers are withheld from the author and from each other. It is for that reason that the APA-style manuscript has the author's name only on the title page and Author Note page—they can be removed prior to sending the manuscript to the reviewers. In practice, however, it is usually possible for the reviewers to figure out who the author is. If the reviewers are highly familiar with the area of research, they likely know who would do research of the kind presented. Additionally, the author often cites his or her own previous work as background. Similarly, an author can sometimes be reasonably sure who is likely to be asked to review the article. For this reason, some editors forego blind review completely. At least one journal editor routinely asks the reviewers whether they wish to be identified to the author and/or to each other.

Manuscript preparation

While most journals in psychology use the *Publication Manual of the American Psychological Society* (2001), most have at least minor alternative requirements. Those "Instructions to Authors" are published in occasional issues of the journal, typically as a single page at the back of the journal, and should be consulted before sending a manuscript to the journal. Most journals also maintain Web sites that include the Instructions to Authors.

Web-based publication

At present, publication of journals is still mostly paper-and-ink, but many journals now make articles available as soon as they have been accepted and formatted for publication, so that the information is available online prior to print publication. This is an important advance given that print publication often comes months after acceptance of an article due to a backlog of articles to get into print.

Fully Web-based publication of journals seems unlikely to become widespread for some time, in part because of the temporary nature of Web sites. Print journals have a permanence that the Web is not yet able to match, though I wouldn't be surprised if that statement needs revision in a few years.

Reviewers

Reviewing of manuscripts is one of the duties of a practicing scientist. Peer review works only if peers review, to make an obvious point. Journal editors try to cultivate persons who can provide reviews from time to time. As noted, reviewers are sometimes suggested by the authors of a manuscript. Reviewers are not paid for their time—again, it is simply a professional duty. Journals typically acknowledge reviewers by publishing a list of their names in the last issue of each volume.

Graduate School in Psychology

Many of the students taking a research methods course are likely to be considering applying to graduate school in some area of psychology to pursue a master's degree or a doctorate. The following discussion is intended to let you know how to find information about graduate schools, how the application process works, and a bit about the nature of graduate school.

One thing worth noting up front: some students, as they near the end of their undergraduate career, are more than a bit tired of school. They may put off graduate school for a few years, or avoid it altogether. But graduate school is not just a continuation of your undergraduate education. It requires taking more courses, true. But it also begins the shift from a concentration on coursework to the *doing* of psychology.

Getting Information About Graduate Programs

General Information. A good web site for general information about graduate school in psychology is maintained by the American Psychological Association (APA) at www.apa.org/student.

The APA's guide to graduate programs. The student in psychology is fortunate in that there is a single source for information about graduate programs. The APA publishes its *Graduate Study in Psychology* every two years. That volume contains information on virtually all of the 500 or so graduate programs in psychology in the United States and Canada. It should be available from your department or your college's library or office of career development/placement. If not, you can order it from the APA (order information is available at www.apa.org/books/student.html).

Graduate Study in Psychology begins with an article on the process of applying to graduate school. The main part contains detailed descriptions of the graduate programs themselves. These are examined in more detail below. Another useful section is an index of programs by areas (Clinical Psychology, Cognitive Psychology, and the like). I recommend that you go through that index just to see the many areas of psychology for which there are special programs. You are likely to discover special topics within psychology of which you were never aware.

Each program listing contains information on where to get application information (usually a departmental Web site where you can either download application forms or apply online), as well as the relevant dates for applications. The listings contain information about each program within that department. They detail the number of applicants in the most recent year, and the number of applicants accepted. One of the most important sections sets out the admission requirements for each program, including the required minimum grade point average (GPA) and Graduate Record Examination (GRE) scores, and the median scores of those admitted. The median scores can give you a reasonable idea whether you are competitive for admission. Keep in mind, though, that by definition half of the persons accepted to those programs had scores below those medians! The relative weights of research experience, work experience, letters of reference, and interviews are also given.

Other information includes tuition, financial assistance, housing.

Your college's Career Development/Placement office. Most colleges and universities have a central location for career development and placement. They will have a collection of college catalogues from your region, as well as information on the GRE—(required for almost all graduate programs) and the Miller Analogies Test (MAT—required mainly for clinical psychology programs). They may also sponsor presentations on graduate school admissions.

The Application Process

Degree options. The principal graduate degree in psychology is the PhD, or Doctor of Philosophy. Some schools offer a Doctor of Psychology, or PsyD, degree. PsyD programs are generally aimed at training practitioners, or professional psychologists, rather than research-oriented scientists. The PsyD is the lesser degree. The PhD degree typically requires five to six years of full-time study after the bachelor's degree. The student usually earns a master's degree along the way (it is sometimes optional).

The master's degree (usually Master of Arts or MA, sometimes Master of Science or MS) is certainly the most common graduate degree in psychology, especially in professional psychology (clinical, counseling, and school psychology), as well as in Industrial/Organizational psychology and Human Factors. Master's-level psychologists usually work under the direction of doctoral-level psychologists. Most of the psychologist positions in public agencies (mental health clinics, psychiatric hospitals, prisons, schools) are at the master's level. The master's degree usually requires three or four semesters of full-time study.

There is an important distinction between master's degrees of which you should be aware. If you are planning to get only the master's degree, you should look for programs that offer a <u>terminal</u> master's degree. (These are listed as MA(T) or MS(T) in *Graduate Study in Psychology*.) Many doctoral programs offer a master's, but only to students who are pursuing the doctorate. Their programs are not aimed at training students for master's-level employment. (Some schools have both terminal master's and PhD programs.)

For professional psychologists, the doctorate is required in order to be fully licensed to work in private practice. Psychologists with the master's degree are required in most states to work under the supervision of a doctorate-level psychologist.

Types of graduate programs. At the top are the major research universities. The faculty members are nearly all regular contributors to the research literature. These are the most selective schools, but have the advantage of providing many research assistantships—most of their students are *paid* to attend graduate school (see the discussion of assistantships later). Most of these schools will admit students only on a full-time basis, and most accept students only for the PhD, though some may also have terminal master's programs. The major research universities accept students on an international basis.

Many more state and private universities are in the second tier of graduate programs. Many of these also offer a high quality of graduate preparation. Typically, they have far fewer assistantships available, so there will be more of a financial burden for the student. These schools are more likely to have terminal master's degrees, and to accept part-time students.

Some universities offer only graduate master's degrees and typically are devoted to professional psychology. These have few, if any, assistantships, but usually accept part-time students. The lower level of research involvement among the faculty means that your exposure to psychology as science will be less thorough than at schools offering doctorate degrees.

Over the past couple of decades a number of private, for profit, schools of professional psychology have opened around the country. These usually offer both terminal master's degrees and PsyD or PhD degrees. Most offer at best a veneer of scientific training in psychology—typically just enough to get by the licensing exams.[1] Because their emphasis is on practice rather than research, the

---

[1]The consequences of training professional psychologists without an adequate background in the science of psychology is well documented in Robyn Dawes' 1994 book, *House of Cards*, which should be required reading for any student interested in becoming a professional psychologist.

schools of professional psychology usually have few, if any, assistantships. Because they do not receive taxpayer support (as the state universities do), the full burden of the cost of the education must be borne by the student, making these a relatively expensive option.

Location. There are graduate schools all over the place, and the quality of the programs is not very closely related to their location. Science is international, and there is no advantage to limiting yourself to just those programs in your own state or region. Obviously, some students have family or other obligations that make it difficult for them to move across country to attend graduate school. But to the extent possible, you should select programs based on their quality and not their location.

Where to apply. If you have the credentials to be competitive for admission to the top schools, you should probably choose to apply schools based on the faculty and their research areas. *Who* you want to study with can be an important part of your decision. If, for example, you are interested in memory, you should seek those graduate programs with the best researchers in memory.

When to apply. Check the listings for the schools you are interested in carefully because the deadline to apply varies. Most of the major PhD programs accept students only for the fall semester and have deadlines for applications typically between January 1 and March 1 for the following fall term. The restriction of admissions to fall only is due to their requirement that all students take a (partly) common first-year curriculum (typically the graduate statistics and research methods sequence). Terminal master's degree programs are more likely to have "rolling admissions" and thus accept students to begin in any term. Some doctoral programs do as well.

Application materials. To begin the application process, download the admissions materials from the universities you are interested in. (E-mail address information is given in the APA guide, or can be found online.) Some schools require a separate application for financial aid, though most have sense enough to treat applications for admission as implying application for financial aid.

Please understand that the admissions process is not casual. You will fill in forms seemingly without end. Many schools, especially in professional psychology, require a personal statement, and you should devote great care to its preparation. It is also a good idea to have the faculty from whom you have requested references read and comment on your personal statement. A few schools require an on-campus interview. You also need to coordinate transcripts, GRE and/or MAT scores (see tests and grades section).

Because parts of your application are sent by others (test scores, transcripts, and sometimes, letters of reference), it is wise to check the status of your application a week or two before the deadline. Some schools do a fine job of notifying applicants when their admission materials are complete (or of any missing information), but others do not. The responsibility is yours.

Tests and grades. Almost all schools require that you have taken the GRE, administered by the Educational Testing Service. The degree of emphasis placed on the test results varies considerably from school to school. The APA guide lists which sub-tests are used and the minimum and median scores. Many schools also require that you take the GRE subject test in Psychology.

Your school's Career Development office will have information about where you can take the GRE and the fees. That information, including on-line registration for the test, is available at www.gre.org.

Many graduate programs in clinical psychology also require that you take the MAT, administered by The Psychological Corporation. This test consists of a large number of analogies. Again, your school's career development office will have application forms and information about locations and dates of testing. On-line information is available at www.tpcweb.org/mat.

In taking either the GRE or the MAT, you should be mindful of the delay in reporting results to the schools to which you are applying (though this is less of an issue with computerized testing). Take the tests in time to get your scores reported before the application deadline.

All graduate schools require that you have official copies of your college transcripts sent to them from each of the colleges and universities you have attended. Most schools send these within a few days of receiving your request. If you have attended other schools before your current one, you can obtain information about ordering transcripts by contacting the registrar's office. Most are now available online; if not, call or write the registrar's office.

Letters of recommendation. Typically, graduate schools require that you have three letters of recommendation sent to them. Most will send you forms and envelopes for this purpose when they send you their application materials. Some have the people writing your references send their letter, sealed and signed on the back, to you. You then forward them with your application. Letters of recommendation should be from faculty, and preferably from faculty who have known you in upper-division (junior/senior) courses. At least two of those faculty members should be from the department of psychology or some allied program. If you have extensive internship experience that involved close work with a professional psychologist, that person could be a useful reference, but in general non-faculty should not be asked.

Writing letters of reference is an expected task for faculty, so do not feel hesitant to ask. The faculty who know you best as a student will be in the best position to write strong letters. Writing reference letters takes time, so you should ask the faculty well in advance whether they are willing to write letters for you. You should be sure to get the materials to your references several weeks before the first letter is due. *Give them a list of schools and dates.* If a school to which you are applying sent you forms and envelopes, you should stamp the envelopes and complete any relevant part of the form. Some schools just ask for a letter from the reference, in which case you should supply a stamped, addressed envelope to the references.

Schools are required by law to permit you to see the letters of recommendation at a later time if you do not sign a waiver of that right. Most schools include such a waiver at the top of their recommendation form. The risk you take in not signing the waiver is that some members of admissions committees may not take a letter as seriously if you have not waived your right to see it. I know of no studies on how much impact this actually has. The safest course is to sign the waiver.

As with other materials, it is your responsibility to check that the letters have been received on time by the schools to which you applied.

Notification and acceptance dates. Member schools of the Council of Graduate Departments of Psychology (COGDOP) have adopted a resolution on acceptance dates. Basically, they agreed to send acceptance letters in time for students to reply by April 15 (for fall admission). That is, if they extend an invitation to you to attend, you must reply by April 15. Once you accept an offer, you are not then free to accept another school's offer without the first school's permission.

The reason for this system is that schools are playing a game of probabilities. They know that if they accept you, it is likely that others have as well. So they usually accept more students than they have spaces for, knowing that not everyone accepted will be attending. But it sometimes happens that on April 15 they have fewer students accepting admissions than they wanted. In this case they will return to the applications and invite several more students. Thus, it is entirely possible that you will receive an invitation as late as May. By agreeing on an April 15 date for all member schools, COGDOP maximizes the ability of schools to extend additional invitations if they did not fill all of their positions in the first round. If a student has not replied by that date, it can be assumed they have decided not to attend. The system thus works to your advantage by making the second round of invitations timely.

If, as you receive invitations to attend, you are accepted at your first-choice school you should immediately notify the other schools to which you applied that you are no longer considering them. That benefits other students who may be just a little further down the list than you were. It is to everyone's advantage to make the system operate efficiently. The opening chapter of the APA guide gives more detail about the notification and acceptance procedures, and you should read that chapter with care.

Expenses of application. Start saving. Most graduate schools charge an application fee of $30 to $50. (Some will waive the fee in hardship cases.) For each application, you will have a fee for transcripts. There is also the expense of taking the GRE (and MAT) and having the scores reported to each school. Campus visits are required by some schools, especially in clinical psychology, where interviews are often required.

Financial Aid

A variety of sources of financial aid are available to graduate students. These include most of the sources available to undergraduates, plus a few more.

Student loans. Student loans for graduate school are available from the same programs that give loans for undergraduate education. In some cases, they permit you to borrow more per year and have a higher maximum amount you can borrow overall. The financial aid office at your current school (and those to which you are applying) should have information on loans.

Assistantships. One major advantage to the larger, research-oriented graduate programs is that they typically have a number of graduate assistantships available. *Teaching assistantships* usually require that you either teach a laboratory section of an undergraduate course or that you grade papers, hold review sessions, and keep office hours for a large lecture course. *Research assistantships* pay you to assist a faculty member in his or her research. The level of your involvement will increase as you gain experience.

Pay for assistantships varies considerably, but the APA Guide gives you some idea of what you can expect. Most assistantships pay you a salary based on 20 hours of work per week. In most cases they also carry a waiver of tuition and some fees. (Note that in that case, the higher tuition many state universities charge for out-of-state students is nullified.) At some schools, assistantships will be quite limited for first-year graduate students.

Traineeships. Traineeships (usually in clinical psychology) are similar to assistantships but pay you for work rendering direct services to clients.

Fellowships. Fellowships are the most prestigious form of support for graduate students. These typically carry the same stipend as an assistantship but with no specific requirement of work in return. Of course, there is a considerable expectation that a student holding such a position will pursue independent research. At most schools, the fellowships are awarded by the faculty, but there is no application process. Fellowships are not usually available to first-year graduate students. Typically, fellowships carry a waiver of tuition and fees.

Scholarships. These are similar to fellowships except that they are for smaller amounts of money.

Tuition and fee waivers. Even students who do not receive stipend support (i.e., a "salary") may be eligible for waivers of tuition and all or some fees. Because most state universities charge higher tuition for out-of-state students, a tuition waiver can be quite valuable.

What to expect of graduate school

By the time you are applying to graduate schools you are likely to be feeling rather burned out about school. If you are a "traditional" student, going straight through, you have now been in school for 15 or 16 years. The prospect of several more sometimes doesn't seem so appealing. Take heart. Graduate education, at least at the PhD level, certainly requires that you take more courses. But most of the coursework of a PhD is finished within a couple of years. After that, you are far more concerned with research than with taking more classes. The graduate courses you take are clearly important, and you have to do well in them— a C is typically a failing grade in graduate school. But if you are considering graduate school you are probably the kind of student who can do the work and *the courses are only a part of what you will be doing.* Assistantships make up a major part of your graduate training. Science is largely learned through apprenticeship—you learn to do science by doing science under the watchful eye of someone who knows more about it than you do.

Many PhD programs now require that you complete a first-year research project. Because the best departments are heavily research oriented, they want you *doing* research from the beginning. Most students also complete a master's degree thesis, usually also involving empirical work in your area. That research (as well as the first-year project) will often grow out of research you are working on with your major professor.

Graduate school can be quite nerve-wracking. As you move through your graduate years and begin work on your dissertation, you are likely to have moments of self-doubt—Am I really good enough to do this? Such doubt is natural, and anyone who doesn't suffer a pang of it is probably living in a dream world. But, if the faculty did not think you were capable of doing the work, they would not have let you in.

Graduate school requires a major investment of time, during which your level of income will be rather modest. It isn't for everyone. But if, after taking a course such as this one, you see science or professional psychology as your calling, go for it!

Writing the APA-Style Paper

The *Publication Manual of the American Psychological Association*, now in its fifth edition, sets out the basic style rules for publication in the journals of the American Psychological Society. In addition, the journals of the American Psychological Society and the Psychonomic Society also generally follow the *Publication Manual*. Many journals in areas as diverse as Sociology, Nursing, and Exercise Science use the *Publication Manual*. This chapter is meant to provide an introduction to the APA publication style that will aid the student in writing laboratory reports and brief papers. It cannot substitute for a close study of the full *Publication Manual* itself, with its 429 pages of detail. Graduate schools in psychology largely assume that the *Publication Manual* has been learned by students at the undergraduate level, and we strongly recommend that you purchase a copy. If you are required to buy the *Publication Manual* for this or some other course, we urge you to avoid the temptation to sell it back to the bookstore at the end of the semester.

This chapter consists of two parts. The first describes the general rules and the various major parts of the APA-style manuscript. The second is a mock manuscript designed to highlight a number of the rules. That mock manuscript reports a really trivial experiment, and is limited to only a few references, which were chosen more as a way to illustrate various types of references than for their direct relevance. It is an aid to learning APA style, rather than a real report of research.

It should be understood that many of the rules for creating a manuscript seem rather peculiar. These are based on the needs of production of the journal. For example, tables and figures are placed at the end of the manuscript, rather than at the place in the text where they are referenced. That is because the production of tables and figures is handled separately from production of text. In producing the article in its published format, the publisher will position the tables and figures appropriately within the body of the text.

Some general rules:

[1] Everything is double-spaced. There are NO exceptions.

[2] Always use 8 1/2" x 11" white bond paper.

[3] Always use a 12-point font, preferably Times Roman or Courier

[4] Always use 1" margins on top, bottom, right, and left.

[5] All pages are numbered except for figures.

[6] Indent the first line of all paragraphs and footnotes.

Levels of headings

There are usually no more than three levels of headings, and often only two. The *main heading* is centered. The second level is the *side heading*, which is flush left, italicized. The main heading and side headings use upper-case letters for all important words. These are illustrated in the mock manuscript.

If a third level is needed (for example if you are reporting the results of two experiments), use the *paragraph heading* which is indented and italicized, ending in a period, with the text following on the same line. The paragraph heading uses upper case for the first word and proper nouns. An example of this, in outline format, follows the mock manuscript.

Citations of references in text

When referring to other studies in the body of the text, list all authors the first time (an exception is noted below). If there are only two authors, list them both every time you cite the paper. If there are three or more, subsequent citations list only the first author, followed by "et al." (not in italics, with a period after "al").[1] Examples:

Bruner, Goodnow, and Austin (1956) found... [first citation]

Bruner et al. (1956) found... [later citations *in new paragraphs*]

Bruner et al. found... [later citations *in the same paragraph* omit the date]

If there are six or more authors, cite only the surname of the first author, followed by "et al." and the year. Do this for the first and subsequent citations. (Omit the date for subsequent citations within the same paragraph.)

---

[1] "Et al." is short for the Latin "et alia"—"and others." The period indicates an abbreviation. Foreign words are usually italicized, but some, such as "et al." have become naturalized citizens, as it were, and are treated as English.

If there are two authors with the same last name, include the first initials of the authors:

B. A. Eriksen and C. W. Eriksen (1974) found...

J. Palmer, Ames, and Lindsey (1993) and S. E. Palmer (1978) investigated...

Any other reference to an article by only one of these authors would also include the initials.

Another approach to references in text is to cite parenthetically. Parenthetical references are treated the same as those shown above, but with minor adjustments:

In their study of change blindness, Simons and Levin (1997) found...
vs.
...as shown by recent studies of change blindness (O'Regan, Rensink, & Clark, 1999; Simons & Levin, 1997).

Note the adjustments:

[1] Replace "and" by an ampersand (&).

[2] If there are several citations within the same parentheses, list them in alphabetical order by the first author's last name.

[3] Separate the author names from the date with a comma. Separate the entries within the parentheses with a semicolon.

You should probably use both types of reference in text to avoid a stilted style.

The Parts of the Manuscript

The parts of the manuscript are discussed in a general way here, but the student should refer to the example paper that follows, which gives many details.

The Title page

The title page gives the *title*, a *page header*, a *running head* that appears at the top of the page in the finished article, and the *authors names and institutional affiliations*. The order of the names is determined by the degree of input each had in the conduct of the research. The title of the article should reflect the variables under investigation, such as "The Effect of Word Length on Recall." Avoid cute titles. It is best to have the title contain the words under which people might search for the article in *PsycINFO*.

The Abstract

The Abstract is a brief (no more than 120 word) overview of the research. It begins on page 2. It should state the main theoretical issue, briefly describe the methodology, and state the principal findings.

The Introduction

The introduction begins on a new page by repeating the title. The first paragraph or two should explain the background of the problem and state the approach being taken to solve it.

The next major part of the introduction is a review of the pertinent literature. Summarize in a very general way what is already known about the area of research. An exhaustive review of the literature, citing every study even remotely pertinent, is usually NOT called for. If a finding or theory is controversial, you must mention that are disagreements. It is unethical to omit reference to research that contradicts your position, though you may merely indicate, with proper references, that an issue is in dispute.

The introduction should end with a development of your own hypothesis and a rationale for how your research will clarify the issues at hand. Especially if you are reporting only one experiment, the last few sentences of the introduction should state in simple terms the nature of the experiment. The Method section will give all the detail. Here, you want to give the reader the condensed version.

The Method section

The Method section gives the details of the research. *The basic rule for this section is that it must give sufficient detail that anyone with the proper training could replicate the experiment.*

This section usually has at least two subheadings, though they will vary quite a bit, depending on the nature of the study. One subsection that is required is "Subjects" or "Participants".[2] This is usually a short section, but it

---

[2] The Fourth Edition of the Publication Manual of the American Psychological Association (1994) mandated that we refer to the persons from whom we obtain data as "participants." The Fifth Edition (2001) once again permits the use of "subjects." "Participant" seems quite appropriate if used for those participating in survey research or the like. However, in an experiment, we prefer the term "subject," because the whole point of doing an experiment is that you, the experimenter, manipulate the independent variable. It is precisely because the person has agreed to temporarily suspend control and let you decide the level of the IV to which they will be exposed, or the order of the levels, that makes the study an experiment. Of course, the subject may remove himself or herself from participation at any time, but for as long as they participate, subjects have allowed you to subject them to the conditions you choose. "Participant" suggests a level of free choice that is not a part of an experiment (beyond the freedom to choose whether or not to participate and to withdraw).

should include the number of subjects, how they were obtained (for example, from advertisements or a human subject research pool), and whether and how much they were compensated. The makeup of the subject group by sex, ethnicity, and age should be reported. Other characteristics should be reported where they may be of importance, or if the study was restricted to a special group. For non-human subjects, specify the species and strain. If any subjects' data were omitted from analyses (for example, because of high error rates in a reaction-time study), the number of such omissions and the reasons for them should be listed.

A subsection labeled "Apparatus" may be appropriate if there was equipment involved in the study. Common apparatus, such as a stopwatch, needs only a mention. More complex equipment, such as an electroencephalogram, should give the brand name and model number, as well as other relevant details. For an experiment using a computer to present a stimulus and collect a response, the refresh rate of the monitor should be reported if very brief displays (less than 100 ms) were used. The size of the monitor should also be reported, as well as the viewing distance and the size of the displays (see the *PsychMate* Chapter 1.6, *Selective Attention and Response Competition* for a further discussion). The specific brand of computer is not usually relevant.

This subsection may instead be titled "Materials," if, for example, the study involved a paper-and-pencil memory experiment, in which details of how the lists of to-be-remembered items were generated may be necessary.

Another subsection is "Procedures," which specifies how the experiment was conducted, including, for example, details of randomization of subjects or stimuli, the timing of the events of the experiment, and any other details necessary for a competent investigator to repeat the study. The general instructions to the subjects should be described. If the instructions formed part of the experimental manipulation, then the relevant sections should be given verbatim.

Where the apparatus or materials are relatively simple, these two subsections can be combined as "Apparatus and Procedures" or "Materials and Procedures." Other subsections can be added if they are needed. We suggest that you peruse a few issues of experimental journals to see the variety of subsections used in Methods sections.

The Results section

The Results section presents the details of the statistical analyses of the data. Discussion of the reporting of statistical analyses is beyond the scope of this example. You would report the data in either a table or a figure, but not both. We have included both in the mock manuscript in order to illustrate how each is presented, and where they appear in the manuscript.

The Discussion section

The Discussion section should begin with a non-technical presentation of the main findings. Depending on the complexity of the research, this might be as long as a paragraph. The section goes on to interpret the results and place them within the framework of theoretical expectations and/or previous findings.

The References

The reference section begins on a new page. Include only those papers, books, or presentations that are actually referred to in the paper.

Cite only those references that you have actually read. If you must cite a secondary source that you have read about, but have not actually read, you indicate that in the text of the paper. For example, if you had read a paper by Adams, that described previous research by Jones, you would describe the research by Jones in this fashion: "Jones (as cited in Adams, 1982) has shown....". You would then include the full reference to Adams (but NOT to Jones) in the reference list. This may seem tedious, but if Adams has incorrectly described the work of Jones—and it can happen—then you have avoided the potential embarrassment of appearing to be guilty of shoddy scholarship and the more immediate problem of academic dishonesty that might result in a grade of F on your paper. Note that if you get the article by Jones and verify for yourself that Adams described it correctly, you could properly cite Jones as a primary source, even if you have not "read" every word of Jones.

The mock manuscript shows the three most frequent types of citations in the reference list—reference to a journal article, a chapter in an edited volume, and a monograph (a entire book by one author or set of authors). A separate sheet at the end of the mock manuscript shows those references in detail.

The Appendix

An appendix is not usually necessary, especially for student papers. You will see them in the published literature most often to report lists of stimulus materials or complex mathematical derivations. We do not include an appendix in the sample paper. If there is an appendix, it begins at the top of a new page.

The Author Note

The author note begins at the top of a new page, and reports the institutional affiliation of each author at the time the research was conducted. If the author has since moved to another institution, there would be a note of this. Acknowledgements of help from others and other special circumstances are indicated, and an address for one of the authors is given.

Content footnotes and copyright permissions

Content footnotes are footnotes that were referenced by number in the text. If you used copyrighted material in your study, that material is acknowledged here. Student papers will seldom need footnotes.

Do NOT use the footnote/endnote function of a word processor for these.

Tables

The mock manuscript gives an example of a fairly simple table. Each table is on a separate sheet with a page number. The table includes its title.

Figure Captions

If there are any figures, the captions to those figures are all given on the figure caption page(s), which are the last numbered pages. Do not use a separate sheet for each figure caption. See the mock manuscript for the format of the figure captions.

Figures

The figures themselves are the last pages of the manuscript. Note that they contain ONLY the figures. Because these are separated from the rest of the manuscript in the process of production of the journal, they must have separate identification. The page header (the brief title in the upper-right corner of each manuscript page) should be hand written on the back of each figure, along with the figure number. They should be written at the edge, away from the figure itself, so that they do not show through when the figure is photographed. If there is any possibility of ambiguity, also write the word TOP on the back, to indicate proper orientation.

Example Manuscript

The pages that follow provide a mock manuscript with comments highlighting important aspects of an APA style manuscript.

Example Manuscript

The *page header* should be no more than 2-3 words, followed by the page number. Page numbering starts on the title page as page 1. In Word, click on *View/Header and Footer* to create a header. You can space over or hit the right-justify button. Click on Insert Page Numbers to add the page number.

The *running head* is the heading printed at the top of the page in the published article. It should be no more than 50 characters.

Mental Rotation 1

Running Head: MENTAL ROTATION OF DIGITS

The title is in upper-case for all important words. It can be more than one line long. It is centered. It should begin in the top half of the page.

List all authors and their institutional affiliations at the time the research was conducted.

The Mental Rotation of Images of Digits

Jane I. Public

University of South Park

Abbreviate where possible. The first time it is used, the term is spelled out and the abbreviation indicated for later use.

Mental Rotation 2

Do not indent the Abstract.

Abstract

This experiment extends the typical study of mental rotation to include digits as the images to be rotated. Reaction time (RT) to decide whether a digit was in normal or mirror-image orientation was measured with human subjects. On each trial, the subject saw a single digit, either upright or rotated 60, 120, or 180 degrees, and was asked to indicate as quickly as possible whether the digit was normal or mirror image. The results confirm the prediction that digits would show the same pattern of results as that found in experiments using letters as stimuli. RT increased with increased levels of rotation ($p = .005$).

Indicate the species.

Only Arabic numerals are used, unless a numeral is used to begin a sentence, in which case it should be spelled out.

Report the significance level for the main finding.

Note use of quotation marks the first time a specialized phrase is used. They are not used subsequently.

When citing parenthetically, use the ampersand ("&"). When citing in text, use "and." Also, the second citation of the same source in a paragraph does not require that the date be repeated.

The title is repeated at the beginning of the introduction.

Mental Rotation 3

The Mental Rotation of Images of Digits

A basic approach to the study of mental images is to examine how they are manipulated during "mental rotation" (Cooper & Shepard, 1973). Cooper and Shepard showed that RT to indicate whether a briefly presented letter was a normal letter or a mirror image increased as the amount of rotation increased. However, we know of no studies that have used digits as stimuli in similar studies. Though it seems likely that mental rotation of digits will function similarly to that of letters, the research reported below is intended to fill this gap in the experimental record.

Other types of materials have been used in mental rotation experiments, with predictable results. Shepard and Metzler (1971) had subjects compare two drawings of 3-dimensional images and make a speeded judgment as to whether the two figures matched or not. One figure was usually rotated relative to the other. They showed that the reaction time (RT) to make the judgment increased as the degree of rotation of the figures increased. Cooper (1975) found similar results with random two-dimensional shapes.

There has been serious debate concerning the nature of imagery. A view developed by Kosslyn strongly supports the semi-perceptual nature of imagery. Pylyshyn is also mentioned here, since he has developed a different approach.

At the end of the introduction, state the basic research question in a non-technical way.

"Data" is a plural noun (singular is *datum*), hence "the data are," though some dictionaries now recognize its usage with a singular verb — "the data is."

Mental Rotation 4

The study of mental imagery has yielded insights into the nature of the cognitive process, and the nature of perceptual representation (Kosslyn, 1994; but see Pylyshyn, 2002). Kosslyn suggests that manipulation of mental images may be part of many cognitive and motor tasks. Wohlschläger (2001) supported this idea with studies of the relation of mental object rotation to planning for actual hand rotation of the real-world objects, and suggest that mental object rotation is an imagined *action* that goes beyond being a pure visual imagery task.

The experiment reported below seeks to extend the study of mental rotation to include rotation of images of digits, which have apparently not been previously studied.

Method

Subjects

Subjects were 12 males and 10 females (mean age 19.3 years) who participated to complete part of a requirement for an Introductory Psychology course. Data from 3 other subjects were omitted, due to error rates in excess of 20%.

Apparatus and Procedures

> For a reaction time experiment, report what happens on each trial and how the trials differed.

Each subject completed 240 trials in a single session. On each

trial, the subject saw a single digit (from the set of 2, 3, 4, 5, 6, and 7 and

their mirror images) presented immediately above a central fixation mark

("+"). The digit remained on the screen until a response was made. If no

response was made within 3 seconds, the trial was terminated and

recorded as an error. The digits and their mirror images were presented

either right-side up or rotated by 60, 120, or 180 degree clockwise or

counterclockwise. The stimuli were 1.2 cm tall and 0.8 cm wide.

Each of the six digits and its mirror image was presented equally

often at each orientation, resulting in 48 types of trials (6 digits x 4

> Report details of counterbalancing and randomization.

rotations x 2 orientations). Each type was repeated 5 times. The

resulting 240 trials were presented in a random order. Subjects were

instructed to indicate whether the stimulus was a normal digit or a mirror

image by pressing the *1* or *2* key on the numeric keypad of the computer

> Report a summary of the instructions. If the instructions were part of the experimental manipulation, report them verbatim.

keyboard. The mapping of keys to responses was counterbalanced by

subject number. Subjects were encouraged to respond as quickly as

possible while keeping errors to a minimum, and were warned if their

In reporting these values, omit the leading zero if the value cannot be above 1 (or below –1). Thus the value of *p* has no leading zero. Nor does the value of *r* (the correlation) reported below. Note that when *F* (or *t* or most other statistics) is below 1, the leading zero is used.

Use one or the other, not both. We include both here to illustrate both a table and a figure.

The Discussion should begin with a brief statement of the principal results in non-technical terms.

Mental Rotation 6

error rate exceeded 10%.

Stimuli were presented on a computer monitor, and stimulus presentation and response recording were controlled by the E-Prime software (Schneider, Eschman, & Zuccolotto, 2002).

Results

The mean correct RT's were compared using a 4 (rotations of 0, 60, 120, or 180 degrees) x 2 (orientations--normal vs. mirror-image) repeated measures ANOVA. The main effect of rotation was significant, $F(3, 63) = 12.36$, $p = .005$, reflecting the generally longer RTs with increased amounts of rotation. The main effect of orientation was not significant, $F(1, 21) = 1.34$, $p = .236$, nor was the interaction, $F(3, 63) = 0.79$, $p = .762$. The increase in RT with increasing rotation was essentially linear, with a correlation between angle of rotation and RT of $r(2) = .954$, p = .002. The cell and marginal means are reported in Table 1 [Figure 1].

Discussion

Comparisons of the mean RTs indicate an increase in RT as digits are rotated farther from right-side up. The increase in RT with increased

Mental Rotation 7

rotation occurred about equally for both normal and mirror-image digits, and no significant difference was found between normal and mirror-image digits.

It is clear that the original experiment, using letters, replicates quite well when digits are substituted. This adds to the types of stimuli known to produce orderly increases in RT with increased amounts of rotation.

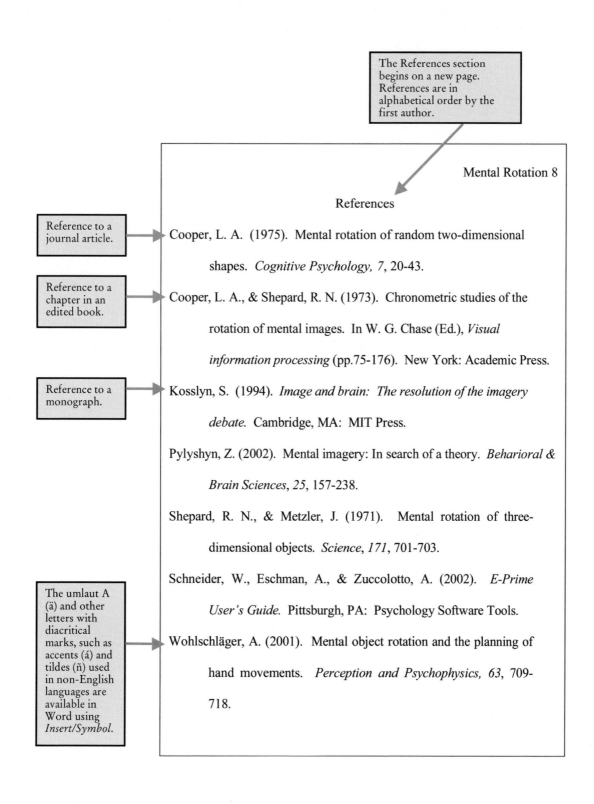

The References section begins on a new page. References are in alphabetical order by the first author.

Mental Rotation 8

References

Reference to a journal article.

Cooper, L. A. (1975). Mental rotation of random two-dimensional shapes. *Cognitive Psychology, 7,* 20-43.

Reference to a chapter in an edited book.

Cooper, L. A., & Shepard, R. N. (1973). Chronometric studies of the rotation of mental images. In W. G. Chase (Ed.), *Visual information processing* (pp.75-176). New York: Academic Press.

Reference to a monograph.

Kosslyn, S. (1994). *Image and brain: The resolution of the imagery debate.* Cambridge, MA: MIT Press.

Pylyshyn, Z. (2002). Mental imagery: In search of a theory. *Beharioral & Brain Sciences, 25,* 157-238.

Shepard, R. N., & Metzler, J. (1971). Mental rotation of three-dimensional objects. *Science, 171,* 701-703.

Schneider, W., Eschman, A., & Zuccolotto, A. (2002). *E-Prime User's Guide.* Pittsburgh, PA: Psychology Software Tools.

The umlaut A (ä) and other letters with diacritical marks, such as accents (á) and tildes (ñ) used in non-English languages are available in Word using *Insert/Symbol.*

Wohlschläger, A. (2001). Mental object rotation and the planning of hand movements. *Perception and Psychophysics, 63,* 709-718.

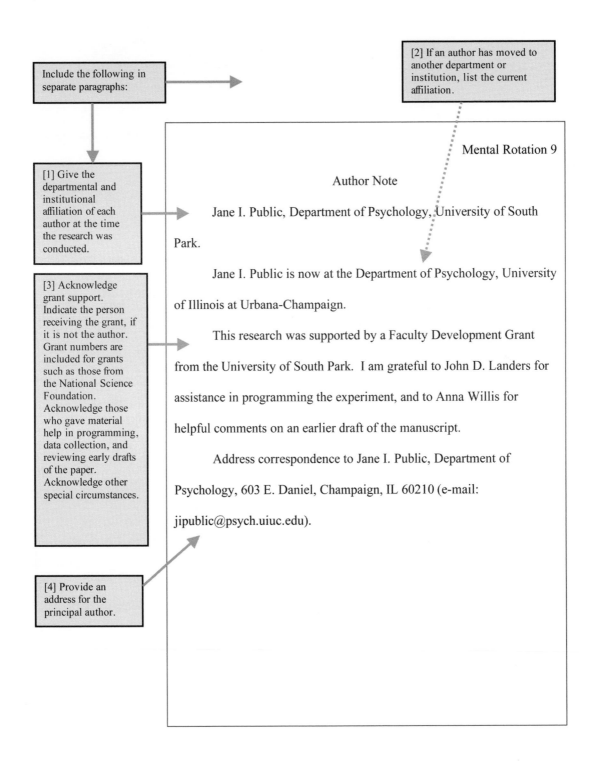

Include the following in separate paragraphs:

[2] If an author has moved to another department or institution, list the current affiliation.

[1] Give the departmental and institutional affiliation of each author at the time the research was conducted.

[3] Acknowledge grant support. Indicate the person receiving the grant, if it is not the author. Grant numbers are included for grants such as those from the National Science Foundation. Acknowledge those who gave material help in programming, data collection, and reviewing early drafts of the paper. Acknowledge other special circumstances.

[4] Provide an address for the principal author.

Mental Rotation 9

Author Note

Jane I. Public, Department of Psychology, University of South Park.

Jane I. Public is now at the Department of Psychology, University of Illinois at Urbana-Champaign.

This research was supported by a Faculty Development Grant from the University of South Park. I am grateful to John D. Landers for assistance in programming the experiment, and to Anna Willis for helpful comments on an earlier draft of the manuscript.

Address correspondence to Jane I. Public, Department of Psychology, 603 E. Daniel, Champaign, IL 60210 (e-mail: jipublic@psych.uiuc.edu).

Each table begins
on a new page.

The title of the
table is in italics,
with no period.
The title should
name the
variables that are
tabled.

Mental Rotation 10

Table 1

Mean Correct RT (ms) as a Function of the Absolute Angle of Rotation

and Whether the Digits were Normal or Mirror-Image

	Absolute Angle of Rotation (Degrees)			
Orientation	0	60	120	180
Normal	1134	1347	1491	1712
Mirror Image	1125	1356	1508	1698

The Figure Caption section begins a new page, and is the last numbered page.

Put the Figure number in italics, but not the caption. The caption ends in a period.

Mental Rotation 11

Figure Caption

Figure 1. Mean correct RT as a function of the absolute angle of rotation

and whether the digits were normal or mirror-image.

The figure caption should state what the variables are that are being displayed.

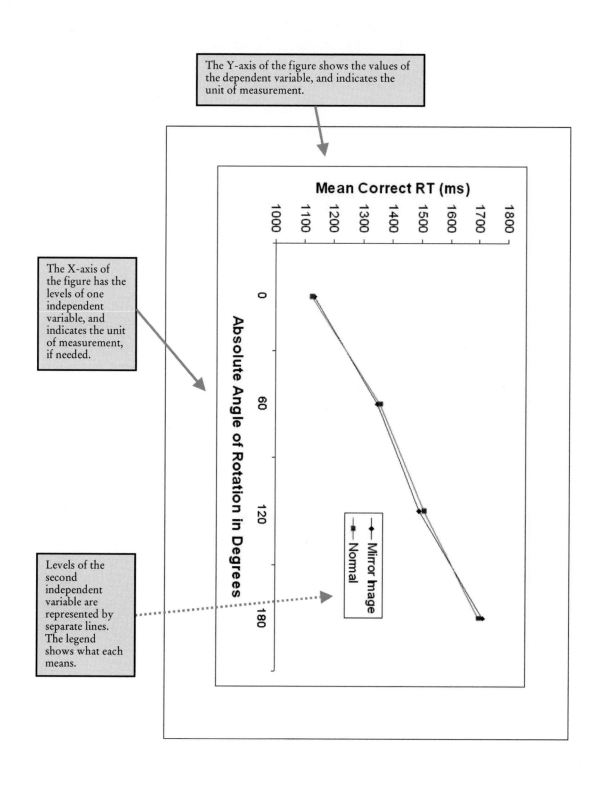

Outline of Sections in a Multi-Experiment Paper.

In the box below is an example, in outline only, of an article with three levels of headings. In this case, it is an article relating two experiments. Note that the text under <u>Subjects</u> and <u>Apparatus and Procedures</u> follows on the same line.

The Mental Rotation of Images of Digits

Experiment 1

Methods

     Subjects.

     Apparatus and Procedures.

Results

Discussion

Experiment 2

Methods

     Subjects.

     Apparatus and Procedures.

Results

Discussion

General Discussion

References

Author Note

Tables

Figure Caption

Details of the common references.

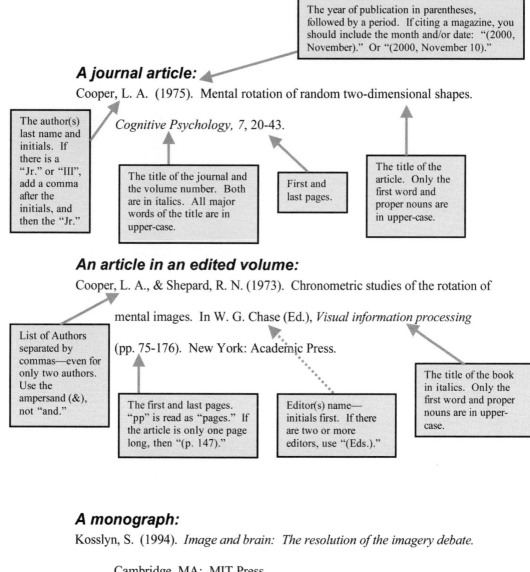

A journal article:

The year of publication in parentheses, followed by a period. If citing a magazine, you should include the month and/or date: "(2000, November)." Or "(2000, November 10)."

Cooper, L. A. (1975). Mental rotation of random two-dimensional shapes.

Cognitive Psychology, 7, 20-43.

The author(s) last name and initials. If there is a "Jr." or "III", add a comma after the initials, and then the "Jr."

The title of the journal and the volume number. Both are in italics. All major words of the title are in upper-case.

First and last pages.

The title of the article. Only the first word and proper nouns are in upper-case.

An article in an edited volume:

Cooper, L. A., & Shepard, R. N. (1973). Chronometric studies of the rotation of

mental images. In W. G. Chase (Ed.), *Visual information processing*

(pp. 75-176). New York: Academic Press.

List of Authors separated by commas—even for only two authors. Use the ampersand (&), not "and."

The first and last pages. "pp" is read as "pages." If the article is only one page long, then "(p. 147)."

Editor(s) name— initials first. If there are two or more editors, use "(Eds.)."

The title of the book in italics. Only the first word and proper nouns are in upper-case.

A monograph:

Kosslyn, S. (1994). *Image and brain: The resolution of the imagery debate.*

Cambridge, MA: MIT Press.

The city of publication and name or abbreviations of the publisher. Give the state if the city is not prominent in published. So—"Cambridge, MA:" but "New York:" or "London:".

References

Adams, J. A. Learning and memory (Rev. ed.).Homewood, IL: Dorsey Press.

Agricola, G. (1950). *De re metallica.* (H. C. Hoover & L. H. Hoover, Trans.). New York: Dover. (Original work published 1556)

Alcock, J. E. (1981). *Parapsychology, science or magic?* Oxford, Pergamon.

Allingham, M. (1964). *Death of a ghost.* London: Heinemann.

American Psychological Association. (2001). *Publication manual of the American Psychological Association.* Washington, DC: American Psychological Association.

Amsel, A. (1989). Behaviorism, neobehaviorism, and cognitivism in learning theory. Hillsdale, NJ: Erlbaum.

Anastasi, A., & Urbina, S. (1988). *Psychological testing* (7th ed.). Upper Saddle River, NJ: Prentice Hall.

Ausubel, D. P. (1960). The use of advance organizers in the learning and retention of meaningful verbal material. *Journal of Educational Psychology, 51,* 267-272.

Bacon, R. (1928). *Opus majus* (R. B. Burke, Trans.). Pittsburgh, PA: University of Pennsylvania Press. Original work published c. 1267.

Barber, T. X. (1976). *Pitfalls in human research.* New York: Pergamon.

Bartlett, F. C. (1932). *Remembering.* Cambridge: Cambridge University Press.

Barzun, J. (2000). *From dawn to decadence.* New York: HarperCollins.

Behar, I., & Adams, C. K. (1966). Some properties of the reaction time ready signal. *American Journal of Psychology,* 79, 419-426.

Bennett, D. J. (1998). *Randomness.* Cambridge, MA: Harvard.

Beveridge, W. I. B. (1957). *The art of scientific investigation* (Rev. ed.). New York: W. W. Norton.

Bierce, A. G. (1881-1906/1946). *The devil's dictionary.* In *The collected writings of Ambrose Bierce.* New York: Citadel Press.

Boring, E. G. (1954). The nature and history of experimental control. *American Journal of Psychology, 67*, 573-589.

Boring, E. G. (1945). The use of operational definitions in science. *Psychological Review, 52*, 243-245.

Boring, E. G. (1952/1963). The validation of scientific belief. In R. I. Watson & D. T. Campbell, Eds.) *History, psychology, and science: Selected papers* (pp. 245-252). New York: John Wiley and Sons.

Borsboom, D., Mellenbergh, G. J., & van Heerden, J. (2004). The concept of validity. *Psychological Review, 111*, 1061-1071.

Bower, G. H., Clark, M., Lesgold, A., & Winzenz, D. (1969). Hierarchical retrieval schemes in recall of categorized word lists. *Journal of Verbal Learning and Verbal Behavior, 8*, 323-343.

Bramel, D. & Friend, R. (1981). Hawthorne, the myth of the docile worker, and class bias in psychology. *American Psychologist, 36*, 867-878.

Brewer. W. F. (1977). Memory for the pragmatic implications of sentences. *Memory & Cognition, 5*, 673-678.

Brewer, W. F., & Treyens, J. C. (1981). Role of schemata in memory for places. *Cognitive Psychology, 13*, 207-230.

Bridgman, P. W. (1927). *The logic of modern physics.* New York: Macmillan.

Bridgman, P. W. (1945). Some general principles of operational analysis. *Psychological Review, 52*, 246-249.

Burghardt, G. M., Wilcoxon, H. C., & Czaplicki, J. A. (1973). Conditioning in garter snakes: Aversion to palatable prey induced by delayed illness. *Animal Learning & Behavior, 1*, 317-320.

Burton, R. F. (1861). *The city of the saints.* New York: Alfred A. Knopf. (Originally published 1963).

Butcher, J. N., Dahlstrom, W. G., Graham, J. R., Tellegen, A., & Kaemmer, B. (1989). *Minnesota Multiphasic Personality Inventory-1 (MMPI-2): Manual for administration and scoring.* Minneapolis, MN: University of Minnesota.

Campbell, D. T., & Stanley, J. C. (1963). *Experimental and quasi-experimental designs for research.* Boston: Houghton Mifflin.

Capron, C., & Duyme, M. (1989). Assessment of effects of socio-economic status on IQ in a full cross-fostering study. *Science, 340*, 552-554.

Carey, B. (2004, October 10). Can prayer heal? Critics say studies go past science's reach. *New York Times*, pp. 1, 32.

Carrell, L. E., Cannon, D. S., Best, M. R., & Stone, M. J. (1986). Nausea and radiation-induced taste aversions in cancer patients. *Appetite, 7*, 203-208.

Chalmers, A. F. (1976). *What is this thing called science?* St. Lucia, Queensland, Australia: University of Queensland Press.

Chase, Stuart (1938). *The tyranny of words.* New York: Harcourt, Brace & World.

Chesterton, G. K. (1905/1963). Straight thinking. *The man who was orthodox.* London: Dennis Dobson.

Clark, H. H., & Chase, W. G. (1972). On the process of comparing sentences against pictures. *Cognitive Psychology, 3*, 472-517.

Collins, A. M., & Quillian, M. R. (1969). Retrieval time from semantic memory. *Journal of Verbal Learning and Verbal Behavior, 8*, 240-247.

Cook, T. D., & Campbell, D. T. (1979). *Quasi-experimentation: Design and analysis issues for field settings.* Chicago: Rand McNally College Publishing.

Cooper, L. A. , & Shepard, R. N. (1973). Chronometric studies of the rotation of mental images. In. W. G. Chase (Ed.), *Visual information processing.* New York, Academic Press.

Dahlstrom, W. G. & Dahlstrom, L. E. (Eds.). (1980). *Basic readings on the MMPI: A new selection on personality measurement.* Minneapolis, MN: University of Minnesota.

Darwin, C. (1859). On the origin of species by means of natural selection; or, The preservation of favoured races in the struggle for life. London: J. Murray.

Darwin, Erasmus (1794). *Zoonomia; or, The laws of organic life.* London: J. Johnson.

Davis, F. J. (2001). *Who is black?: One nation's definition* (10th anniversary edition). University Park, PA: Pennsylvania State University Press.

Deffenbacher, K. A., & Loftus, E. F. (1982). Do jurors share a common understanding concerning eye-witness behavior? *Law and Human Behavior, 6*, 15-30.

Diaconis, P. (1978). Statistical problems in ESP research. *Science*, 201, 131-136.

Diaconis, P. (1979). Rejoinder to Edward F. Kelly. *Zetetic Scholar*, 5, 29-34.

Dobzhansky, T. (1973). Nothing is biology makes sense except in the light of evolution. *American Biology Teacher, 35,* 125-129.

Doyle, A. Conan(1928). Sherlock Holmes: The complete short stories. London: John Murray.

Duhem, P. (1962). *The aim and structure of physical theory.* New York: Atheneum.

Ebbinghaus, H. (1913). *Memory* (H. A. Ruger & C. E. Bussenius, Trans.). New York: Teacher's College, Columbia University (Original work published in 1885.)

Eriksen, B. A., & Eriksen, C. W. (1974). Effects of noise letters upon the identification of a target letter in a nonsearch task. *Perception and Psychophysics, 16,* 143-149.

Eriksen, C. W. (1995). The flankers task and response competition: A useful tool for investigating a wide variety of cognitive problems. *Visual Cognition, 2,* 101-118.

Fink, A. (1995). *How to sample in surveys.* Thousand Oaks, CA: SAGE.

Fisher, R., & Yates, F. (1963) *Statistical tables* (6th ed.). London: Oliver and Boyd.

Fisher, R. A. (1925). *Statistical methods for research workers.* London: Oliver and Boyd.

Fisher, R. A. (1960). *The design of experiments* (7th ed.). London: Collier MacMillan. (Originally published 1935).

Franke, R.H. & Kaul, J.D. (1978). The Hawthorne experiments: First statistical interpretation. *American Sociological Review, 1978, 43,* 623-643.

Gallo, E. (1991). Nature faking in the humanities. *Skeptical Inquirer,* 15(4), 371-375.

Galton, Francis. (1885). Regression towards mediocrity in hereditary stature. *Journal of the Anthropological Institute,* 15, 246-262.

Garcia, J., & Koelling, R. A. (1966). Relation of cue to consequence in avoidance learning. *Psychonomic Science,* 4, 123-124.

Garner, W. R., Hake, H. W., & Eriksen, C. W. (1956). Operationism and the concept of perception. *Psycholgoical Review, 63,* 149-159.

Gazzaniga, M. S., Ivry, R. B., & Mangun, G. R. (2002). *Cognitive neuroscience: The biology of the mind.* New York: W. W. Norton.

Glanzer, M., & Cunitz, A. R. (1966). Two storage mechanisms in recall. *Journal of Verbal Learning and Verbal Behavior, 5,* 351-369.

Glass, G. V., & Stanley, J. C. (1970). *Statistical methods in education and psychology.* Englewood Cliffs, NJ: Prentice-Hall.

Gould, S. J. (1999). *Questioning the millenium.* Rev. Ed. New York: Harmony.

Granit, R. (1977). *The purposive brain.* Cambridge, MA: MIT Press.

Greene, R. L. (1992). *Human memory: Paradogms and paradoxes.* Hillsdale, NJ: Lawrence Erlbaum Associates.

Grice, G. R. (1966). Dependence of empirical laws upon the source of experimental variation. *Psychological Review, 661, 488-498.*

Grice, G. R., & Hunter, J. J. (1964). Stimulus intensity effects depend upon the type of experimental design. *Psychological Review, 71,* 247-256.

Griggs, R. A. & Cox, J. R. (1982). The elusive thematic-materials effect in Wason's selection task. *British Journal of Psychology, 73,* 407-420.

Gross, P. R., & Levitt, N. (1994). *Higher superstition.* Baltimore, MD: The Johns Hopkins University Press.

Gross, P. R., Levitt, N., & Lewis, M. W. (Eds.) (1996). *The flight from science and reason.* NY: New York Academy of Sciences.

Gustavson, C. R., Kelly, D. J., Sweeney, M., & Garcia, J. (1976). Prey-lithium aversion I: Coyotes and wolves. *Behavioral Biology,* 17, 61-72.

Halpern, D. (2000). Sex differences in cognitive abilities (3rd ed.). Mahwah, NJ: L. Erlbaum Associates.

Harré, R. (1960). *An introduction to the logic of the sciences.* London, MacMillan.

Heathcote, A., Brown, S., & Mewhort, D. J. K. (2000). The power law repealed: The case for an exponential law of practice. *Psychonomic Bulletin and Review, 7,* 185-207.

Hebb, D. O. (1949). *The organization of behavior.* New York: John Wiley & Sons.

Hick, W. E. (1952) On the rate of gain of information. *Quarterly Journal of Experimental Psychology, 4,* 11-26.

Hintzman, D. L. (1991). Why are formal models useful in psychology? In W. E. Hockley & S. Lewandowsky (Eds.), *Relating theory and data: Essays on human memory in honor of Bennet B. Murdoch, Jr.* (pp. 39-56). Hillsdale, NJ: Erlbaum.

Hyman, R. (1953). Stimulus information as a determinant of reaction time. *Journal of Experimental Psychology, 45,* 188-196.

Jaffe, E. (2005). How random is that? Students are convenient research subjects but they're not a simple sample. *Observer, 18,* 20-30.

Jastrow, J. (1935). *Wish and wisdom, episodes in the vagueries of belief.* New York: D. Appleton-Century.

Jefferys, W. H. & Berger, J. O. (1992). Ockham's Razor and Bayesian analysis. *American Scientist, 80,* 64-72.

Julesz, B. (1995). *Dialogues on perception.* Cambridge, MA: MIT.

Kahneman, D. (1973). *Attention and effort.* Englewood Cliffs, NJ: Prentice-Hall.

Kempthorne, O. (1976). The analysis of variance and factorial design. In D. B. Owen (Ed.), *On the history of probability and statistics* (pp. 29-54). New York: Marcel Dekker.

Kendall, P. (1994, November 25). Chemist has the power to tame skunk's spray. *Chicago Tribune,* Inside section 2, Chicagoland, p. 1 and 10.

Kennedy, J. L. (1952). An evaluation of extra-sensory perception. *Proceedings of the American Philosophical Society,* 96, 513-518.

Keppel, G. (1982). *Design and analysis* (2nd ed.). Englewood Cliffs, NJ: Prentice-Hall.

Kihlstrom, J. F. (2002). Demand characteristics in the laboratory and the clinic: conversations and collaborations with subjects and patients. *Prevention & Treatment,* 5. Retrieved September 1, 2004, from http://journals.apa.org/prevention/volume5/pre0050036c.html.

Kintsch, W. (1971). Models for free recall and recognition. In D. A. Norman (Ed.), *Models of human memory.* New York: Academic Press.

Koerth, W. (1922). A pursuit apparatus: Eye-hand coordination. *Psychological Monographs, 31,* 288-292.

Kosslyn, S. M. (1994). *Image and brain: The resolution of the imagery debate.* Cambridge, MA: MIT Press.

Kosslyn, S. M, Pascual-Leone, A., Felician, O. & Camposano, S. (1999). The role of area 17 in visual imagery: Convergent evidence from PET and rTMS. *Science, 284,* 167-170.

Krosnick, J. (1999). Survey research. *Annual Review of Psychology, 50,* 537-567.

Kuhn, T. S. (1970). *The structure of scientific revolutions* (2nd ed.). Chicago, IL: University of Chicago.

Lashley, K. (1960). In search of the engram. In F. Beach, D. O. Hebb, C. T. Morgan, & H. W. Nissen (Eds.). *The neuropsychology of Lashley* (pp. 478-505). New York: McGraw-Hill.

Le Bihan, D., Turner, R., Zeffiro, T. A., Cuenod, C. A., Jezzard, P., & Bonnerot, V. (1993). Activation of human primary visual cortex during visual recall : A magnetic resonance imaging study. Proceedings of the National Academy of Sciences USA, 90, 11802-11805.

Likert, R. (1932). A technique for the measurement of attitudes. *Archives of Psychology, 140.*

Lippa, R. (1991). Some psychometric characteristics of gender diagnosticity measures: Reliability, Validity, Consistency across domains, and relationship to the "Big Five." *Journal of Personality and Social Psychology, 61,* 1000-1011.

Lipton, P. (2005). Testing hypotheses: Prediction and prejudice. *Science, 307,* 219-221.

Loftus, E. F. (1993). Psychologists in the eyewitness world. *American Psychologist, 48,* 550-552.

Logan, G. (2002). An instance theory of attention and memory. *Psychological Review, 109,* 376-400.

Lord, F. M. (1953). On the statistical treatment of football numbers. *American Psychologist, 8,* 750-751.

Lykken, D. T. (1968). Statistical significance in psychological research. *Psychological Bulletin, 70,* 151-159.

Magnussen, D. (1967). *Test theory.* Reading, MA: Addison-Wesley.

Marcus, A. D. (2004, June 8). Fighting cancer with a sugar pill. *Wall Street Journal, 243*, pp. D1, D9.

Masling, J. (1966). Role-related behavior of the subject and psychologist and its effects upon psychological data. In D. Levine (Ed.) *Nebraska symposium on motivation* (pp. 67-103). Lincoln, Nebraska: University of Nebraska Press.

McDaniel, M. A., & Pressley, M, (1984). Putting the keyword method in context. *Journal of Educational Psychology, 76*, 598-609.

Michell, J. (1990). A*n introduction to the logic of psychological measurement.* Hillsdale, NJ: Lawrence Erlbaum.

Mill, J. S. (1843). *A system of logic, ratiocinative and inductive: Being a connected view of the principles of evidence and the methods of scientific investigation.* London: J. W. Parker

Mitroff, I. I. (1974, November 2). Studying the lunar-rock scientist. *Saturday Review/World, 2*, 64-65.

Moore, J. A. (1993). *Science as a way of knowing: The foundations of modern biology.* Cambridge, MA: Harvard.

Morgan, C. T. (1965). Physiological psychology. New York: McGraw-Hill.

Mynatt, C. R., Doherty, M. E., & Tweney, R. D. (1978). Consequences of confirmation and disconfirmation in a simulated research environment. *Quarterly Journal of Experimental Psychology, 30*, 395-406.

Murchison, C. A. (Ed.). (1927). *The case for and against psychical belief.* Worcester, MA: Clark University.

Nairne, J. S. (2002). Remembering over the short-term: The case against the standard model. *Annual Review of Psychology, 53*, 53-81.

Neisser, U., Bardoo, G., Bouchard, T. J., Jr., Boykin, A. W., Brody, N., Ceci, S. J., et al. (1996). Intelligence: Knowns and unknowns. *American Psychologist, 51*, 77-101.

Oaksford, M. & Chater, N. (1994). A rational analysis of the selection task as optimal data selection. *Psychological Review, 101*, 608-631.

Orne, M. T. (1962). On the social psychology of the psychological experiment: With particular reference to demand characteristics and their implications. *American Psychologist*, 17, 776-783. (Also reprinted in *Prevention & Treatment*, 5. Retrieved September 1, 2002, from http://journals.apa.org/prevention/volume5/pre0050035a.html.)

Parsons, H. M. (1974). What happened at Hawthorne? *Science, 183*, 922-931.

Pesare, P. J., Bauer, T. J., & Gleeson, G. A. (1950). Untreated syphilis in the male Negro: Observation of abnormalities over 16 years. *American Journal of Syphilis, Gonorrhea, & Venereal Disease, 34*, 201-213.

Pitt, B., Zannad, F., Remme, W., Cody, R., Castaigne, A, Perez, A., et al. (1999).The effect of spironolactone on morbidity and mortality of patients with severe heart failure. *The New England Journal of Medicine, 341*, 709-717.

Popper, K. (1959). *The logic of scientific discovery.* Toronto, Ontario: University of Toronto Press. (Originally published 1935).

Quine, W. V. O. (1961). Two dogmas of empiricism. In W. V. O. Quine (Ed.), *From a logical point of view* (pp. 20-46). New York: Harper and Row.

RAND Corporation. (1955). *A million random digits with 100,000 normal deviates.* New York: Free Press.

Randi, J. (1980). *Flim-Flam!* NY: Lippincott and Crowell.

Recommendations guiding physicians in biomedical research involving human subjects. Adopted by the 18th World Medical Assembly, Helsinki, Finland, June 1964, amended by the 29th World Medical Assembly, Tokyo, Japan, October 1975, and the 35th World Medical Assembly, Venice, Italy, October 1983.

Reichle, E. D., Carpenter, P. A., & Just, M. A. (2000). The neural bases of strategy and skill in sentence-picture verification. *Cognitive Psychology, 40*, 261-295.

Rhine, J. B. (1974). A new case of experimenter unreliability. *Journal of Parapsychology, 38*, 215-255.

Rivers, E., Schuman, S. H., Simpson, L., & Olansky, S. (1953, April). Twenty years of followup experience in a long-range medical study. *Public Health Reports, 68*, 391-395.

Rosch, E. (1975). Cognitive representations of semantic categories. *Journal of Experimental Psychology: General, 104*, 192-233.

Rosenthal, R., & Rubin, D. B. (1978). Interpersonal expectancy effects: The first 345 studies [with replies]. *The Behavioral and Brain Sciences, 1*, 377-416.

Rosnow, R. L. (2002). The nature and role of demand characteristics in scientific inquiry. *Prevention and Treatment, 5*. Retrieved September 1, 2004, from http://journals.apa.org/prevention/volume5/pre0050037c.html.

Rothman, K. & Michels, K. (1994). The continuing unethical use of placebo controls. *The New England Journal of Medicine, 331*, 394-398.

Ruby, L. (1954). *The art of making sense.* New York: J. B. Lippincott.

Shepard, R. N., & Metzler, J. (1971). Mental rotation of three-dimensional objects. *Science, 171*, 701-703.

Shettleworth, S. J. (1972). Constraints on learning. In D. S. Lehrman, & R. A. Hinde (Eds.). *Advances in the study of behavior: IV* (pp. 1-69) Oxford, England: Academic Press, 1972.

Silverman, I. (1977). *The human subject in the psychological laboratory.* New York: Pergamon.

Skinner, B. F. (1938). The behavior of organisms: An experimental analysis. Englewood Cliffs, NJ: Appleton-Century-Crofts.

Snow, J. (1965). *Snow on cholera; being a reprint of two papers.* New York: Hafner. (Original work published 1845 and 1855).

Solomon, R. L. (1949). An extension of control group design. *Psychological Bulletin*, 46, 137-150.

Solomon & Lessac (1968). A control group design for experimental studies of developmental processes. *Psychological Bulletin*, 70, 145-150.

Spirer, H. F., & Spirer, L. (1993). *Data analysis for monitoring human rights.* Washington, DC: American Association for the Advancement of Science.

Spirito, A., Overholser, J., Ashworth, S., Morgan, J., & Benedict-Drew, C. (1988). Evaluation of a suicide awareness curriculum for high school students. *Journal of the American Academy of Child and Adolescent Psychiatry, 27*, 705-711.

Squire, L. R. (1995). Biological foundations of accuracy and inaccuracy in memory. In D. L. Schacter (Ed.) *Memory distortion: How minds, brains, and societies reconstruct the past* (pp. 197-225). Cambridge, MA: Harvard.

Sternberg, S. (1966). High-speed scanning in human memory. *Science, 153*, 652-654.

Sternber, S. (1969). The discovery of processing stages: Extension of Donder's method. *Acta Psychologica, 30*, 276-315.

Stevens, S. S. (1951). Mathematics, measurement, and psychophysics. In Stevens, S. S. (Ed.), *Handbook of experimental psychology* (pp. 1-49). New York: Wiley.

Stewart-Williams, S. (2004). The placebo puzzle: Putting together the pieces. *Health Psychology, 23,* 198-206.

Symons, C. S. & Johnson, B. T. (1997). The self-reference effect in memory: A meta-analysis. *Psychological Bulletin, 121,* 371-394

Targ, R., & Puthoff, H. E. (1974). Information transfer under conditions of sensory shielding. *Nature, 251,* 602-607.

The Nuremberg Code (1947) In: Mitscherlich A, Mielke F. *Doctors of infamy: the story of the Nazi medical crimes.* New York: Schuman, 1949: xxiii-xxv.

"Trials of War Criminals Before the Nuremberg Military Tribunals Under Control Council Law No. 10", Vol. 2, Nuremberg, October 1946 - April 1949. (Washington, DC: US Government Printing Office, 1949). pp 181-182.

Tulving, E. & Thomson, D. M. (1973). Encoding specificity and retrieval processes in episodic memory. *Psychological Review, 80,* 352-373.

Tversky, A., & Kahneman, D. (1974). Judgment under uncertainty: Heuristics and biases. *Science, 185,* 1124-1131.

Tweney, R. D. (1998). Toward a cognitive psychology of science: Recent research and its implications. *Current Directions in Psychological Science, 7,* 150-154.

Ulrich, R., & Miller, J. (1994). Effects of truncation on reaction time analysis. *Journal of Experimental Psychology: General, 123,* 34-80.

Uraneck, K. (2001). New federal privacy rules stump researchers. *The Scientist, 15,* 33.

U.S. Food and Drug Administration. (1998). Exception for informed consent for studies in emergency settings: Regulatory language and excerpts from preamble. www.foa.gov/oc/ohrt/irbs/except.html

Van Selst, M., & Jolicoeur, P. (1994). A solution to the effect of sample size on outlier elimination. *Quarterly Journal of Experimental Psychology, 47A,* 631-650.

Wagenaar, W. A. (1969) Note on the construction of digram-balanced Latin squares. *Psychological Bulletin, 72,* 384-386.

Wang, A. Y., & Thomas, M. H. (2000). Looking for long-term mnemonic effects on serial recall: The legacy of Simonides. *American Journal of Psychology, 113*, 331-340.

Wason, P. C., & Johnson-Laird, P. N. (1970). A conflict between selecting and evaluating information in an inferential task. *British Journal of Psychology, 61*, 509-515.

White, A. D. (1899). *A history of the warfare of science with theology in Christendom.* New York, D. Appleton.

Wilcoxon, H. C., Dragoin, W. B., & Kral, P. A. (1971). Illness-induced aversions in rat and quail Relative salience of visual and gustatory cues. *Science*, 171, 826-828.

Winch, W. H. (1908). The transfer of improvement of memory in school children. *British Journal of Psychology*, 2, 284-293.

Wolpert, L. (1992). *The unnatural nature of science.* Cambridge, MA: Harvard University Press.

Woodruff, Guy, & Premack, David (1979). Intentional communication in the chimpanzee: The development of deception. *Cognition, 7*, 333-362.

Woodworth, R. S. (1938). *Experimental psychology.* New York: Henry Holt.

Yerkes, R. M., & Dodson, J. D. (1908). The relation of strength of stimulus to rapidity of habit-formation. *Journal of Comparative Neurology and Psychology, 18*, 459-482.

Ziman, E.J. (1968). *Public knowledge: An essay concerning the social dimension of science.* Cambridge: Cambridge University Press.

Ziman, J. (1981). *Puzzles, problems, and enigmas.* New York: Cambridge University Press.

Index

Index of Names

Index of *PsychMate* References